The Role of Informal Economies in the Post-Soviet World

There is a widely held belief within policy circles and some academic disciplines that in the former Soviet states the transition to a market economy is complete and that the formal economy is the dominant factor in everyday economic life. This is linked to broader discussions around the discourse of the formal economy's dominance in everyday life. After critiques of these two arguments the book then provides in-depth discussions on the nature and importance of informal practices in Ukraine and Moscow.

While academics and policy makers often note that the forms of market economy in post-Soviet states take many different forms, they still conclude that the transition is complete. Furthermore, there is a lack of understanding of what this means for those living through such monumental economic and social changes. It is clear that marketisation has posed many challenges for the people of Russia and Ukraine, with levels of economic marginalisation still extremely high even though more than 20 years have passed since the Soviet Union's collapse. Informality and corruption are entwined within daily life, and in short the lived experience of transition is, for many, very different to that predicted by those who led the reforms.

Based on extensive ethnographic and quantitative research conducted in Ukraine and Russia between 2004 and 2012, this book's central argument is that for many people the informal economy, such as cash-in-hand work, subsistence production and the use of social networks, is of great importance to everyday life. Formal work is both a facilitator of such processes and is often supported by them, as people can only afford to undertake low-paid formal work as a result of their informal incomes. By looking at the informal nature of formal work and practices, informal practices, gift giving, volunteer work and the economies of the household, the book is one of the first to give an overview of the nature of the informal economy in all spheres of everyday practice.

Colin C. Williams is Professor of Public Policy at the Management School at Sheffield University, UK.

John Round is Lecturer in Human Geography at Birmingham University, UK.

Peter Rodgers is Lecturer in Strategy and International Business, Management School, University of Sheffield, UK.

Routledge studies in the modern world economy

1 **Interest Rates and Budget Deficits**
A study of the advanced economies
Kanhaya L. Gupta and Bakhtiar Moazzami

2 **World Trade after the Uruguay Round**
Prospects and policy options for the twenty-first century
Edited by Harald Sander and András Inotai

3 **The Flow Analysis of Labour Markets**
Edited by Ronald Schettkat

4 **Inflation and Unemployment**
Contributions to a new macroeconomic approach
Edited by Alvaro Cencini and Mauro Baranzini

5 **Macroeconomic Dimensions of Public Finance**
Essays in honour of Vito Tanzi
Edited by Mario I. Blejer and Teresa M. Ter-Minassian

6 **Fiscal Policy and Economic Reforms**
Essays in honour of Vito Tanzi
Edited by Mario I. Blejer and Teresa M. Ter-Minassian

7 **Competition Policy in the Global Economy**
Modalities for co-operation
Edited by Leonard Waverman, William S. Comanor and Akira Goto

8 **Working in the Macro Economy**
A study of the US labor market
Martin F.J. Prachowny

9 **How Does Privatization Work?**
Edited by Anthony Bennett

10 **The Economics and Politics of International Trade**
Freedom and trade: volume II
Edited by Gary Cook

11 **The Legal and Moral Aspects of International Trade**
Freedom and trade: volume III
Edited by Asif Qureshi, Hillel Steiner and Geraint Parry

12 **Capital Markets and Corporate Governance in Japan, Germany and the United States**
Organizational response to market inefficiencies
Helmut M. Dietl

13 **Competition and Trade Policies**
Coherence or conflict
Edited by Einar Hope

14 **Rice**
The primary commodity
A.J.H. Latham

15 **Trade, Theory and Econometrics**
Essays in honour of John S. Chipman
Edited by James C. Moore, Raymond Riezman and James R. Melvin

16 **Who Benefits from Privatisation?**
Edited by Moazzem Hossain and Justin Malbon

17 **Towards a Fair Global Labour Market**
Avoiding the new slave trade
Ozay Mehmet, Errol Mendes and Robert Sinding

18 **Models of Futures Markets**
Edited by Barry Goss

19 **Venture Capital Investment**
An agency analysis of UK practice
Gavin C. Reid

20 **Macroeconomic Forecasting**
A sociological appraisal
Robert Evans

21 **Multimedia and Regional Economic Restructuring**
Edited by Hans-Joachim Braczyk, Gerhard Fuchs and Hans-Georg Wolf

22 **The New Industrial Geography**
Regions, regulation and institutions
Edited by Trevor J. Barnes and Meric S. Gertler

23 **The Employment Impact of Innovation**
Evidence and policy
Edited by Marco Vivarelli and Mario Pianta

24 **International Health Care Reform**
A legal, economic and political analysis
Colleen Flood

25 **Competition Policy Analysis**
Edited by Einar Hope

26 **Culture and Enterprise**
The development, representation and morality of business
Don Lavoie and Emily Chamlee-Wright

27 **Global Financial Crises and Reforms**
Cases and caveats
B.N. Ghosh

28 **Geography of Production and Economic Integration**
Miroslav N. Jovanović

29 **Technology, Trade and Growth in OECD Countries**
Does specialisation matter?
Valentina Meliciani

30 **Post-Industrial Labour Markets**
Profiles of North America and Scandinavia
Edited by Thomas P. Boje and Bengt Furaker

31 **Capital Flows without Crisis**
Reconciling capital mobility and economic stability
Edited by Dipak Dasgupta, Marc Uzan and Dominic Wilson

32 **International Trade and National Welfare**
Murray C. Kemp

33 **Global Trading Systems at Crossroads**
A post-Seattle perspective
Dilip K. Das

34 **The Economics and Management of Technological Diversification**
Edited by John Cantwell, Alfonso Gambardella and Ove Granstrand

35 **Before and Beyond EMU**
Historical lessons and future prospects
Edited by Patrick Crowley

36 **Fiscal Decentralization**
Ehtisham Ahmad and Vito Tanzi

37 **Regionalisation of Globalised Innovation**
Locations for advanced industrial development and disparities in participation
Edited by Ulrich Hilpert

38 **Gold and the Modern World Economy**
Edited by MoonJoong Tcha

39 **Global Economic Institutions**
Willem Molle

40 **Global Governance and Financial Crises**
Edited by Meghnad Desai and Yahia Said

41 **Linking Local and Global Economies**
The ties that bind
Edited by Carlo Pietrobelli and Arni Sverrisson

42 **Tax Systems and Tax Reforms in Europe**
Edited by Luigi Bernardi and Paola Profeta

43 **Trade Liberalization and APEC**
Edited by Jiro Okamoto

44 **Fiscal Deficits in the Pacific Region**
Edited by Akira Kohsaka

45 **Financial Globalization and the Emerging Market Economies**
Dilip K. Das

46 **International Labor Mobility**
Unemployment and increasing returns to scale
Bharati Basu

47 **Good Governance in the Era of Global Neoliberalism**
Conflict and depolitization in Latin America, Eastern Europe, Asia and Africa
Edited by Jolle Demmers, Alex E. Fernández Jilberto and Barbara Hogenboom

48 **The International Trade System**
Alice Landau

49 International Perspectives on Temporary Work and Workers
Edited by John Burgess and Julia Connell

50 Working Time and Workers' Preferences in Industrialized Countries
Finding the balance
Edited by Jon C. Messenger

51 Tax Systems and Tax Reforms in New EU Members
Edited by Luigi Bernardi, Mark Chandler and Luca Gandullia

52 Globalization and the Nation State
The impact of the IMF and the World Bank
Edited by Gustav Ranis, James Vreeland and Stephen Kosak

53 Macroeconomic Policies and Poverty Reduction
Edited by Ashoka Mody and Catherine Pattillo

54 Regional Monetary Policy
Carlos J. Rodríguez-Fuentez

55 Trade and Migration in the Modern World
Carl Mosk

56 Globalisation and the Labour Market
Trade, technology and less-skilled workers in Europe and the United States
Edited by Robert Anderton, Paul Brenton and John Whalley

57 Financial Crises
Socio-economic causes and institutional context
Brenda Spotton Visano

58 Globalization and Self Determination
Is the nation-state under siege?
Edited by David R. Cameron, Gustav Ranis and Annalisa Zinn

59 Developing Countries and the Doha Development Round of the WTO
Edited by Pitou van Dijck and Gerrit Faber

60 Immigrant Enterprise in Europe and the USA
Prodromos Panayiotopoulos

61 Solving the Riddle of Globalization and Development
Edited by Manuel Agosín, David Bloom, George Chapelier and Jagdish Saigal

62 Foreign Direct Investment and the World Economy
Ashoka Mody

63 The World Economy
A global analysis
Horst Siebert

64 Production Organizations in Japanese Economic Development
Edited by Tetsuji Okazaki

65 The Economics of Language
International analyses
Edited by Barry R. Chiswick and Paul W. Miller

66 Street Entrepreneurs
People, place and politics in local and global perspective
Edited by John Cross and Alfonso Morales

67 Global Challenges and Local Responses
The East Asian experience
Edited by Jang-Sup Shin

68 Globalization and Regional Integration
The origins, development and impact of the single European aviation market
Alan Dobson

69 Russia Moves into the Global Economy
Breaking out
John M. Letiche

70 The European Economy in an American Mirror
Barry Eichengreen, Michael Landesmann and Dieter Stiefel

71 Working Time Around the World
Trends in working hours, laws, and policies in a global comparative perspective
Jon C. Messenger, Sangheon Lee and Deidre McCann

72 International Water Treaties
Negotiation and cooperation along transboundary rivers
Shlomi Dinar

73 Economic Integration in the Americas
Edited by Joseph A. McKinney and H. Stephen Gardner

74 Expanding Frontiers of Global Trade Rules
The political economy dynamics of the international trading system
Nitya Nanda

75 The Macroeconomics of Global Imbalances
European and Asian perspectives
Edited by Marc Uzan

76 China and Asia
Economic and financial interactions
Edited by Yin-Wong Cheung and Kar-Yiu Wong

77 Regional Inequality in China
Trends, explanations and policy responses
Edited by Shenggen Fan, Ravi Kanbur and Xiaobo Zhang

78 Governing Rapid Growth in China
Equity and institutions
Edited by Ravi Kanbur and Xiaobo Zhang

79 The Indonesian Labour Market
Shafiq Dhanani, Iyanatul Islam and Anis Chowdhury

80 Cost–Benefit Analysis in Multi-level Government in Europe and the USA
The case of EU cohesion policy and of US federal investment policies
Alessandro Ferrara

81 **The Economic Geography of Air Transportation**
Space, time, and the freedom of the sky
John Bowen

82 **Cartelization, Antitrust and Globalization in the US and Europe**
Mark LeClair

83 **The Political Economy of Integration**
Jeffrey Cason

84 **Critical Issues in Air Transport Economics and Business**
Rosario Macario and Eddy Van de Voorde

85 **Financial Liberalisation and Economic Performance**
Luiz Fernando de Paula

86 **A General Theory of Institutional Change**
Shiping Tang

87 **The Dynamics of Asian Financial Integration**
Edited by Michael Devereux, Philip Lane, Park Cyn-young and Wei Shang-jin

88 **Innovative Fiscal Policy and Economic Development in Transition Economies**
Aleksandr Gevorkyan

89 **Foreign Direct Investments in Asia**
Edited by Chalongphob Sussangkarn, Yung Chul Park and Sung Jin Kang

90 **Time Zones, Communications Networks, and International Trade**
Toru Kikuchi

91 **Miraculous Growth and Stagnation in Post-War Japan**
Edited by Koichi Hamada, Keijiro Otsuka, Gustav Ranis, and Ken Togo

92 **Multilateralism and Regionalism in Global Economic Governance**
Trade, investment and finance
Edited by Junji Nakagawa

93 **Economic Growth and Income Inequality in China, India and Singapore**
Trends and policy implications
Pundarik Mukhopadhaya, G. Shantakumar and Bhanoji Rao

94 **Foreign Direct Investment in China**
Spillover effects on domestic enterprises
Deng Ziliang

95 **Enterprise Forms and Economic Efficiency**
Capitalist, cooperative and government firms
Kazuhiko Mikami

96 **Diversity and Transformations of Asian Capitalism**
Edited by R. Boyer, H. Uemura and A. Isogai

97 **Knowledge Transfer in the Automobile Industry**
Global–local production networks
Dessy Irawati

98 **Exchange Rates and Foreign Direct Investment in Emerging Asia**
Selected issues and policy options
Ramkishen S. Rajan

99 **Singapore, the Energy Economy**
From the first refinery to the end of cheap oil, 1960–2010
Ng Weng Hoong

100 **China–India Economics**
Challenges, competition and collaboration
Amitendu Palit

101 **Case Studies on Chinese Enterprises**
Edited by Donglin Xia

102 **Argentina's Economic Growth and Recovery**
Michael Cohen

103 **The Korean Labour Market After the 1997 Economic Crisis**
Edited by Joonmo Cho, Richard B. Freeman, Jaeho Keum and Sunwoong Kim

104 **China and India**
The quest for energy resources in the 21st century
Zhao Hong

105 **Beyond the Global Crisis**
Structural adjustments and regional integration in Europe and Latin America
Edited by Lionello Punzo, Carmen Aparecida Feio and Martin Putchet Anyui

106 **The Global Economic Crisis in Latin America**
Impacts and responses
Edited by Michael Cohen

107 **The Processes and Practices of Fair Trade**
Trust, ethics and governance
Edited by Brigitte Granville and Janet Dine

108 **Regional Development through Ecological Business**
Unique cases in Japanese rural regions
Makoto Hirano

109 **Aging and Economic Growth Potentials in the Pacific Region**
Edited by Akira Kohsaka

110 **Crises of Global Economy and the Future of Capitalism**
An insight into the Marx's crisis theory
Edited by Kiichiro Yagi, Nobuharu Yokokawa, Shinjiro Hagiwara and Gary A. Dymski

111 **The Financial History of the Bank for International Settlements**
Kazuhiko Yago

112 **Freight Transport and the Modern Economy**
Michel Savy and June Burnham

113 **Thoughts on Economic Development in China**
Edited by Ma Ying and Hans-Michael Trautwein

114 **China's Ethnic Minorities**
Social and economic indicators
Rongxing Guo

115 **Globalization, Outsourcing and Labour Development in ASEAN**
Shandre Thangavelu and Aekapol Chongvilaivan

116 **The Role of Informal Economies in the Post-Soviet World**
The end of transition?
Colin C. Williams, John Round and Peter Rodgers

The Role of Informal Economies in the Post-Soviet World

The end of transition?

Colin C. Williams, John Round and Peter Rodgers

Routledge
Taylor & Francis Group
LONDON AND NEW YORK

First published 2013
by Routledge
2 Park Square, Milton Park, Abingdon, Oxon OX14 4RN

Simultaneously published in the USA and Canada
by Routledge
711 Third Avenue, New York, NY 10017

Routledge is an imprint of the Taylor & Francis Group, an informa business

British Library Cataloguing in Publication Data
A catalogue record for this book is available from the British Library

Library of Congress Cataloging in Publication Data
A catalog record has been requested for this book

ISBN: 978-0-415-56721-3 (hbk)
ISBN: 978-0-203-76896-9 (ebk)

Typeset in Times New Roman
by Wearset Ltd, Boldon, Tyne and Wear

FSC www.fsc.org MIX Paper from responsible sources FSC® C013056

Printed and bound in Great Britain by
TJ International Ltd, Padstow, Cornwall

This book is dedicated to
Alexander George

Contents

Illustrations

Figures

Tables

Acknowledgements

Gratitude is expressed by the authors to the following for their much appreciated financial support for this project: the ESRC (grant number: RES -000-22-0985), the Leverhulme Trust (SAS/2005/0055) and the Leicester University's School of Management. More broadly, the authors would also like to thank the various institutions (Leicester University's School of Management, The Management School at the University of Sheffield, the University of Birmingham's School of Geography, Earth and Environmental Sciences, the National Research University, Higher School of Economics' Faculty of Sociology and Centre for Advanced Studies, and the Slavic Research Centre at the University of Hokkaido) for providing the time and the intellectual environments in order to facilitate the writing of this book.

Words of thanks are also given to the many participants in Russia and Ukraine, without whose generous contributions this book would not have seen the light of day. Special thanks go to Natalya Dmitrevna in Kiev, Sergei Viktorovich in Kharkiv and Emilia Kosterina in Moscow. John Round would also like to give great thanks to his partner, Irina Kuznetsova, and their daughter Anastacia, for their never-ending support during the writing of this book.

1 Introduction

In a village just outside Moscow's city limits, a house stands out from all the others in the vicinity in that it is impeccably maintained and has a very well cultivated garden. Given that the owner's only income is her pension, the immaculate condition of her house seems somewhat at odds with her economic circumstances, especially when it is compared with the others surrounding it in the village. It transpires that the owner 'rents' rooms in her house to Chechen migrants who, wary of working in Moscow city centre as they are without the correct documentation, work as labourers in this rural fringe area of Moscow, building homes for Russia's rich. Eager to send as much money home as possible and to save money for the winter months when work is scarce, her lodgers wish to reduce their outgoings as much as possible. Therefore, rather than pay rent to her, they steal materials from the building sites on which they work and use them to renovate her house. They also help her plant, tend and harvest her vegetable garden, and when there is produce to sell, they drive her to the local market and pick her up on their return home in the evening. Here at the market, she sells the food produced in her vegetable garden informally on the edge of the market as she does not want to pay the bribe and annual fee for a licence to sell formally. To ensure she does not have any trouble from the owners of the market, she gives some of her produce to the police who operate in the vicinity. Back in her village, she also makes a small annual payment to the local police who are aware of the migrants' presence, in order to ensure that there are no problems. Indeed, this practice of receiving such informal payments is quite lucrative for the local police chief since he also receives an annual payment from the caretaker of the local school so that a blind eye is turned when he turns the school's sports hall into a temporary hostel for migrants during the summer months. Not all of this income is kept by the local chief of police, however, as he has to make payments 'upwards' to ensure that he keeps his position and can continue to operate without interference. In consequence, from the house owner renting out rooms in her home, through the entrepreneurial behaviour of the migrants and the interactions of the residents with the state in the form of the police and licences, to the production and selling of the foodstuffs, all of these processes are wholly informal exchanges. The only formal component in this woman's totality of livelihood practices is the pension which just about covers her communal charges, utility bills and the informal payments she has to make to obtain her medicines that are supposedly free.

This example of a participant's livelihood practices gathered during the field-work for this book conveys the commonality of informal practices in everyday life for many people in post-Soviet economies. Far from the informal economy being some minor residue in contemporary post-Soviet economies or a leftover from some previous system of exchange that is steadily disappearing from view, this example displays how informal exchanges remain a persistent and integral feature of the livelihood practices of a large segment of the population in post-Soviet societies and well beyond. As Standing (2011: 261) points out, the informal economy is one of the key defining features of the contemporary global economy, and contrary to the assumption that there is a universal formalisation of economies, it is more the informal economy that has 'become pervasive'. Of course, estimating the true size of the informal economy is a difficult, if not impossible, task since by its very nature such work is hidden from the state's gaze. Using indirect proxy indicators, however, Schneider *et al.* (2010) have suggested that the size of the 'shadow economy' globally is equivalent to about 34 per cent of global GDP. Obviously, however, there are marked differences in its size between countries, with estimates ranging from 67 per cent of GDP in Bolivia to 8.4 per cent in Switzerland, and with the two countries that are the focus of this book – Russia and Ukraine – both sitting at the higher end with their shadow economies estimated to be equivalent to 46 and 52 per cent of GDP, respectively. This shadow economy, moreover, is purported to be increasing, not decreasing, in size relative to the official economy on a global level, especially during the current economic crisis (Kulikov and Blyzniuk 2010). To ignore the informal economy when providing accounts of the 'economic' and 'economy', therefore, would be to overlook a major, if not the dominant, segment of the whole economy in many countries.

In this book, in consequence, our aim is to start to bring out of the shadows the important role that informal economies play in people's livelihood practices. In order to do so, we here focus our attention on the role of informal economies in the post-Soviet/socialist world in general, and Ukraine and Russia in particular. To achieve this, our intention is to first re-think not only the discourse of 'transition' in the post-Soviet world, but also the meanings of the 'economic' and 'economy' in the contemporary world, and following this, to develop an analytical lens which enables the totality of work relations to be understood when studying the economy and the trajectories of development in different places. To show the outcomes of adopting this 'whole economy' perspective, we will then chart in some detail the full range of economic practices in Ukraine, as well as in Russia's capital city of Moscow, in order to understand the role that informal economies play in the contemporary post-Soviet world. This will provide critical insight into the so-called transformation or transition process in post-Soviet economies and the meanings of the economic and economy in lived experience in such spaces by examining the full range of livelihood practices pursued by people. This will reveal not only that studying the formal economy alone fails to fully capture the lived experiences of people's economic practices, but also, and more importantly, that unless the full repertoire of the economic practices pursued by people are evaluated, it is impossible to understand the meaning of the economic and economy or the trajectory of economic development in the world today.

At the heart of this book is a critique of the notion that economic transition is at an end in Russia and Ukraine and that the move from the command system to the market economy is complete. The term transition implies a movement from one place, or state, to another, a defined starting and end point. Within the context of post-Soviet/socialist states, this refers to the movement away from the command economy system, with the state controlling all aspects of planning, production, distribution and sale, to the neo-liberal system where 'the market knows best'. For most Soviet and socialist countries, this process began between 1989 and 1991 and was 'completed' either by joining the European Union, the bestowing of 'market status' by other countries or entry into the World Trade Organisation (for discussion on 'the end of the transition paradigm', see Carothers 2002). A full discussion of this transition literature is provided in Chapter 2. It is important to highlight at the outset, nevertheless, that the concept of economic transition from one state to another is highly simplified. As will be shown through the lens of everyday life, there was never any 'pure' command economy system where the state controlled all aspects of planning, production, distribution and sale. Neither is it the case that all post-Soviet/socialist states have now moved to some 'pure' ideal-type market economy, which after all only exists in textbooks and is in lived practice nowhere apparent. Instead, through examining the lived experience of how people achieved and achieve their livelihoods, it quickly becomes apparent that all economies are composed of a diverse repertoire of labour practices, and that if the 'economic' and 'economy' are to be understood, it is necessary to move beyond such simplified accounts where one mode of production or another assumes a hegemonic status and all other systems of exchange disappear. Rather, what happens is that economies are sometimes involved in processes of transformation whereby there is a shift in the balance afforded to different systems of exchange and that these transformations involve multiple development paths and trajectories being pursued from different starting points (Abbott and Wallace 2009; Brown *et al.* 2012; Pickles and Smith 1998; Round *et al.* 2010; Smith and Timár 2010; Sýkora and Bouzarovski 2012). By exploring the importance, role and nature of informal economies in post-Soviet economies, both in the past and present, in consequence, this book disputes not only the past hegemony of the command economy system, but also the primacy of the formal market economy in the present along with the view that there is a universal linear development path being pursued towards a hegemonic formal market economy system.

To move beyond an understanding of the economic and economy which is centred on the impending hegemony of a formal market economy and to gain greater understanding of the role that informal economies continue to play in people's livelihood practices, a 'whole economy' perspective will be used here. This is achieved by adopting an analytical lens for understanding the multiple labour practices which exist in contemporary economies that conceptualises a spectrum from formal-oriented to informal-oriented labour practices, which is cross-cut by another spectrum ranging from wholly monetised to wholly non-monetised labour practices. The resultant outcome is to capture the plurality of labour practices that exist in post-Soviet societies in a manner which shows how they all seamlessly merge into each other. Having developed this theoretical and conceptual framework for understanding the plurality of labour practices in economies, the intention in the second part of the book is to apply this to understanding the multifarious practices used in post-Soviet societies.

To achieve this, we will here report the findings of fieldwork conducted since 2005 in Ukraine and Moscow. Indeed, the fieldwork in the post-Soviet world on which this book is based has been a long time in gestation. Prior to conducting the research for this book, one of the authors had been researching the informal economy in western economies for well over two decades before turning his attention to analysing the informal economies of the post-Soviet world in order to write this book, while the other two authors had realised for more than a decade prior to writing this book the importance of informal economies in the post-Soviet world. Indeed, many of the research questions on which the eventual fieldwork for this book was based emerged from the lessons learned from these dual experiences of studying this phenomenon in the western world and from researching aspects of the informal economy in post-Soviet countries for doctoral research on the coping practices of senior citizens in Russia and identity formation in Ukraine.

It is also important to realise that we as authors have had many formative experiences gained during extended periods living in post-Soviet households that drove our curiosity to understand the role played by informal economies in everyday life. For example, on arrival in Russia to conduct his doctoral research on the coping practices of senior citizens in Russia, one of the authors of this book opened the front door on his first morning in Russia and found a large jar of caviar on the doorstep. When he asked the owner of the apartment what it was doing there, he was told that it was in return for a favour. That evening as the owner was leaving the flat he said 'I am just going out to pay my "tax" (i.e. an informal payment) to get out of military service.' Such first impressions of post-Soviet everyday life have been formative in realising the important role that informal economies play in daily life and have provided the motivation to want to conduct the research for this book.

It was, however, only some years later that we began our more 'formal' research into the role that informal economies play in livelihood practices in the post-Soviet world. Between 2005 and 2007 both quantitative and qualitative empirical research was undertaken into this phenomenon. On the one hand, this involved a structured questionnaire conducted on a face-to-face basis at the household level with 600 participants in Ukraine and 313 participants in Moscow. On the other hand, it involved some 75 follow-up semi-structured qualitative interviews across the two countries, with participants selected using maximum variation sampling in order to gain a richer and more textured understanding of the role informal economies play in livelihood practices. The Ukraine research, it must be mentioned, was funded by the Economic and Social Research Council (ESRC), while the funding to replicate the research in Moscow was provided by the School of Management at the University of Leicester. The findings reported in this book are from this fieldwork, the methodology of which will be introduced in greater depth in Chapter 4. Since 2007 when this quantitative and qualitative research was completed, a further 96 in-depth face-to-face interviews have been conducted in Ukraine and Russia between 2008 and 2012, mostly in order to bring greater clarity to our understanding of the role played by informal economies in livelihood practices in these countries. The opportunity to conduct these 96 in-depth interviews has arisen, it should be stated, because one of the authors had being living in Ukraine for almost three years up until 2011, while another of the authors has spent the last two years since 2011 living and working on a full-time basis in Moscow.

Indeed, these extended periods living and working in Ukraine and Moscow between 2008 and the present day have provided the opportunity for a great deal of ethnographic observation to be undertaken to further understand the role played by informal economies in daily life. To take just one small example of how ethnographic observation becomes an inherent part of daily life when living in post-Soviet societies and an integral part of the research process, we here recount a recent experience on the Moscow metro. While queuing to buy a metro ticket at a local station during 2011, one of the authors observed that a large number of people were seemingly shaking hands with an elderly woman overseeing the barriers. It became clear that what was actually happening was that money was being given to the woman who was then letting people through without a ticket. When the author tried to instigate this transaction himself, much to his embarrassment, it was refused. Somewhat red-faced, he returned to the back of the queue to purchase his metro ticket and when he later recounted this story to a local resident, it turned out that the woman working the metro station was an acquaintance of the resident and she arranged for the author to have an interview with her so he could understand this practice.

On interviewing her, it turned out that her wage was so low, she argued, that she had no choice but to take money in this manner and that those paying her were getting a cheaper ride on the metro (tickets are not required to exit the system), but she only did so with those she knew and trusted. She then went on to discuss that she could not survive on her official salary as she had to pay for medicines that were supposed to be free, that her apartment was in a poor condition and that she had to pay for someone to undertake the repairs. She also highlighted how the builders employed to do the repairs for her were also being paid in cash, as were those being sub-contracted by them to do some of the work in her home, such as the electricians. Indeed, she even offered to arrange an interview with them if the author so desired. From this single ethnographic observation, therefore, not only did an interview eventually result, but also a much deeper understanding of the role of informal economic activity, the motivations underpinning it and the social relations involved.

This example, furthermore, highlights another important point regarding research on the role played by informal economies. While it might be assumed by those who have not engaged in research on this phenomenon that people will be reticent about discussing such practices, given that there is illegality involved, the opposite is more often than not the case. As Round (2006) discusses, the interviewees often take great pride in discussing the practices they engage in as these practices enable the household to cope in the face of perceived government indifference, and the participants are therefore often more than willing to discuss them in-depth (see also Pavlovskaya 2004). We found the same in the research for this book. Far from displaying any reticence, the participants often took great pride in telling us about their exploits and how they managed to secure a livelihood using a multiplicity of informal practices.

It is also important to state that by living in the areas in which the fieldwork has been conducted, this has enabled not only a diverse variety of observations to be made, but also for trust to be built up with many of the residents in the localities. Indeed, over time, living in many of the districts studied has resulted in friendships being made with potential participants in the research, and although we have been open about our role as academics, care has had to be taken with respect to how we have dealt with casual conversations about this phenomenon. As a general rule, information gained from such casual conversations has not been included in the findings reported in this book. However, if something extremely relevant was mentioned during casual conversation, then afterwards permission has been asked regarding whether we could include it in our research findings for this book. Nevertheless, it is impossible to forget things one has heard in casual conversation, and on some occasions these conversations have provided the basis for lines of questioning during more formal interviews with others as our knowledge of the role informal economic practices play in everyday life in these countries has improved (for further discussion of this issue, see Essers 2009).

It also needs to be pointed out that some of the interviews conducted for this book have been at times emotionally challenging for the researchers. There have been numerous discussions of upsetting events, especially with regards to the informal payments required in the healthcare system as discussed in Chapter 5, and there also have been times when the participants saw the authors as 'privileged' western academics and therefore capable of resolving various problems with the state for them. These have proven very difficult situations to negotiate and sometimes interviews could not continue because of the assumptions of the interviewee (for further discussion on the emotional impact of such research, see Lee and Lee 2012 or Dickson-Swift *et al.* 2007). The overall lesson, nevertheless, from conducting research over a seven-year time span for this book is that despite the popular assumption that it is difficult to talk to people about the role played by informal economic practices in securing a livelihood, this has not been found to be the case in the post-Soviet countries we have studied. As will become apparent throughout this book, participants have been not only open with us about the informal economic practices they undertake, but have sometimes gone to great lengths to help us understand how such practices are used by them to secure a livelihood.

Structure of the book

In order to understand the role that informal economic practices play in securing a livelihood in post-Soviet spaces, Part I provides the theoretical and conceptual framework for understanding this issue. In Chapter 2 we revisit the recurring question of transition in order to dispute not only the past hegemony of the command economy system, but also the notion that there is a universal linear trajectory of development in post-Soviet spaces towards a hegemonic formal market economy system as some end point. Instead, we call for a more nuanced argument to be adopted that recognises the transformation of post-Soviet economies in different ways from different starting points and along different economic development trajectories. This is reinforced in Chapter 3. This re-theorises the 'economic' by providing evidence of the shallow and uneven permeation of the formal market economy in the post-Soviet/socialist world and the persistence of informal economic practices. Given the recognition of the persistence of informal economic activities in these societies, Chapter 4 then outlines an analytical lens for capturing the plurality of labour practices that exist in post-Soviet societies and applies this to understanding the multifarious labour practices used in Ukraine and Russia. The outcome will be to begin to reveal not only the shallow permeation of the formal market economy in Ukraine and Russia that have been supposedly undergoing a 'transition' to formal market economies, but also the existence of diverse work cultures across different populations along with marked socio-spatial variations in the nature of individual labour practices.

This sets the scene for Part II of the book, which unravels the lived experiences of transition in these post-Soviet societies. To begin to develop a deeper understanding of these socio-spatial variations in individual labour practices, each of the eight spheres of labour used in post-Soviet societies are then reviewed in turn. Chapter 5 examines formal employment and, more precisely, how in post-Soviet societies the formal economy is so infused with informality that it is difficult, if not impossible, to differentiate formal and informal labour practices. Chapter 6 then evaluates the role played by informal employment in securing a livelihood in post-Soviet societies; Chapter 7 investigates the roles played by paid favours, reimbursed family work and one-to-one unpaid labour; Chapter 8 evaluates two forms of labour practice that have been seldom, if ever, before considered, namely formal unpaid employment and informal unpaid employment; while Chapter 9 evaluates the prominent role played by self-provisioning. Chapter 10 then pulls the findings together to provide an overview of the prominent role played by informal economies in the post-Soviet world and the implications of this for re-theorising not only the process of 'transition' but also the 'economic'. The outcome will be to show that it is not only time to move beyond the assumption of the impending hegemony of the formal market economy by recognising the persistence and importance of other labour practices in securing a livelihood, but also to open up the future to the possibility of alternative economic futures beyond market hegemony in post-Soviet spaces.

Part I

(Re)theorising transition economies

2 Re-visiting the recurring question of transition

Everything the Communists told us about communism was a complete and utter lie. Unfortunately, everything the Communists told us about capitalism turned out to be true.

A popular joke in Moscow during the early 1990s, as recounted by John Nelis, then of the World Bank

Introduction: the durability of transition theory

All forms of economic reform led by global institutions are, at their heart, aimed at marketisation. The creation, or realigning, of economies towards the market has been the cornerstone of meta-global policy from Latin America in the early 1980s, to Eastern Europe later in the decade, in the post-Soviet states during the 1990s and to the responses to Europe's financial crisis from 2008 onwards. This is because there is a fundamental belief that market-led reforms such as the deregulation of the economy, the withdrawal of state involvement and the opening up of the market will lead to both growth and a 'trickle down' of the benefits to the majority. In return for financial assistance from organisations such as the International Monetary Fund (IMF), often desperately needed to pay debt obligations or social welfare transfers such as pensions, countries agree to wide-ranging market-oriented reforms. Almost always the reforms involve measures such as the privatisation of state assets, the liberalisation of the economy, deregulation and austerity.

From the mid-1980s, states undertaking such reforms came to be known as 'transition' countries as they were moving from one economic system, be it from military-based governance, a command economy or a mismanaged state heading towards bankruptcy, towards a market economy. In other words, they were transiting from one economic form to another, with a starting and an end point when the reforms are complete. The role of this chapter is to provide a critique of the notion of transition, concentrating on three interlocking points. First, the very idea of transition is extremely flawed as it suggests that the concept of the perfectly working market economy actually exists outside of the textbook (for a discussion on the varieties of capitalism in operation, see Lane 2007). From this, therefore, there is an end point at which reforms will be complete. It also suggests that all starting points are the same, and that economic geographies and histories are irrelevant. Second, the social costs of such reforms are almost always ignored. While there is an acknowledgement that there will be short-term social 'costs', it is assumed that as the market develops, the majority will benefit. As this book shows, depending on the criteria you take, this is simply not the case. Finally, and perhaps most importantly, the role of informal practices within everyday life is simply not acknowledged in such reforms. This is the case at all scales, be it the practices used by business people to grab the benefits of privatisation schemes or the informal coping practices used in everyday life by the economically marginalised.

Given that within the social sciences there has been considerable critique of transition theory, it might seem that the book is setting up a 'straw man' to knock down. Here, therefore, it is important to demonstrate why discussions on its use are still of vital importance to understanding everyday life in post-Soviet spaces and the nature of informal practices. Pickles and Smith (1998: 2) were among the first to develop a systemic critique of transition theory. As they state,

> Transition is not a one-way process of change from one hegemonic system to another. Rather, transition constitutes a complex reworking of old social relations in the light of processes distinct to one of the boldest projects in contemporary history – the attempt to construct a form of capitalism on and with the ruins of the communist system.

Key within this quote is the notion that transition is based on the ruin and relations of the old system, which vary according to location, and that the economies that emerged were a *form* of market economies. Such theorisations became extremely influential in studies of economic reform and understanding the practices of everyday life (e.g. Golubchikov and Phelps 2011; Pavlovskaya 2004; Round *et al.* 2010; Smith and Swain 2010; Stenning and Hörschelmann 2008; Yeung and Lin 2003). These discussions led to re-theorisations of the form of economy that has developed within post-Soviet states rather than the textbook market system springing 'forth like a *deus ex machina*' (Burawoy 1998: 303), as displayed by discussions of systems of 'economic involution' (Burawoy *et al.* 2000), 'chaotic capitalism' (Lane 2000), 'hybrid' capitalism (Hanson and Teague 2007), 'anti-modern' economies (Rose 2009) or a 'virtual economy' (Gaddy and Ickes 1998). When discussing the 'varieties of capitalism' that have developed in post-Soviet spaces, Pickles (2008: 6) states in relation to 'transition theory':

> From the side of cultural studies, social theory, post-structuralism and post-colonialism, contemporary social sciences are now suspicious of the use of meta-narratives to explain social and economic processes, and political economy itself has developed a thorough-going critique of transitology.

From such rejections of meta-narratives, the term transformation has come to be used as a more nuanced term to describe and theorise reforming economies as it recognises that there are a multitude of starting points and that there is no fixed, pre-determined outcome. In other words, and as the current economic crisis amply demonstrates, we simply do not know the future for economic systems, growth or behaviour.

However, the concept of transition is still widely used in economics and management studies (e.g. Aristei and Perugini 2012; Bruck and Lehmann 2012; Frye 2011; Lehmann and Muravyev 2012; O'Brien *et al.* 2011; Perlman and Balabanova 2011; Turley and Luke 2010; Winiecki 2012), especially in relation to the economies of former socialist countries. Its uncritical usage within economics is particularly problematic as it is from such studies that the policies of international lending agencies are based. This is primarily because of the continuing assumption that economic behaviour can be modelled (Morgan and Knuuttila 2012) and that reforms and economic development can be measured quantitatively (Fine and Milonakis 2011). Therefore, it was possible for the deputy director of the IMF to state in July 2012 that Eastern and Central Europe 'has been through a lot in the last two decades. It has successfully transitioned from planned to market economy' (Shafik 2012: 1).

The European Bank for Reconstruction and Development (EBRD), set up in 1991 to assist the former Soviet and socialist countries in the reform process, has a journal called *Economics of Transition* which states on its opening page that it 'fosters transition to market economies in countries from central and eastern Europe to central Asia and north Africa'. The inclusion of north Africa in this statement demonstrates further why critiques of transition theory are still relevant today. Even though, as shown above, there is a whole body of work highlighting the term's problematic nature, it continues to be applied to regions undergoing socio-economic crisis (Saif 2011). The director of the IMF's Middle East and Central Asia Department, Masood Ahmed (2012), for example, talks about financial support for Arab countries in 'transition'. Such discussions are more nuanced than the approach taken towards Russia, for example, in 1991, but are still couched in terms of the transition to the neo-liberal democratic market economy. Within such discussions, other forms of economic development, based on, for example, religious beliefs or alternative economic practices, are not even allowed space for discussion.

Such thinking is also evident in approaches aimed at solving Europe's current economic crisis. In the mid-2000s, a discussion emerged about whether large organisations such as the IMF were still needed, given economic growth in many regions and the ability of private financial institutions to provide lending facilities to states (Maier 2007). Obviously the banking crisis and the subsequent recession in many mature economies led to such thinking being quickly abandoned. The IMF again came to global prominence, providing loans to Greece, for example, in order to insure against the default on sovereign debt. In return for such loans, recipients have to undertake stringent austerity measures, deregulate their economy and reduce social protection obligations (Katsimi and Moutos 2010; Matsaganis 2012). In other words, they have to transit their economy to the textbook neo-liberal market economy ideal. Thus, two decades after the socially disastrous reforms began in Russia, the same approaches are now being seen within the EU, signalling how the study of transition theory remains pertinent today. The remainder of this chapter details how economic reform was enacted in Russia and Ukraine, demonstrating the short-sightedness of the transition approach and the resulting diverse economies that arose.

The Soviet Union and its informal economies

It is common that the Soviet Union's command economy is presented as a monolith, with the state in control of all of its functions (Rutland 2009). However, as Ledeneva (2006: 1) states,

> The Soviet system was not a planned economy. It was meant to be, but those living within its borders found that they had to counteract its over-centralization and its ideological limitations through intricate schemes of informal exchange, regional and industrial lobbying, and a variety of practices for cheating the system.

There were also marked geographical variations in how the command economy was enacted. As many commentators highlight, the countries that formed the command economy all had different starting points from, for example, the relatively industrialised Czech Republic to the mainly agricultural Russia and Ukraine (Pickles and Smith 1998; Round 2009; Smith 2000; Verdery 1991). Within the system, Moscow had dominance and different regions of the Union were given prominence in different sectors, such as food production in Ukraine and agricultural machinery production in Belarus (Shaw 1999; Sokol 2001). Five-year plans were produced, to which each enterprise had to adhere, despite Moscow having imperfect information about local conditions, such as which land was suited to different types of agricultural production (Shmelev and Popov 1990). As Davies (2001) states, massive divisions existed between ministries who were competing for resources and power within the government, rather than working for a common social good, and overall there was not a culture of innovation (Berliner 1978). The lack of investment in mass communications and information technology made it increasingly difficult for the centre to know what its branches were doing (Colton 1986), and often managers would simply falsify information to be sent to Moscow (Anderson and Boettke 1997). As Ledeneva (2006) states, the system could be cheated in many ways.

In short, the system did not work as planned, there were huge geographical differences within it and it was not able to move towards intensive modes of production (Ofer 1987). Furthermore, and as McAuley (1979) notes, there were wide differences in pay within the Soviet Union, which belied the system's commitment to equal reward for labour (Round 2006). Overall, the command economy operated differently to the way suggested in textbooks and there were significant variations within it.

Officially, poverty could not exist within the Soviet system as this would undermine the ideological superiority of the socialist system (Matthews 1986).

Furthermore, as those of working age were, unless categorised as unable to work, legally bound to undertake paid employment and as the state, through enterprises, provided a comprehensive 'cradle to the grave' welfare system (Ashwin 1999), it would have been a major failing of the system if poverty did exist. It was commonplace in the early literature examining post-Soviet social marginalisation to state that poverty was at a very low level at the Soviet Union's collapse, with often the Goskomstat figure of 1.8 per cent of the population living in poverty in 1991 cited when comparisons are made to post-Soviet levels of poverty (Klugman and Braithwaite 1998). However, the reality was markedly different. In the early Soviet period, 60,000 families were monitored and analysts were allowed to publish material from the data. However, in the late 1920s this was stopped and words such as poverty and slum were officially banned (Matthews 1986). This is not to say that the Soviet authorities were not aware of the problems of everyday life and the term 'under provisioning' was coined as a more ideologically palatable alternative to 'poverty' (Round and Kosterina 2005). Under this schema, which was only introduced in the early 1970s, social transfers were made to those whose household income was below a certain level, mainly those with more than one child. It was, of course, extremely difficult given the secrecy and lack of data on the issue to ascertain a true poverty figure for the Soviet Union. Sarkisyan and Kuznetsova (1964) calculated that the average household income with two workers was 178 roubles per month. For a family with two children, the subsistence figure was 205 roubles per month, suggesting that the average family would be experiencing serious economic marginalisation.

As Mathews (1986: 2) asserted, 'Soviet poverty is nothing like Third World poverty but its scope is breathtaking.' He discusses how the state calculated that the average Soviet household spent 3 per cent of their income on housing. However, surveys of émigrés suggested that the figure was closer to 10 per cent. Sarkisyan and Kuznetsova (1964) discuss how as many as 20 per cent of the population did not have a suitable winter coat, and points out that the true cost of household repairs were far above the state-set costs, which meant many struggled to make such repairs. Matthews' (1967) émigré survey saw 45 per cent reporting that they had seen people begging. Estimations of realistic Soviet poverty levels, understandably, vary greatly. Urlanis (1966) noted that only 3.8 per cent of single people and 5 per cent of couples without children could be considered poor, but 21 per cent of families with children and 25 per cent of single-parent families. Rimashevskaya (2006: 120) suggests the level was even higher when she states: 'Our studies showed that in the late 1960s the share of under-provisioned ('poor') made 29.7% of the total population, in the late 1970s 32.1%, and in the late 1980s 38.9%.'

What is clear is that given the closeness of the average wage and the poverty line, many families lived extremely close to economic marginalisation (Rimashevskaya and Onikov 1977). Compounding this situation was the shortage of food and consumer goods. As Alexeev (1986) notes, the need to queue for goods was an alternative form of inflation. As the state controlled prices, their cost could not reflect their demand and thus people had to queue for them (Nordhaus 1990). Most anthropological work on the Soviet era notes the role of the queue and the time that, mostly women, had to devote to securing enough food for the household (Bogdanov 2012; Humphrey 2002; Shevchenko 2009). While there is no data available for the amount of time that was spent queuing, interviewees for this book who were old enough to do so during the Soviet period all discussed how it was a major drain on their time. As one interviewee said,

> After a day at work and a long journey home I had to pick up the children from their grandparents and then begin to think about preparing dinner. Even though we both had to work my husband did very little around the house and rarely shopped or cooked. I would almost every day have to queue for the most simplest of products. It was extremely tiring and frustrating.

Shortages were not confined to food, with the vast majority of consumer goods, from clothing to windscreen wipers, in short supply (Morton 1980). As Ledeneva (1998: 28) states, from personal experience, queues were an 'omnipresent' part of everyday life. Therefore, it was commonplace in the Soviet Union for households to suffer from both economic marginalisation and a shortage of goods. To cope, they often turned to the informal economy.

Informality in the former Soviet Union

It is somewhat of a cliché that the Soviet Union was typified by high levels of state control of the everyday. However, managers at all levels realised that if serious attempts were made to constrain the informal economy, then social unrest would soon follow (Matthews 1967). Although it is difficult in all economies to ascertain the size of the informal sector, this was especially difficult in the Soviet Union as it officially did not exist and there were strict controls on the forms of research that academics could undertake (Weinberg 1974). It is clear, however, that informal practices were an extremely important part of everyday life and were culturally different to informal practices in market economies.

First, informal practices were often undertaken for free, or for exchange, as money had relatively little value given the shortage of goods to purchase. It was much more important to have a wide network of friends and acquaintances that could be called upon in a time of need, and a commonly heard phrase at the time was 'it is better to have a hundred friends than a hundred roubles'. The Russian term for this use of connections is *blat*, which implies an obligation to repay the favour when someone has helped you, such as when they need assistance to acquire a good or service (Ledeneva 2006). The second difference between informal practices in Soviet compared with western economies was its omnipresent nature. Ledeneva (2008: 123) discusses how *blat* was needed to negotiate almost all aspects of life, from the 'everyday' such as obtaining food, through 'periodical events' such as holidays and 'life-cycle' events such as obtaining kindergarten places, to helping others. As she states, 'blat were required to satisfy all four types of needs. Their pervasive use as a "safety-net" or "survival kit" made involvement in informal practices compulsory rather than voluntary' (Ledeneva 2008: 123).

Grossman (1977) argues that the need to engage in the informal economy increased as economic stagnation took hold of the Soviet economy from the early 1970s. Although *blat* was extremely important to everyday life, there were also instances of informal work undertaken for cash in hand. The majority of such work was nominally illegal as only certain practices were allowed under Soviet law, such as the sale of domestically grown food, tutoring and the repairing of clothes. Wage labour for other activities and individuals was not permitted and nor was the buying and reselling of goods for profit. Using Soviet family budget surveys and national accounts, Kim (2003) estimates that between 1969 and 1990 the average percentage of informal income as a proportion of total income was 16.3 per cent. This he notes equated to 6.8 per cent of Soviet GNP and that there were sizable differences in informal activity between Soviet states. Bartlett (1990) suggests that the figures were even higher, ranging from 38 per cent in Soviet Russia to 67 per cent in Belarus. In the sphere of housing, O'Hearn (1980) estimates that 70 per cent of home repairs were conducted in the informal economy. Therefore, it is clear that the informal economy was a key part of Soviet life.

A sizable share of informal work was undertaken through the workplace. This took the form of either stealing products for exchange within *blat* networks (Sampson 1987) or using company time to undertake informal work or to queue for goods (Ashwin and Clarke 2003; Gregory 1987; Zaslavskaia 1987). The state turned a blind eye to such practices because, as Sampson (1987: 120) notes, 'The second economy helps to alleviate consumer shortages and bureaucratic bottlenecks in all these societies. It also acts as a social mollifier, channelling dangerous political frustrations into consumerism, swindling, or petty corruption.'

Furthermore, as Harrison (2002) notes, there simply was not the capability or capacity within the state system to monitor it effectively. Thus, the state had the choice of either spending enormous resources on monitoring systems, or accepting that there would be theft. Given the Soviet Union's economic slowdown, the former was never a realistic option. Both Kiblitskaya (2000) and Ashwin (1998) discuss how the shortage of skilled labour also empowered workers, allowing them to be absent in the knowledge that their employer could not afford to dismiss them. Such practices led to the oft-heard phrase 'you pretend to pay us and we pretend to work', indicating the almost tacit bargain that as long as workers were there when plans needed to be fulfilled, managers would turn a blind eye to informal practices during quieter periods. Labour turnover was high as workers moved between enterprises looking for the most favourable conditions, both in terms of pay and benefits, but also for *blat* opportunities. Gregory and Stuart (1994) estimate that approximately 20 per cent of the workforce changed employment per year, with those who moved often in search of informal opportunities termed 'rolling stones'.

People interviewed during the course of the fieldwork for this book who had worked in the late Soviet period all recounted how they had to spend increasing amounts of time acting informally as consumer shortages increased. As one asserted,

> It seemed like we were spending all of our time either queuing for things or doing work and favours for people in return for goods. It would be for really simple things such as meat or washing powder but there was no other way of getting the things we needed. Of course sometimes I did work for cash in hand as it was always nice to be able to buy a beer but overall it was a lot of work for simple things.

There are many reasons why the Soviet Union and the state collapsed, but there is little doubt that the form of its economy was a significant cause (Åslund 1995; Beissinger 2002; Graham 1993; Sakwa 1999; Suny 1994). As Sampson (1987) perceptively noted, tolerating such high levels of informal activity for social reasons did not help the formal economy in the long term as it only replicated its problems. What is also clear is that the Soviet Union's economic form at its collapse was a long way from the textbook definition of a command economy. Informal practices were rife and there were wide geographical variations in both the formal and informal spheres across the Union. Therefore, it is possible to state that as the Soviet Union collapsed, there was not a single point from which the move towards a market economy began, but rather a multitude of histories, geographies, legacies and competing practices.

The Soviet Union's collapse and the rise of the Washington Consensus

While there were myriad reasons for the Soviet Union's collapse, the rapidity of its disintegration was a surprise (Strayer 1998), despite the plans for radical economic reform developed in the late 1980s, such as Shatlin and Yavlinsky's '500-day plan' aimed at the economy's liberalisation. The failure of the command economy was met with triumphalism among western politicians and economists and was, now infamously, declared as the 'end of history' as it demonstrated the superiority and inevitability of the western neo-liberal economic model (Fukuyama 1992). As Wedel (2001: 2) notes 'The thinking of the day was that "we" had a once in a lifetime window of opportunity to effect change', and post-Soviet states were now seen as a *tabula rasa* from which it was expected that a market economy would 'spring forth like a *deus ex machina*' (Burawoy 1998: 303).

As well as demonstrating the west's economic superiority, the collapse was also seen as an ideological vindication for the Cold War. Therefore, it was seen as crucial that in the newly independent states, and especially in Russia, given its leading role in the Soviet Union and its nuclear capability, that the communists could not come back into power at any cost. The Soviet collapse was also seen as an opportunity for western firms. It was assumed that new, lucrative markets would open up in Russia's resource-rich regions and that it represented a 'wild frontier' ripe for exploitation (Freeland 2000; Sidaway and Power 1995). However, while espousing free-market rhetoric towards the east, western countries were rapidly erecting barriers to ensure that their markets were not flooded with cheap imports from the former Soviet republics (Christiansen *et al.*, 2000).

How, though, could a market economy be created in the post-Soviet spaces? As Stenning (2005) notes, there were numerous implausible internal plans to transit to the market within 100 days of the Soviet Union's collapse. However, given the political turmoil, together with the economic crisis engulfing the region, outside assistance was always going to be required. From 1989, the countries of Eastern Europe had been moving towards market-based systems with the assistance of organisations such as the World Bank and IMF (Rodrik 2006). The policy prescriptions broadly followed those which had been implemented earlier in the decade in South American countries such as Argentina and Brazil in attempts to reduce budget deficits, liberalise economies and encourage privatisation. The package of policies were termed the Washington Consensus as they were ideologically led, as well as financed and consulted upon, by US economic officials and the IMF and World Bank, all of whom are based in Washington (Stiglitz 1998). Williamson (2009), who is credited as the first to use the term in 1989 before a congressional hearing, stated that the consensus coalesced around ten points regarding how economies should be reformed: fiscal discipline; the reordering of public expenditure priorities; tax reform; liberalising interest rates; a competitive exchange rate; trade liberalisation; the liberalisation of inward foreign direct investment; privatisation; deregulation; and secure property rights. In short, the state should divest itself of control of the economy and countries should open up to international competition. In return for loans, which were desperately needed to pay social benefits, recipient countries had to agree to undertake reforms based around these ten points.

Given the reforms' relative economic success in South America, it was 'logical' that they be transposed onto the newly independent countries of Eastern and Central Europe (Lane 2007; Rodrik 2006). As Gabrisch and Hoslscher (2006) note, the political reforms of the time were looking for an economic basis and the Washington Consensus provided this. With Central and Eastern Europe undertaking the above-mentioned reforms, it was again 'logical' that as the Soviet Union collapsed and began desperately to look for new economic forms and financial support, that the Washington Consensus move even further east (Kolodko 1999; Solimano 1998; Smith and Swain 1998). As noted above, western economic thinking on the reform of centrally planned economies ignored their diversity and thus reforms were introduced in a blanket fashion (McCleery and De Paolis 2008; Suzuki 2001). For example, Poland had experience of the market economy prior to its submergence into the socialist system. Therefore, when it began its move towards the market it had legislation that it could immediately re-enact. While such legislation was not ideal, it provided a basis around which market-based relations such as property rights could be developed. Such countries were thus able to adopt a market framework very quickly, whereas in Russia and elsewhere across the former Soviet Union, such institutions had to be developed from scratch.

This would be difficult enough under normal circumstances, but given the political turmoil, economic collapse and the developing oligarchy who wished to steer institutional development to their benefit, it was an almost impossible task (Wedal 1998). Notwithstanding this, Russia began the reform process based around the 'four pillars of transition' (Gros and Steinherr 1995; Round 2009), namely:

1 Liberalisation:

- The freeing of the economy from state control and political influence. The state can no longer dictate what, where and how much is produced or where it can be sold.
- Prices are to be determined by the laws of supply and demand. Subsidies on goods must be removed and prices for services brought into line with world levels.
- Regional subsidies must be curtailed.
- The use of barter between enterprises should be eliminated.

2 Stabilisation:

- As the state withdraws from the economy it must also curb its expenditure. This entails a reduction in the size of the state apparatus and a decrease in spending on social safety nets.
- The state should avoid excessive borrowing and living beyond its means.
- It should implement a strict monetary policy to control inflation and create a stable currency.
- Myriad laws are implemented for the whole system to work, making it an extremely complex and time-consuming process.

3 Privatisation:

- The state must divest itself of ownership of the means of production. This is to be achieved through privatisation schemes, open to both foreign and internal competition.
- The state should create conditions for the formation of new private enterprises.
- It is preferable that employees have the opportunity to become stakeholders in their enterprises through voucher privatisation schemes.
- Monopolies are to be dismantled.

4 Internationalisation:

- The domestic economy must be opened up to international competition.
- Conditions must be created to encourage foreign investment, such as legal norms, property rights and a trust culture.

- International standards for accounting, custom duties and tax must be developed.
- A stable, convertible currency must be introduced.

Perhaps the biggest ideological issue was the timing of the reforms. Gradual reforms, and continued state involvement in the economy, would protect the population from the worst impacts of economic reforms, known as the 'Chinese model' (Burawoy 1996). However, this was rejected by the reformers primarily because of a concern that if the reforms were not enacted as a 'big bang', then the communists would be voted back into power by an electorate disaffected by the social outcomes of transition (Burawoy and Verdery 1999). Furthermore, as Stenning (2005) states, it was assumed that every aspect of the Soviet system would have to be disregarded.

The focus of both domestic and international policy was on erasing and ignoring the institutions, practices and geographies of socialism, which were deemed to have failed, and building a new social, economic and political system 'from scratch'. Such approaches rested on viewing East-Central Europe and the former Soviet Union as a *tabula rasa*, primed for 'capitalism by design'. It was assumed that the power of the market would automatically lead to the rapid rise of the institutions, regulations, cultures and practices that are necessary for the efficient functioning of a neo-liberal market (Smith and Swain 1998). Even the most optimistic of reformers acknowledged that there would be considerable social costs. However, they assumed that it would only be temporary and that economic growth would bring prosperity to the majority in a short space of time (for critiques of such approaches, see Berardi 2001; Escobar 1995; Pender 2001). However, as Crisp and Kelly (1999: 534) state:

> Regardless of their macroeconomic results, the burden of adjustment would be borne disproportionately by the poorest sectors of developing societies. The removal of price supports, declining exchange rates, diminishing government spending, and loss of public employment all impacted the poor inordinately. Government price controls and purchasing subsidies usually focused on energy and foodstuffs, which are relatively large parts of people's budgets.

The Russian 'big bang' was enacted in January 1992 and the social impacts were immediate. In Russia price liberalisation led to hyperinflation, over 2,600 per cent in 1992, wiping out savings and real incomes and wages and social transfers went unpaid for extended periods. Concurrently, life expectancy for men fell from 64 to 58 years old within a decade, with suicide, murder and alcohol abuse rates all soaring (Syrinov 2003). Ukraine suffered arguably even more severe impacts, as by 1993 inflation had reached almost 10,000 per cent per annum (Åslund 2002), again destroying savings and real wages; and, epitomising the chaos, it was not until 1996 that the first post-Soviet bank notes were introduced (Wilson 2005). As one Ukrainian interviewee recalled,

> I just cannot imagine now how we survived. Our wages were worthless a day after we received them. We just went and bought whatever we could whenever we had money whether we needed it or not. We did not know from one day to the next what was going to happen, it was complete chaos. We did not know if we would be able to feed our children. As the changes were happening so quickly we could not even begin to understand what was happening, all we were concerned with was surviving.

Given the complexity, unpopularity, scale and general chaos surrounding the reforms, it is no surprise that the 'big bang' was only partially enacted. As noted above, price liberalisation was introduced, but in both Russia and Ukraine, regional governments attempted to control prices and subsidies remained in place in order to provide some form of social protection (Koen and Phillips 1992). Attempts at macro-stabilisation were deeply flawed, with money supply constricted simply by not paying state employees, suppliers or pensions, with the failure to enforce hard budget constraints allowing bankrupt enterprises to continue operating (Broadman 1998; Freeland 2000; Hoffman 2011). Internationalisation was also stymied as foreign trade and investment remained heavily regulated and the financing of imports by export credits and foreign investment regulations were at best opaque.

On one level it seemed as if Russia's privatisation schemes were successful. By the end of 1992, over 60,000 enterprises were privately owned, compared with only 70 in 1991, and by the end of the following year two-thirds of all state assets had been transferred to private enterprises. However, as Wedel (2001), Lane (2000), Hoffman (2011) and Freeland (2000) all discuss at length, the privatisation processes were deeply flawed and the main concern was the divestiture of assets to ensure the communists could not return to power. To whom, how and for how much the assets were sold was of secondary concern. This was crucial as the reforms' increasing unpopularity saw communist politicians, sensing that they might be able to regain power, withdrawing their support for the process, and by the end of 1992 it appeared that the reform process would grind to a halt. It was only revived when Yeltsin won a nationwide referendum on his position and policies in 1993, though gaining only 53 per cent support for the reform process (Åslund 2011). However, the Russian government was at this point effectively economically bankrupt. In order to pay wages and pensions it borrowed money from Russian entrepreneurs in return for the lender 'managing' the enterprises that were exploiting the country's natural resources. As the government was unable to repay, the 'loans became shares' and control of the country's natural resources was passed to a new oligarch class (Freeland 2000). This led to the creation of, rather than a market economy, what has been variously described as systems of 'economic involution' (Burawoy *et al.* 2000), 'chaotic capitalism' (Lane 2000), 'virtual economies' (Gaddy and Ickes 1998) and 'a Weberian political capitalism' (Hanson and Teague 2007). These are rather different to visions of the 'messianic reforms' that were implemented in the early 1990s with the faith that market reform would occur (Burawoy 2001).

The end of transition?

Despite this variety of capitalisms developing in former socialist and Soviet countries (Lane 2007), the international economic community still felt able to ascertain whether they had 'achieved' market status. Åslund (2007: 277) argues that the 'empirical evidence is strong' that Russia 'became a market economy after a couple of years of transition'. He argues (emphasis added) that

> The most relevant measure of a country's degree of market economy is the EBRD's transition index, ranking countries from no market economy (0) to a *normal Western* market economy (1). From 1992 to 1995, Russia was an intermediary market economy, in the interval 0.5–0.7, and in 1996 it reached 0.7, the level of a full-fledged market economy.
>
> (Åslund 2007: 278)

Language such as 'normal Western' reiterates the notion that the transition project assumed that post-Soviet states should become more like the west, despite the many varieties of capitalism they could have followed. It is quite incredible that a country with an inflation rate of approximately 2,500 per cent, as Russia endured in 1992, could be classed as 'an intermediary market economy'. The EBRD (2012) produces scorecards on transition indicators, macroeconomic indicators, structural change indicators, transition development snapshots and now uses a range of 1 to 4+ 'where 1 represents little or no change from a rigid centrally planned economy and 4+ represents the standards of an industrialised market economy'. Large-scale privatisation, for example, is measured thus:

1 little private ownership;
2 comprehensive scheme almost ready for implementation – some sales completed;
3 more than 25 per cent of large-scale enterprise assets in private hands or in the process of being privatised (with the process having reached a stage at which the state has effectively ceded its ownership rights), but possibly with major unresolved issues regarding corporate governance;
4 more than 50 per cent of state-owned enterprise and farm assets in private ownership and significant progress with corporate governance of these enterprises;
4+ standards and performance typical of advanced industrial economies – more than 75 per cent of enterprise assets in private ownership with effective corporate governance.

Russia is currently rated at 3, as is Ukraine (EBRD 2011), which recognises the issues surrounding corporate governance in both countries. However, in the mid-1990s the former enjoyed a rating of 4. The issue here is that while such rankings provide interesting comparisons between countries, they reveal little about the actual workings of the processes and practices they rank. As Myant and Drahokoupil (2012: 71) note,

> the EBRD was quick to give a positive assessment to the Russian and Czech Republic voucher privatizations (scores of 4 and 3, respectively, by 1994), implicitly praising the speed of transformation into formally private ownership, but overlooking the negative consequences. In both cases, the results of voucher privatization were chaotic ownership structures in which large sums of money could be made and exported without creating a viable business structure.

There is nothing in such ratings about the scale and nature of informal practices and almost nothing about the social impacts of the reforms. The main reflections on social change can be found in the 'transition development snapshots' which look at expenditure on health and education as a share of GDP, household spending on power and water and poverty levels. While all are problematic, the latter is particularly so; for both Russia and Ukraine the poverty levels are stated as 3.7 per cent. This figure seems impressive until the methodology is revealed, as it is based on the UN's $2 per day calculations. For Russia this equates to approximately 1,900 roubles per month, which is three times lower than the already unrealistic state subsistence minimum figure, and therefore has no relevance at all to realistic conceptualisations of poverty in Russia.

Why does this matter? First, such rankings reiterate that there is an end point to reforms, that transition is complete when a certain 'score' is reached. Indeed, the authors of this book were in Ukraine when the EU bestowed market economy status on the country, after it met certain quantitative criteria (Kuzio 2006). This was met with some bemusement from interviewees at the time who saw on a daily basis that their economic practices were often far from the market. The market status was erroneously used by the state to imply that EU membership could be achieved soon, a powerful political tool among voters. Such statements were popular but not as popular as the government thought. Rather than reflecting the progress the country was making, interviewees saw it as a way to leave the country to live and work in a 'more normal economy'. As one stated,

> I would leave today if I could. The rules of the game change here so often and I am tired of working informally with no security and in a country where there is so much corruption. I work hard and I just want to have a normal life which I will never have here.

Russia was granted market status in 2001 but did not gain entry to the World Trade Organisation (WTO) until 2012.

Second, there is no room for the informal economy in such discussions, apart from the fact it is a sign of progress if its share of the economy declines. As the above quote shows, informality, in the form of corruption, was, and still is, a major part of everyday post-Soviet life, but scorecards and other such mechanisms struggle to incorporate such issues.

Third, they do not reflect the social outcomes of the reforms. Russia privatised quickly, but the way in which it did so placed the country's wealth in the hands of a few individuals. Attempts were made to ensure that employees shared the spoils of privatisation, but very few did. A voucher scheme gave employees shares in their enterprise but few understood the mechanism and/or they were so desperate for money to feed their families they sold their shares as quickly as possible. This allowed those with some capital to quickly take overall control of enterprises and the vast majority of the general public saw little benefit (Freeland 2000; Hoffman 2011). As Gilman (2010) argues, the reforms took place in a vacuum where political, economic and social relations were being reformulated almost daily and hyperinflation rendered savings meaningless. As one interviewee asserted,

> My dad was working abroad when the Soviet Union collapsed and when he returned he had a few US dollars and some video recorders. He traded our one-room flat for a two-roomed one in the centre of the city by bartering some of his goods. We literally got a bigger flat by having some video recorders to trade! It was chaos, without our dacha to grow food and my dad's dollars as none of us got paid for months and when they did pay us by then the value of the back pay was worthless.

As Wilson (2005) notes, it was easy for enterprises to make a profit if they 'forgot' to pay their workers or paid them late, allowing inflation to reduce the value of what they had to pay. However, if the enterprise was privatised, it was seen as progress by organisations such as the EBRD.

As the 1990s progressed and the socio-economic problems Russia and Ukraine faced as a result of the shock-therapy approach showed no signs of abating, the Washington Consensus' theoretical underpinnings came under increasing scrutiny. It was now recognised that the market reforms could not be expected to work *deus ex machina* without strong institutions to guide them. Gilman (2010), the IMF's senior advisor to Russia between 1996 and 2000, argues that another key problem was the state's weakness, which occurred as the reforms happened in a vacuum, with the state reconstituted alongside and often behind the economy. The lack of strong state functions and institutions ensured, for example, that corruption flourished (Levin and Satarov 2000), political patronage superseded the legal process (Hoffman 2011) and that the oligarch class had undue power over the political everyday (Wedel 2001). The World Bank acknowledged that it had been too simplistic to expect fully functioning market economies to form without state guidance, with Stiglitz (1998: 1), then the World Bank's chief economist, stating in 1998:

> The policies advanced by the Washington Consensus are not complete, and they are sometimes misguided. Making markets work requires more than

> just low inflation; it requires sound financial regulation, competition policy, and policies to facilitate the transfer of technology and to encourage transparency. States can improve their capabilities by reinvigorating their institutions. This means not only building administrative or technical capacity but instituting rules and norms that provide officials with incentives to act in the collective interest while restraining arbitrary action and corruption.

Furthermore, given the chaos of the early reform period, it was totally unrealistic that the benefits of the reforms would reach the majority quickly. As Gilman (2010: 7) states, 'we suffered a collective myopia in believing that a few years would be sufficient in turning things around'. The publication of 'Beyond the Washington Consensus: Institutions Matter' (Burki and Perry 1998) was the beginning of international aid agencies taking a more micro-economic approach to market reforms, with an emphasis on reducing corruption and strengthening the institutions which guide market development. It also saw a recognition that geography matters, which was crucial because, as McCleery and De Paolis (2008: 23) argue in their 'post-mortem' of the Washington Consensus,

> If, as we argue, all countries are different, and the magnitude, timing, or even existence of potential gains from liberalization depends on a myriad of factors.... It is impossible for a 'one size fits all' policy to promote equitable development in all of the world's diverse developing countries.

The policies arising from this theoretical shift became known as the post-Washington Consensus, where it was recognised that the state did have a role to play in market economies, with particular reference to the regulation of financial markets and areas where the market struggles, such as education and healthcare (Cowling and Tomlinson 2011). This shift coincided with one of the longest periods of overall global economic growth, and the role of institutions such as the IMF was beginning to be questioned as states often preferred now to turn to the market to raise capital (Maier 2007). On the basis of high oil revenues, Russia became a 'middle-income' country and a net donor of international aid, vindication that the transition path was complete and that it had been the correct one to take (Sutela 2012).

Conclusions

This chapter has argued that the transition or transformation debate is reduced by some to merely a semantic argument. Its relevance, however, has been brought sharply back into focus at the onset of the current global economic crisis. This enables us to pose a provocative question: are we all Russians now? Virtually overnight, austerity reforms within the majority of EU states saw notions of education, work and retirement change, conceptually at least. The removal of security, the decreasing real worth of pensions, the absence of 'decent' work, and subsequently the need to find alternative forms of income, leading to a rise in informal practices within the EU, is eerily reminiscent of the early post-Soviet period. While there is not the same level of political upheaval, there is a political stasis as technocrats come into power with the remit of withdrawing the state from society. Perhaps most perturbing, however, is the return of institutions such as the IMF without debate or reflection. In order to obtain loans, countries such as Greece and Spain have had to agree to far-reaching reforms, such as the slashing of public spending and privatisation of state assets. This seems to be a return to the Washington Consensus form of reform, with the ideas of the post-Washington ideology, such as the stronger role of institutions to help regulate the market and to protect the most vulnerable, being forgotten with no reflection on the social costs that this ideology produced in the post-Soviet spaces or the forms of economy that emerged post-reform.

Güven (2012: 869–870) argues that although the then IMF's managing director Dominique Strauss-Kahn described the crisis of 2008 as a 'year of humility', the response of such organisations can be seen as 'paradigm renewal'. Labelling the current reforms a Berlin–Washington Consensus, Fitoussi and Saraceno (2012: 2) argue that 'the European Union has gone farther than any other country or institution in internalizing the prescriptions of the Washington Consensus'. It is clear, therefore, that the transition/transformation debate is much more than a semantic discussion. Within the current reform prescriptions there is no discussion of the variety of capitalisms that exist across the globe or the role of informal practices within everyday life, bar that the informal economy plays a negative role in economic development. Therefore, it is imperative that debates on the nature of economic reform are kept alive and that lessons are learned from previous outcomes. With this in mind, the book now turns to re-theorising 'the economic' before exploring in depth the informal practices that have developed as a response to the post-Soviet reforms implemented in the early 1990s.

3 Re-theorising the economic

Introduction

Every society has to produce, distribute and allocate the goods and services required by its citizens. All societies, in consequence, have an economy of some type. Economies, however, can be organised in various ways. To depict how an economy is structured, three modes of delivering goods and services have been commonly differentiated, namely the 'market' (private sector), the 'state' (public sector) and the 'community' (informal or third) sector (Boswell 1990; Giddens 1998; Gough 2000; Polanyi 1944; Powell 1990; Putterman 1990), even if different labels are sometimes attached to these realms, with Polanyi (1944) referring to 'market exchange', 'redistribution' and 'reciprocity', and Giddens (1998) discussing 'private', 'public' and 'civil society'. Taking these three modes of delivering goods and services as our starting point, the aim of this chapter is to begin to challenge the widespread consensus which exists regarding the trajectory of economic development in post-Soviet spaces, namely that the transition to the market economy is complete. This discourse relies on two assumptions. First, in all economies it is believed that goods and services are being increasingly produced and delivered through the formal (market and state) sphere rather than through the community or informal sphere (henceforth known as the 'formalisation' thesis); and second, that this formal production and delivery of goods and services is increasingly occurring through the market sector, rather than by the public sector (the 'marketisation' thesis). In other words, there is a belief that post-Soviet spaces, as Chapter 2 showed, are moving towards the production and delivery of goods and services through the formal economy in general and the formal market economy more particularly.

The intention of this chapter is thus to evaluate empirically this narrative on the direction of post-Soviet economies. It starts by analysing the two meta-narratives about the trajectory of economic development, namely formalisation and marketisation. Then, in order to challenge the widely accepted view that the transition to the market is complete, the following section presents discussion of how this has started to be empirically and theoretically challenged. This sets the scene for the book's following chapters, which seek to re-read the configuration of the economic and economy in contemporary post-Soviet spaces.

The formalisation thesis

The formalisation thesis asserts that goods and services are increasingly provided through the formal economy (the state and market spheres) and that the informal economy is in demise (for further discussion see Williams 2005a, 2007). Here, the intention is to reveal how this vision of the trajectory of economic development both dominates thought and practice in the post-Soviet world, as Chapter 2 showed, and constrains what is considered feasible and valid as possible futures for post-Soviet spaces. This powerful discourse, however, does not only describe the direction of change, hierarchically ordering countries in the present and informing them of their trajectory (as in the EBRD's scorecards), but also serves to shape thinking about what action is required by supranational institutions, national governments, economic development agencies and individuals themselves. For example, the whole thrust of post-Soviet/socialist economic policy, based upon the Washington Consensus, has been focused upon how to facilitate the 'transition' to a formal market economy. Grounded in this grand narrative that details what constitutes 'progress', governments of post-Soviet/socialist states have tended to concentrate near enough exclusively on developing the formal economy and viewed informal work as, at best, playing a supporting role and, at worst, deleterious to development and something to be formalised so as to allow this trajectory of economic development to be implemented. This is revealed by state discourses on the nature of 'the informal' as when the authors discussed the issue with political and economic elites the common answer is that people act in this manner purely 'to cheat the state out of tax revenues'. There is almost no discussion on how such practices are part of a range of livelihood tactics, that they support and are implicitly interlinked with the formal or how they are created in response to the forms of capitalism that have developed in these countries.

As noted in the previous chapter, the reforms enacted in the post-Soviet world were aimed at creating an economy that only exists in textbooks. However, as Carrier and Miller (1998: 225) discuss, this was of little importance to those leading the reforms as 'economic models are no longer measured against the world they seek to describe, but instead the world is measured against them, found wanting and made to conform'. Arguing that we now live in a time of economic virtualism (for example, economic models and/or the Washington Consensus), Carrier (1998: 8) argues that there was a

> conscious attempt to make the real world conform to the virtual image, justified by the claim that the failure of the real to conform to the idea is a consequence not merely of imperfections, but is a failure that itself has undesirable consequences.

In this so-called 'virtualism', the formal economy in the formalisation thesis represents progress, modernity and advancement, while the informal economy is indicative of backwardness, under-development and traditionalism (Peck 2010). Through this, Wacquant (2012: 66) sees 'neoliberalism as an articulation of state, market and citizenship that harnesses the first to impose the stamp of the second onto the third'. In other words, it is more than an economic approach and one which attempts to destroy anything that is outside of its realm, i.e. the informal.

As such, the formalisation thesis depicts the formal and informal economy as what Derrida (1967) calls a 'binary hierarchy'. For him, western thought is dominated by a hierarchical binary mode of thinking that, first, conceptualises objects/identities as stable, bounded and constituted via negation, and second, reads the resultant binary structures in a hierarchical manner where the first term in any dualistic opposite (the superordinate) is endowed with positivity and the second term, the subordinate (or subservient) 'other', with negativity. Read through this lens, the depiction of the formal and informal economy in the formalisation thesis is one in which the informal economy represents the subordinate 'other' endowed with negativity, while the formal economy is read as a superordinate and is attributed with positivity (see also Routh 2011). As McFarlane and Waibel (2012: 5) state, the formal is normally seen as 'rule based, structured, explicit ... and regular'.

Indeed, to see how the informal economy is read in this dominant narrative as a subservient 'other' endowed with negativity, whose meaning is established solely in relation to its superordinate opposite (the formal economy), one needs look no further than the numerous adjectives to denote this sphere. As Latouche (1993: 129) recognises, 'most of them simply qualify – either directly or indirectly – whatever is meant, in a negative way' (see also Cooper and May 2012). Variously referred to as 'non-structured', 'unpaid', 'non-official', 'non-organised', 'a-normal', 'hidden', 'a-legal', 'black', 'submerged', 'non-visible', 'shadow', 'a-typical' or 'irregular', this sphere is thus denoted as 'bereft of its own logic or identity other than can be indicated by this displacement away from, or even effacement of, the "normal"' (Latouche 1993: 129). It is described by what it is not – what is absent from, or insufficient about, such work – relative to the formal sphere, and this absence or insufficiency is always viewed as a negative feature of such work (for further discussion on the terminology of informal work and its negative reading see Webb *et al.* 2012). Overall, as Lemaitre and Helmsing (2012: 747) note, the 'non-market' is most often discussed in reference to 'market failures'.

It is not simply the adjectives used to denote this sphere, however, that display how the formal/informal economy is represented as a binary hierarchy. The narrative of what constitutes progress in the formalisation thesis similarly privileges the superordinate over the subordinate other. The informal sector is read as primitive or traditional, stagnant, marginal, residual, weak, and about to be extinguished; a leftover of pre-capitalist formations that the inexorable and inevitable march of formalisation will eradicate. As McFarlane and Waibel (2012) discuss, moreover, there is also often assumed to be a spatial hierarchy, with informal areas such as the 'slum' seen as totally separate from formal spaces such as the 'market'. Indeed, a universal natural and inevitable shift towards the formalisation of goods and services provision is envisaged as post-Soviet societies become more 'advanced'. The persistence of supposedly traditional informal activities, therefore, is taken as a manifestation of 'backwardness' (e.g. Geertz 1963) and it is assumed that such work will disappear with economic 'progress' (Lewis 1959). As the rest of the book shows, these prognoses have simply not come to pass. However, the informal is still often seen as a 'means of refuge' for those unable to succeed in the formal economy. Venkatesh's (2006: 385) extremely interesting work on informal practices in disadvantaged neighbourhoods in Chicago highlights its positive elements, but still portrays it as a binary which cannot be bridged, when he says:

> The underground economy enables poor communities to survive but can lead to alienation from the wider world.... On the one hand, the underground economy is a space forged by exclusion from the social mainstream. Much of the reason for lending to one another, hiring off the books, and solving crimes without the aid of the police is that banks discriminate against the poor, mainstream employers and unions do not do effective outreach to the poor and minorities, and law enforcement does not provide adequate service to the inner city. On the other hand, however meaningful and satisfactory it may be for those involved, this kind of adjustment does little over time to bring about improvement in credit availability, labor force participation, and policing. It does little to leverage more stable and productive relationships with the institutions of the wider world.

Informal work is thus read as existing in the interstices, or as scattered and fragmented across the economic landscape (Günther and Launov 2012). Formal work, by contrast, is still represented as systematic, naturally expansive and coextensive with the national or world economy (White and Williams 2012).

Such a hierarchical and temporal sequencing of formal and informal work in the formalisation thesis, therefore, focuses upon the imminent destruction of the informal economy, its proto-capitalist qualities, its weak and its determined position, viewing it either as 'the mere vestige of a disappearing past [or as] transitory or provisional' (Latouche 1993: 49). Rarely is the informal sector represented as resilient, ubiquitous, capable of generative growth, or as driving economic change in the formalisation thesis. Nor is it represented as part of a multitude of different forms of work co-existing in the contemporary world but instead is always positioned in a temporal sequence where the informal sphere is characterised as a remnant of the past and 'backward', while the formal sphere is characterised as 'modern' and 'progressive'. There is also almost no discussion on the symbiotic relationships between the two spheres – for example, on how informal practices enable households to perform their formal work, or the role that informal labour plays in global production chains (Phillips 2011). Rather, the informal sphere is near enough always viewed as possessing wholly negative attributes while the 'progressive' formal sphere is assumed to possess positive features. For example, Bayat (2007: 579) argues that 'informal life', as typified by 'flexibility, pragmatism, negotiation, as well as constant struggle for survival and self-development' is the 'habitus of the dispossessed'. Through this the spaces which the informal processes themselves take place in can be cast in a negative fashion with a need to reclaim them for 'the formal'. As Roy (2011: 233) describes:

> The valorization of elite informalities and the criminalization of subaltern informalities produce an uneven urban geography of spatial value. This in turn fuels frontiers of urban development and expansion. Informalized spaces are reclaimed through urban renewal, while formalized spaces accrue value through state-authorized legitimacy. As a concept, urban informality therefore cannot be understood in ontological or topological terms. Instead, it is a heuristic device that uncovers the ever-shifting urban relationship between the legal and illegal, legitimate and illegitimate, authorized and unauthorized.

Many political economists, recognising that the informal sector is persistent and growing, have portrayed it as a new form of work emerging in late capitalism as a direct result of the advent of a deregulated, open world economy, which is encouraging a race-to-the-bottom. In this reading, informal workers are viewed as sharing the same characteristics subsumed under the heading of 'downgraded labour': they receive few benefits, low wages and have poor working conditions (Field 2012; Routh 2011). In sum, the depiction is of the informal sphere as a pre-modern sector composed of workers engaged in exploitative and oppressive work, and thus a hindrance to 'progress'. This is encapsulated in the International Labour Organisation's (ILO) campaign to reduce informal work which, as Lerche (2012) discusses, is dubbed the 'decent work approach'. Obviously this implies that informal work is 'indecent' (this is not a criticism of the campaign per se, or to suggest that exploitation does not take place, but rather a reflection on how such work is labelled and categorised). Seldom are positive attributes assigned to the informal sphere, such as how this work is autonomous and often rewarding in nature for its participants and the role it plays in general economic development (see Philips 2011).

One notable exception is, however, put forward by Sassen (2009: 30) who, similar to Standing (2011), argues that globalisation has led to an increase in informalisation. She argues that this is not just confined to the global South or to the margins of big cities, but is integral to all global cities. Casting informal modes of production as a means of creative freedom, she discusses how an

> often overlooked trend has been the proliferation of an informal economy of creative professionals in these cities. Comprised of artists, architects, designers, and software developers, this new informal economy greatly expands opportunities and networking potentials for people to operate in the interstices of urban and organizational spaces that are usually dominated by large corporate actors. It also allows these artists and professionals to escape the corporatization of creative work. In this process they contribute a very specific feature of the new urban economy: its innovativeness and a certain type of frontier spirit.

This far more nuanced approach begins to reveal the relationships between the formal and informal as much more than a binary hierarchy. However, such arguments are rare within academic debates, especially within economics and management (see Godfrey 2011, for further discussion on how the informal is a 'new' space for research), and even more so within policy discussion and construction. The outcome in post-Soviet spaces and beyond is that the dominance of the formalisation thesis results in the possibilities for the trajectory of economic development to be closed off from anything other than formalisation. In other words it is argued that there is only one future for economic development and it is one in which there is a linear path towards a formalisation of work.

Yet despite the widespread acceptance of this thesis and its normative propositions, little evidence is ever brought to the fore to corroborate that this is indeed the direction of change and that formal work possesses positive attributes and informal work negative features. Instead, it is simply assumed that this is the case. Given that other ideas in the social sciences are seldom, if ever, accepted without evidence, there is a real need for a rigorous investigation of this thesis, especially when it is recognised that it not only seeks to reflect lived practice but also acts as a narrative that is being used to shape the direction of economic development. This will be returned to below. First, however, the fact that it is a particular type of formal economy that is widely seen to be coming to the fore needs to be discussed.

The marketisation thesis

It is not only the narrative of an ongoing formalisation of work whereby goods and services are increasingly produced and delivered through the formal (market and state) sphere rather than using informal work that has dominated thought regarding the direction of post-Soviet economies. It is a particular type of formalisation that is seen to be occurring. The widely held view is that the formal production and delivery of goods and services is increasingly occurring through the market sector (rather than by the public sector). This is here termed the marketisation thesis, but might also be termed the 'commercialisation' or 'commodification' thesis.

At the present moment in history, the near-universal belief is that of the three modes of delivering goods and services, the market is expanding while the other two spheres are contracting (e.g. Lee 2000; Polanyi 1944; Scott 2001; Smith 2000; Watts 1999). Indeed, so dominant is this narrative that few can imagine a future for post-Soviet spaces other than the further encroachment of the market. This, therefore, severely curtails what is considered feasible, valid and possible regarding the direction of economic development. As Flavin *et al.* (2011: 252) state:

> The study of the market economy is as old as social science itself. This is hardly surprising given that since the emergence of capitalism, market principles have come to structure economic production and exchange, and

> thereby to permeate the wider social order through that structuring. Whatever their ultimate judgment on capitalism, from advocates (such as Adam Smith or Milton Friedman) to opponents (e.g. Marx or Bourdieu) to those who are both (say, J. S. Mill or even John Rawls), social theorists widely agree that once introduced, the market ultimately comes to influence the entire social order.

How, therefore, does the marketisation thesis view the trajectory so far as the production and delivery of goods and services is concerned? Breaking this thesis down into its component parts, first, the belief is that goods and services are increasingly produced for exchange; second, these exchanges are seen to increasingly take place on a monetised basis; and third and finally, this monetised exchange is viewed as increasingly occurring for the purpose of profit. For adherents to the marketisation thesis, therefore, profit-motivated monetised exchange is seen to be expanding into new spheres of everyday life while non-market economic practices (i.e. the public and informal spheres) are contracting. As Crouch (2012: 366–337) argues:

> In recent decades objections to political attempts to impose a moral framework on economic life have become increasingly triumphant, as neoliberal ideas about the superiority of markets and corporations over government action have become dominant. The same ideology has also encouraged us to bring more and more areas of life within the compass of this economic reasoning. Fields like health and education, which in the past were seen as having their own sets of values, have been brought into the market.

As he goes on to suggest, as profit maximisation is 'the sole goal of corporations' it became seen that 'no other institutions in society should try to establish alternative goals'. This notion of the impending hegemony of marketisation has been asserted to be happening in many realms (Wacquant 2012), including education (Natale and Doran 2012; Newman and Jahdi 2009; Tilak 2009) and healthcare (Burau 2012; Jensen 2011; Sturgeon 2010). As Eikenberry (2009: 592) notes, marketisation now even 'pervades thinking and practice in non-profit and voluntary organisations today'; Ciscel and Heath (2001: 401) argue that capitalism is transforming 'every human interaction into a transient market exchange'; and Jessop (2012) discusses how this narrative is interwoven within uncritical discourses of globalisation. Within this framework Harvey (2011: vi) states that capital is seen as 'the lifeblood that flows through the body politic of all of those societies that we call capitalistic, spreading out, sometimes as a trickle and other times as a flood, into every nook and cranny of the inhabited world'. As Dicken (2003: 579–580) puts it in the context of the command economy's collapse and China's economic reforms:

> More than at any time in the past 50 years, virtually the entire world economy is now a *market economy*. The collapse of the state socialist

> systems at the end of the 1980s and their headlong rush to embrace the market, together with the more controlled opening-up of the Chinese economy since 1979, has created a very different global system from that which emerged after World War II. Virtually all parts of the world are now, to a greater or lesser extent, connected into an increasingly integrated system in which the parameters of the market dominate.

The outcome, in the eyes of a leading neo-liberal economist, is that 'Capitalism stands alone as the only feasible way rationally to organize a modern economy' (De Soto 2001: 1), and this leads him to assert that 'all plausible alternatives to capitalism have now evaporated' (De Soto 2001: 13). It is not just neo-liberals, however, who view this to be the case, and there is much criticism of the 'hegemonic left-liberalism' which, it is argued, uncritically adopts 'the mantra that there is no alternative to the capitalist market' (Cremin 2012: 46). As Hickel and Khan (2012: 205) forcefully argue:

> As a result, neoliberal ideology has become a totalizing way of life, a world-view that furnishes the terms for everyday praxis and representation, creates its own forms of political participation and activism, and promotes a virtually unassailable notion of morality. It is not just a manipulative ploy to appropriate surplus value, *but a regime in the truest sense of the term*—a cultural logic that insinuates itself into every aspect of lived experience. Neoliberal logic cuts across class divides, religious and cultural affiliations, and political loyalties. It is articulated not only on the trading floors of the New York Stock Exchange, not only in university economics departments, not only in the marble halls of the World Bank and International Monetary Fund (IMF), but also—crucially—in the politics of progressive institutions like the United Nations Development Program (UNDP), by the fashionable environmentalists doing the rounds in American universities, by gender and racial justice advocacy groups, and by charitable philanthropists of all stripes [emphasis added].

Thus, for adherents to the narrative of marketisation, one mode of exchange is replacing all others. The formal market economy is becoming *the* economic institution rather than one mode of producing and delivering goods and services among many. The notion that the formal market economy is expanding and all other realms shrinking has today taken on the aura of an uncontested fact, with the only debate being the pace, extent and unevenness of marketisation. For some, the process is rather more complete and the formal market economy more hegemonic than for others. Comeliau (2000: 45), for example, talks of 'its almost exclusive use to solve the great majority of economic and social problems' while Thrift and Walling (2000: 96) asserts that 'What is certain is that the process of commodification has reached into every nook and cranny of modern life'. For others, however, there is still seen to be some distance to travel before the total marketisation of working life is absolute (Gough 2000; Watts 1999). As Watts (1999: 312) puts it,

> The process by which everything becomes a commodity – and therefore everything comes to acquire a price and a monetary form (commoditization/commodification) – is not complete, even in our own societies where transactions still occur outside of the marketplace. But the reality of capitalism is that ever more of social life is mediated through and by the market.

Among such commentators, therefore, there is no questioning of marketisation. The only debate is over the extent to which it has so far colonised the production and delivery of goods and services and the distance that needs to be travelled before the process is complete. Despite the predominance of this narrative, scholars rarely offer more than some broad-brush qualitative judgement. None attempt to measure, even in the crudest terms, the extent or pace of its encroachment or even its unevenness. As Harvey (2000: 68) posits with regard to what he considers a highly uneven process,

> if there is any real qualitative trend it is towards the reassertion of early nineteenth-century capitalist values coupled with a twenty-first century penchant for pulling everyone (and everything that can be exchanged) into the orbit of capital while rendering large segments of the world's population permanently redundant in relation to the basic dynamics of capital accumulation.

Indeed, this is the consensus. Even if the formal market economy is forever stretching outward to pull in more spheres of life and colonise areas previously untouched by its hand, this is widely regarded as a highly uneven process. Few, however, doubt that the overarching global trajectory is towards the hegemony of the formal market economy. Nor is there much difference between right- and left-wing political discourses. Both sides of the political spectrum concur that the overarching process is towards the dominance of the formal market economy, even if their reasons for asserting this and normative views on its consequences vary considerably. As Cremin (2012) notes, this even extends into discussions which should be especially critical of the discourse, such as debates on environmental issues and social justice. For a brief moment in time at the credit crunch's apogee, it appeared that there might be space for discussion on alternative pathways for 'the economy'. With people protesting on the streets against the return of Washington Consensus-style approaches in the majority of countries in the global North, debate seemed inevitable. However, the moment was fleeting and as Jessop (2011: 17) states:

> Much mainstream commentary has read the crisis from the viewpoints of capital accumulation rather than social reproduction, the global North rather than the global South, and the best way for states to restore rather than constrain the dominance of market forces.

Therefore, market solutions to market problems magically appeared to be the only way out of the crisis and for future development. However, besides the aforementioned discussions on the pace, extent and unevenness of the process of commodification, such protests and debate highlight that there are contrasting normative positions about, first, whether marketisation is to be celebrated or not, and second and often inextricably inter-related, whether it is a 'natural' and 'organic' or a 'socially constructed' process. Each issue is here considered in turn.

Towards a formal market economy: positive or negative?

Different stances exist on whether this turn towards the formal market economy is to be celebrated or not. At one end of the spectrum are those neo-liberals for whom marketisation is positive because it results in liberation, freedom and progress from the irrational constraints of tradition and collective bonds, creating a social order from the market-coordinated actions of free and rational individuals. This advocacy of marketisation is often inextricably tied to a view of market-oriented behaviour as the natural basis for all social life. Depicted for instance in Thatcherism, a cultural and political revolution is seen to be required to remove from social life anything that might reduce the centrality of market models as the basis of social order.

As Block (2002) points out, this celebratory view of capitalism in neo-liberal thought has taken on board many of the tenets of what originally was a critical Marxian discourse. On the one hand, the very term 'capitalism', that until the late 1960s was unused in polite company, has now been adopted by neo-liberals in a much more positive sense to convey the type of society being sought. On the other hand, the core Marxist idea that economic organisation sets the basic frame for the larger society, previously considered objectionable and rejected as 'vulgar materialism', is now widely accepted by neo-liberals. The result is that today capitalism is the name the business media uses and the idea that the structure of the economy determines the wider society has been transformed from 'vulgar materialism' to common sense. More importantly, the fundamentally Marxian claim that capitalism as an economic system is global, unified and coherent was embraced by Margaret Thatcher, Ronald Reagan and other apostles of neo-liberal ideology in order to encourage their goals of privatisation, deregulation and public sector retrenchment. In an increasingly global capitalist economy, it was asserted that countries had no choice but to follow such a path.

For many on the left of the political spectrum, meanwhile, marketisation is again accepted, but this process is seen more negatively. For them, the increasing penetration of the formal market economy is highlighted, but so as to display how it leads to an eroding of communal life and has deleterious consequences for social values that might stand above the merely economic measure of price (e.g. Comelieau 2002; Slater and Tonkiss 2001). As Comelieau (2002: 45) states,

> wherever market rationality acquires dominance, it transforms *social relations in their entirety*. Resting as it does upon private appropriation and

> competition, it entails individualist rivalry far more than mutual support as the basis for relations among the members of a society. It thus has a destructive impact upon the 'social fabric' itself.

This highlighting of the deleterious impacts of commodification, of course, is by no means new. Indeed, Beveridge (1948: 322), widely recognised as the founder of the modern welfare state, was seriously concerned about the emergence of what he called the 'business motive'. For him, there was a need to hold onto 'something other than the pursuit of gain as the dominant force in society. The business motive ... is ... in continual or repeated conflict with the Philanthropic Motive, and has too often been successful.' He concludes that 'the business motive is a good servant but a bad master, and a society which gives itself up to the dominance of the business motive is a bad society'. The negative view of marketisation therefore depicts the implementation of an implacable logic of quantification and formal rationality as producing inequality, social disorder, loss of substantive values and a destruction of both individual and social relations. As Carroll (2010) argues, this even extends into development programmes to the global South which, wrapped up in the guise of the post-Washington Consensus, amount to little more, he argues, than 'deep marketisation' rather than pathways to social justice.

The formal market economy: natural or constructed?

Directly related to this debate on the virtues of the formal market economy is a discussion concerning whether such a trajectory of economies is 'natural' and 'organic', or 'socially created'. For neo-liberals, marketisation is commonly viewed as a natural or organic process, while for those critical of the consequences it is more commonly viewed as socially constructed. Before analysing these contrasting positions, however, it is necessary to reiterate the shared 'buying into' the meta-narrative of marketisation by both bodies of thought. As Slater and Tonkiss (2001: 3–4) assert, 'political and economic orthodoxies treat markets as self-evident, permanent and incontestable'. In the 'natural' or 'organic' view, this trajectory towards capitalist hegemony is portrayed as inevitable, all-powerful and all-conquering, even an unstoppable supernatural force.

Indeed, this force of nature is even sometimes assigned human characteristics and emotions. In the business media, for example, markets are often depicted as calm, depressed, expectant, hesitant, nervous and sensitive. Sometimes the pound sterling, euro or US dollar has a good day, at other times it is ailing or sinking fast. Markets seem, therefore, to be ascribed with human attributes beyond the control of mortals. They are superhuman god-like figures. This is more than simply a discourse to make them comprehensible to the public by financial journalists. It is imbuing markets with the force of nature, giving them a divine will. The outcome is that 'there is no alternative' but to obey the logic of this all-powerful force. Seen in this manner, capitalism is constructed as existing outside of society or even above it. Reflecting the stance of many economists and formal anthropologists, the economy becomes a separate differentiated sphere. Instead of economic life being part of broader social relations, these relations become an epi-phenomena of the market; there is an economisation of culture. For those more critical of marketisation, however, this 'un-embedded' organic view of capitalism is rejected. For them, the formal market economy is socially constructed and although the momentum is towards an ever more marketised world, this does not mean it cannot be stopped. Following Polanyi (1944: 140), it has been widely recognised that 'the road to the free market was opened and kept open by an enormous increase in continuous, centrally organized, and controlled interventionism' and as such, that the formal market economy is a created system rather than a natural or organic one.

One way in which this view of the formal market economy as a created system has come to the fore, albeit implicitly, is in the literature on the 'varieties of capitalism' (Coates 2002; Thelen 2012; Whitley 2002) that has developed into discussions on variegated capitalisms (Bruff and Horn 2012; Dixon 2011; Jessop 2012). The contention that different varieties of capitalism developed in Anglo-Saxon countries, within the EU and East Asia for example, displays that there is no one single variety with one uniform logic, but a multiplicity of strains reflecting the different social systems in which they are created. The key problem with this varieties-of-capitalism literature, however, is that it has been largely silent on the critical issue of capitalism as a natural system (Bruff and Horn 2012). Although implicit is the idea that there is no single unified system that operates like a force of nature, it is seldom explicit. The outcome is the persistence of a view that capitalism is some natural or organic system beyond the control of the societies in which it exists. Nevertheless, even when portrayed as created rather than organic, the validity of the inevitable drift towards the formal market economy is still not widely questioned. A marketisation of economic life is still seen to be taking place. Although in principle, social constructionists need not argue this since they recognise that marketisation is not inevitable, in practice, few do so. To transcend the marketisation thesis, in consequence, it is necessary to highlight more explicitly the lack of evidence to support this meta-narrative concerning the direction of economic development.

The formal market economy: a delusion?

Given the widespread assumption that capitalism is penetrating ever more deeply into post-Soviet spaces, one might think that there would be voluminous evidence supporting this view of the trajectory of economic development. Yet a worrying and disturbing finding once one starts searching for the evidence is that hardly any is ever provided. For example, pronouncements by authors such as Rifkin (2000: 3) that 'The marketplace is a pervasive force in our lives', and from Gudeman (2001: 144) that 'markets are subsuming greater portions of everyday life' are offered to the reader with no supporting evidence. Similarly, the assertion by Carruthers and Babb (2000: 4) that there has been 'the near-complete penetration of market relations into our modern economic lives' is justified by nothing more than the statement that 'markets enter our lives today in many ways "too numerous to be mentioned" ' and the spurious notion that the spread of marketised 'ways of viewing' signals how marketisation is becoming hegemonic. Watts (1999: 312), in the same vein, supports his belief that although 'commodification is not complete ... the reality of capitalism is that ever more of social life is mediated through and by the market', merely by pointing out how subsistence economies are rare.

Such thin evidence is by no means exceptional. Few commentators move beyond what Martin and Sunley (2001: 152), in another context, term 'vague theory and thin empirics'. Perhaps because it is a widely accepted canon of wisdom, evidence is seldom deemed necessary. Indeed, perhaps the growing hegemony of the formal market economy is so obvious to all that there is no need to provide evidence. Perhaps, however, it is not. No other ideas in the social sciences are accepted without corroboration and there are no grounds for exempting the formalisation and marketisation theses. Perhaps the only reason for exempting them is if one believes they are irrefutable facts. If so, then interrogating that this is indeed the case should be welcomed, especially given the paucity of evidence so far provided.

Why, therefore, is evidence not sought? One principal reason is perhaps that a 'way of viewing' has become confused with a lived reality. To take an example, recent years have seen the advent of discussions of a 'marriage market' whereby people seek out and take decisions on partners much like any other profit-oriented investment. Yet just because this endeavour can be read in a formal marketised manner does not mean that this endeavour is now marketised; just because one can read marriage and partnership as a formal market transaction does not mean that everybody is doing so, marrying and choosing partners for profit-motivated purposes. Just because the language of the formal market realm is now colonising more and more areas of human existence, reaching far into inviolable sanctuaries, such that we can now talk of emotional investments, erotic capital and of the returns on our relationships, does not mean that this is now always the lived practice. Making a friendship might pay dividends, be profitless, rewarding, cost us dear, we may shop around for new friendships, be in the market for a new relationship, have the assets of our youth, intellect or energy so that we can make capital out of them, there may be pay-offs, bonuses to be had and meagre returns from friendships, and we may all have our price, but this language does not mean that there is a marketisation of everything.

Indeed, even if this marketised 'way of viewing' has become more common, commentators must know that this does not necessarily translate into lived practice. They live in post-Soviet societies and understand the social mores that prevail. They must know that seeking monetary profit in all social transactions is widely deemed unacceptable and inappropriate. Even if one acts in a market-like manner in commercial transactions, the same cannot apply to exchanges between friends and kin where reciprocity, altruism and charity should and must prevail. Different exchange relations are appropriate and acceptable in different social situations. Doing a favour for kin, friends or neighbours is very different to selling a service to a client, and disputes over whether something is a favour or a service is a dispute over whether the relationship is friendship or commerce. Just because an altruistic favour can be read as market-like and profit-motivated does not make it so.

Moreover, such commentators must know that there are well-defined socially constructed boundaries it is unacceptable to cross, or what Block (2002) calls 'blockages to commodification'. Domains can be identified where, although money may not be completely excluded, its use is often highly constrained, as in the example of exchanging gifts. Although the giving of gifts is a universal trait, its pattern and meaning varies cross-culturally (Bloch and Parry 1989). In many post-Soviet societies, gift exchange tends to be personal and altruistic relative to impersonal and self-interested commodity exchange. As Gregory (1982: 12) states, 'commodity exchange is an exchange of alienable things between transactors who are in a state of reciprocal independence.... Non-commodity (gift) exchange is an exchange of inalienable things between transactors who are in a state of reciprocal dependence.' Gift exchange establishes and/or maintains a social relationship between the giver and recipient. A gift invokes an obligation – a relationship of indebtedness, status difference, or even subordination. As such, the meaning of the gift must be appropriate to the relationship. And in contemporary post-Soviet societies, money is seldom seen as an appropriate gift. Furthermore, one would never offer money to somebody who invited you to dinner as a substitute for returning the favour. The debt is personal and direct and must be repaid in kind. Norms of exchange evolve, however, and are not timeless and unchanging. What is inappropriate at one time period or place can become acceptable later or elsewhere.

The point quite simply is that blockages are always present. Although these blockages change over time and space, there are always blockages of one form or another. The argument of exponents of the hegemony of the formal market economy, therefore, can be read as contending that the spheres subject to blocked exchanges are dwindling in number over time as the tentacles of formalisation and marketisation stretch ever deeper and wider. Until now, no evidence has been provided of whether this is the case. The strong consensus, nevertheless, is that the formal market economy is increasingly totalising, hegemonic, all encompassing and universal.

De-centring the formal market economy

Ever since the command economy's collapse, the recurring narrative, as Chapter 2 showed, has been that the post-Soviet/socialist spaces of East-Central Europe are in transition to a formal market economy, reflecting and reinforcing the broader worldwide process whereby an all-conquering capitalism stretches its wings wider across the globe and penetrates deeper into every crevice of everyday life. The demise of the state as a direct provider of goods and services in favour of the formal market economy, even if the state continues to regulate, albeit in poorer ways and with less developed and appropriate legislation than in western economies (Neef 2002; Sik 1993, 1994; Wallace and Haerpfer 2002), is often taken as evidence. However, such a trend towards privatisation within the formal economy is insufficient to inform an understanding of whether or not a formal market economy is becoming hegemonic. If, for example, the informal economy were growing relative to the formal economy, then the formal market economy would not be becoming increasingly hegemonic.

To question this discourse of marketism that serves the vested interests of capitalism (by constructing the formal market economy as a natural and inevitable future) and closes off discussion of alternative futures for economic development, the degree to which post-Soviet/socialist societies are witnessing the advance of the formal market economy is here evaluated critically. At first glance it might seem like a fruitless exercise to raise doubts about the incursion of the formal market economy into the post-Soviet/socialist world. Here, however, we wish to show that this is far from the case.

To evaluate the validity of this view that the formal market economy is becoming ever more dominant in the post-Soviet/socialist world, on the one hand, it can be indirectly assessed using the proxy measure of formal employment participation rates. If relatively few goods and services were produced, sold and distributed through the formal economy, then few people would be in formal jobs. However, as more goods and services are exchanged in this manner, then a growth in the employment participation rate would be witnessed, culminating in a state of 'full-employment'. On the other hand, and perhaps more accurately, the extent of formalisation and how this is changing over time can be directly evaluated by comparing the volume and value of formal and informal work in different time periods using measures of either the inputs into, or outputs of, such work. Each measure of formalisation is here evaluated in turn.

A proxy measure: evaluating the shift towards full(er) employment

Analysing the degree to which citizens in the post-Soviet/socialist world are immersed in the formal labour market, as stated, is a proxy measure of the degree of formalisation, and evaluating the extent to which they are immersed in formal employment in the private sector is a broad proxy measure of the advent of the formal market economy. Examining solely the employment participation rate of the working-age population (aged 15–64 years old), the ILO (2012) report that in Central and Southeastern Europe (non-EU) and the Commonwealth of Independent States (CIS), the employment participation rate was 58.8 per cent in 2000, 57.7 per cent in 2005 and 59.2 per cent in 2010. Four in every ten people of working age in the post-Soviet/socialist world were therefore jobless in 2010. To achieve full participation, two new jobs are required for every three in existence (a 69 per cent increase in the number of jobs). Table 3.1 displays the results for various post-Soviet/socialist countries. This reveals that even if the 'jobs gap' is narrower in some nations than others, all are far from a state of full employment. Contrary to the hyperbole and rhetoric of politicians who often assert that full employment is nearly achieved, even Kazakhstan, the country with the

Table 3.1 Labour force participation rate (15–64 years old), 1990–2010 in post-Soviet/socialist societies

Country	*1990*	*1995*	*2000*	*2005*	*2010*	*Growth (+) or decline (–) or no change (0) 1990–2010*
Albania	67.9	68.1	67.1	66.3	66.5	–
Armenia	72.7	72.0	71.5	67.0	63.7	–
Bosnia and Herzegovina	49.5	49.6	51.3	51.4	54.5	+
Bulgaria	69.5	67.4	64.6	62.4	67.0	–
Croatia	65.0	64.5	64.3	65.3	64.5	–
Czech Republic	71.2	72.2	71.5	70.4	69.7	–
Estonia	78.7	72.2	69.9	70.4	74.0	–
Georgia	68.0	68.8	66.3	67.2	67.7	–
Hungary	65.7	59.3	59.7	61.2	62.3	–
Kazakhstan	75.7	76.4	76.1	76.3	77.4	+
Kyrgyzstan	71.3	71.1	69.5	69.4	69.9	–
Latvia	78.8	71.9	67.2	69.4	73.7	–
Lithuania	75.7	73.4	71.1	68.3	70.7	–
FYR Macedonia	60.1	61.0	60.3	60.7	64.4	+
Moldova, Republic of	75.1	71.4	65.4	53.9	46.4	–
Poland	70.2	66.5	64.7	63.9	65.6	–
Romania	67.5	70.1	69.9	62.4	63.8	–
Russian Federation	76.9	71.1	71.1	70.9	72.9	–
Serbia and Montenegro	60.0	61.4	62.9	64.2	63.5	+
Slovakia	76.3	69.4	69.7	68.9	68.7	–
Slovenia	60.5	68.4	67.5	70.6	71.2	+
Tajikistan	70.6	70.9	70.2	68.8	68.7	–
Turkmenistan	63.4	63.6	64.0	64.0	63.6	0
Ukraine	72.8	71.0	66.8	66.7	67.2	–
Uzbekistan	62.7	62.6	63.0	63.3	63.9	+

Source: ILO Key Indicators of the Labour Market (KILM), http://kilm.ilo.org/kilmnet.

highest employment participation rate (77.4 per cent), requires one new job for every three existing jobs in order to achieve full employment.

Is it the case, nevertheless, that employment participation rates are moving closer to full employment over time? As Table 3.1 displays, this is not the case. Over the past two decades, few nations have managed to close their 'jobs gap'. Indeed, just five nations in this table made any progress at all. Over this two-decade period, Slovenia managed to raise employment participation rates from 60.5 per cent to 71.2 per cent, Serbia and Montenegro from 60 per cent to 63.5 per cent, Uzbekistan from 62.7 per cent to 63.9 per cent, Kazakhstan from 75.7 per cent to 77.4 per cent and Bosnia and Herzegovina from 49.5 per cent to 54.5 per cent. In most nations, however, the 'jobs gap' widened. Some falls were quite dramatic. For example, employment participation rates in the Republic of Moldova fell from 75.1 per cent in 1990 to 46.4 per cent by 2010. The view that there is a long-term universal trend towards fuller employment, therefore, must be treated with considerable caution. It is not borne out by the evidence. Across the post-Soviet/socialist space, in sum, a wide gap exists between current employment levels and a situation of full participation, and the trend is not on the whole narrowing over time in most nations.

Employment participation rates thus provide no evidence of a universal process of formalisation in post-Soviet/socialist economies over the past two decades. However, this is perhaps a very poor proxy indicator. Analysing formal employment alone tells us nothing about whether and how the balance is altering between formal and informal work. For example, increased participation in employment is not always accompanied by a decline in informal work. It may be accompanied by a quicker or slower growth in informal work, a decline in informal work or a similar growth rate, resulting in no change in the overall balance of formal and informal work. Unless both formal and informal work is analysed, therefore, whether there is a process of formalisation will not be known.

More direct measures of the permeation of the formal market economy

To evaluate whether a formalisation of work has taken place in post-Soviet/socialist economies, in theory, one could evaluate the volume and value of the formal and informal spheres in terms of either their inputs or outputs (Goldschmidt-Clermont 1982, 1998, 2000; Gregory and Windebank 2000; Luxton 1997). In practice, it is only data on the volume and value of the inputs that are readily available in the form of time-budget data (Gershuny 2000; Murgatroyd and Neuburger 1997; Robinson and Godbey 1997). Here, participants fill in diaries of what they do, and by analysing the data the time that they spend in formal employment and in other forms of work can be calculated (Gershuny and Jones 1987; Gershuny *et al.* 1994; Juster and Stafford 1991).

Table 3.2 collates the findings of time-budget studies conducted in some post-socialist societies. This reveals that unpaid work occupies 45.6 per cent of all working time, meaning that the tentacles of the formal economy are far shorter than expounded by proponents of formalisation. Unpaid work, although for so

Table 3.2 The paid/unpaid work balance in post-socialist economies

Country	*Paid work (minutes)*	*Unpaid work (minutes)*	*Percentage of work time spent on unpaid work*
Hungary	345	254	42.4
Poland	332	244	42.4
Bulgaria	285	245	46.2
Czechoslovakia	320	272	45.9
East Germany	298	276	48.1
Ex-Yugoslavia	308	292	48.7
Mean	314	263	45.6

Source: derived from Gershuny (2000: table 7.1).

long considered a marginal 'other', is in fact larger than paid work, measured in terms of the amount of time spent carrying it out. This, however, should come as no surprise. When Polanyi (1944) depicted well over half a century ago 'the great transformation' from a non-market to a market society, he strongly emphasised that this was merely a shift in the balance of economic activity between these spheres. He never suggested it was a total transformation. Even if some have since then portrayed the shift towards a formal market economy as rather more total than Polanyi wanted to portray (e.g. Harvey 1982, 1989), this table demonstrates that Polanyi was quite correct not to over-exaggerate the encroachment of the formal market economy.

It is not only time-budget diaries that provide a direct measure of the degree of penetration of the formal market economy. There are also some very useful direct surveys, including the New Democracies Barometer (NDB) surveys conducted between 1992 and 1998 (Rose and Haerpfer 1992; Wallace and Haerpfer 2002). Given the rather dated evidence provided by these surveys, we here report a survey conducted in eight countries, namely Armenia, Belarus, Georgia, Kazakhstan, Kyrgyzstan, Moldova, Russia and Ukraine, during 2001 from the Living Conditions, Lifestyles and Health Project funded by the European Union under the INCO-Copernicus programme (see Abbott and Wallace 2009).

For those who perhaps assume that the formal economy in general and capitalist activity in particular has stretched its tentacles ever wider and deeper, Table 3.3 displays that this is far from the case. First, and examining the main source of income of households, it displays that on average just under half of all households rely on formal employment for their main income, just under one-quarter on pensions, one-fifth rely on non-exchanged work, one-tenth on the cash economy and just over 3 per cent on the social economy. This means that

Table 3.3 Primary sphere relied on by households to secure their livelihood in CIS countries, 2001

Country	*Percentage of households primarily dependent on:*				
	Formal economy: employment	*Formal economy: pension*	*Cash-in-hand economy*	*Unpaid exchange*	*Self-provisioning*
Armenia	28	27	14	6	25
Belarus	61	26	3	2	8
Georgia	35	12	11	4	38
Kazakhstan	57	20	8	4	11
Kyrgyzstan	26	13	14	2	44
Moldova	33	23	14	3	27
Russia	56	28	5	2	10
Ukraine	41	32	7	3	16
Average	43	24	9	3	21

Source: derived from Abbot and Wallace (2009: table 2).

for two-thirds of households the main income is from the formal economy, which includes employment in the public, private and third sectors, and not all of which is therefore formal capitalist endeavour.

However, there are significant variations between countries. Over 60 per cent of households receive their main source of income from formal employment in Belarus and over half in Kazakhstan and Russia compared with just one-third in Moldova and Georgia and one-fifth in Armenia and Kyrgyzstan. Two groups of countries, therefore, can be distinguished. In the first group, comprising Russia, Belarus, Kazakhstan and Ukraine, the vast majority of households (three-quarters or more) received their main income from the formal sector (wages or pensions). In the second group of countries, comprising Armenia, Georgia, Moldova and Kyrgyzstan, there is a much higher reliance on the informal economy, with nearly two-thirds of households' main income being from the informal economy in Kyrgyzstan and around half in the other three countries.

It might be asserted, of course, that those reliant on the cash-in-hand economy are reliant on capitalist endeavour, albeit of a completely unregulated and illegitimate variety. Recently, however, a growing literature unpacking the motives and work relations underpinning cash-in-hand work has revealed that over half of such work is conducted for friends, neighbours and acquaintances, often for not-for-profit reasons, such as to redistribute money to friends, neighbours and acquaintances in a way that avoids any connotation of charity or to build social support networks (Williams 2004c). As such, households primarily reliant on cash-in-hand work cannot all be assumed to be engaged in capitalist (i.e. profit-motivated monetised exchange) practices, albeit of an illegitimate variety. Although this might be the case for some, this cannot be assumed for all such households. For others, reliance on cash-in-hand work is likely to reflect their overarching dependence on friends, neighbours and kin for their means of livelihood and to be grounded in work relations more akin to mutual aid than profit-motivated capitalist practices.

Nevertheless, the important point is perhaps that only for around two-thirds of households in these CIS, formal income sources (employment or pensions) is the primary income source used to secure their livelihood, intimating that the transition to capitalism has been by no means all-encompassing, especially when one considers that some of this dependence on the formal sphere for livelihoods is through employment in the public or not-for-profit sectors or through redistributive state provision (pensions) rather than the profit-motivated capitalist sphere. Even this finding that examines solely the main sources of income, however, perhaps exaggerates the degree to which capitalism has become more central to livelihoods. As Table 3.4 reveals, when households were also asked for the second most important sphere that contributes to their livelihoods, the finding was that just 8 per cent of households cite the formal sphere as being both the first and second most important sphere and just 18 per cent relied on pensions and formal jobs alone for their income. Instead, 64 per cent of households relied on some combination of both formal and informal practices while 18 per cent relied on non-formal sources alone. To refer to these CIS as

Table 3.4 Primary and second most important spheres households rely on for their standard of living in CIS countries, 2001

Primary sphere relied on	*Percentage of all households*	*Of which second most important sphere is (%)*				
		Self-provisioning	*Unpaid exchanges*	*Cash-in-hand*	*Formal job*	*Pension*
Self-provisioning	21	1	1	7	6	6
Unpaid exchange	3	1	1	<1	<1	<1
Cash-in-hand	9	2	2	3	1	1
Formal job	43	16	5	10	8	4
Pension	24	11	4	3	2	4

Source: derived from Abbot and Wallace (2009: table 4).

capitalist societies is thus a grave misnomer. Less than one-fifth of households define themselves as reliant on the formal sphere (which, to repeat, is composed of not only the capitalist sphere but also the public and not-for-profit sectors).

For the vast majority of households, in consequence, a multiplicity of economic practices are used to secure a livelihood, as many smaller-scale qualitative studies have previously displayed in rich detail (Arnstberg and Boren 2003; Burawoy and Verdery 1999; Burrell 2011; Pavlovskaya 2004; Shevchenko 2009; Ghodsee 2011). Indeed, even when the formal sector is cited as being either the principal or second most important contributor to their living standard, it is usually combined with informal economic practices, meaning that a heterogeneous portfolio of work practices is the norm rather than the exception. Indeed, around 90 per cent of households cite sources other than the formal sphere as either most important or second most important to their standard of living. These data thus clearly delineate the limited contribution of the formal sector (i.e. where goods and services are provided through paid employment), never mind the capitalist economy (where this formal provision is conducted by private sector firms for profit-motivated purposes rather than the public or not-for-profit sectors).

Indeed, Table 3.5 further reinforces this shallow permeation of capitalism. It displays that one in four households in these CIS at the time of the survey received no income from the formal economy. Nevertheless, there are some cross-national variations. In a first group of countries (Russia, Belarus and Ukraine), well over three-quarters of households receive income from the formal economy, while in a second group (Armenia, Georgia and Kyrgyzstan) one-third have no connection to the formal economy. Kazakhstan and Moldova, meanwhile, both have just over two-thirds of households receiving income from the formal economy.

In sum, the majority of households in the CIS do have some connection with the formal economy, but the importance of the formal realm is far from being hegemonic. Instead, the vast majority of households rely principally on a plurality of economic practices to secure their livelihood and capitalist economic

Table 3.5 Share of households not receiving income from the formal economy, by country

Country	*Percentage of households receiving income from formal economy*	*Percentage of households receiving no income from formal economy*
Armenia	67.2	32.9
Belarus	89.6	10.4
Georgia	61.1	38.9
Kazakhstan	70.8	29.2
Kyrgyzstan	56.0	44.0
Moldova	72.2	27.8
Russia	87.4	12.6
Ukraine	82.6	17.4
Average	75.1	24.9

Source: derived from Abbot and Wallace (2009: table 5).

practices are just one among many that are employed in order to get by. There are, nevertheless, differences between countries. One group of countries, namely Russia, Ukraine, Belarus and Kazakhstan, has a greater reliance on formal modes of production to secure their livelihood than another group that is notably more dependent on other economic practices.

The role of informal economies in post-Soviet societies

Given the shallow and uneven penetration of the formal market economy in post-Soviet/socialist societies, there appears to be a need to rethink the 'economic' and 'economy' in these spaces. To start to achieve this, the theories behind the role of the informal must be considered, before they are tested empirically throughout the rest of the book. As will be revealed, for many decades a residue thesis was adopted which depicted informal economic activities as left-over and disappearing from view. The recognition of the persistence of informal economic activities, however, has led to the emergence of various competing perspectives that variously seek to explain their role in post-Soviet spaces, namely structuralist, neo-liberal and post-structuralist theorisations which respectively view informal economic activities as a by-product, alternative and complement to the formal market economy. Here, each theorisation is briefly reviewed in turn.

Modernisation theory: the informal sector as a residue

For many decades, the informal sector was depicted as a residue that was gradually disappearing from view, with economic 'advancement' and 'modernisation' (Geertz 1963; Lewis 1959). This formalisation thesis, therefore, temporally sequences the formal and informal work existing in post-Soviet spaces today.

The formal economy is the emergent mode of work organisation and positively depicted as representing 'progress', 'development', 'modernity' and 'advancement', while the informal economy is the receding mode of work organisation and negatively portrayed as representing 'under-development', 'traditionalism' and 'backwardness' (Geertz 1963; Lewis 1959).

Here, therefore, informal economic activities are 'the mere vestige of a disappearing past [or as] transitory or provisional' (Latouche 1993: 49). Never are they represented as resilient, ubiquitous, capable of generative growth, or as driving economic change. Nor are they even represented as part of a multitude of different forms of work co-existing in the contemporary post-Soviet world, but instead, are always positioned in a historic sequence as a remnant of the past. The outcome is that the trajectory of economic development is closed. There is only one trajectory and it is one in which there is an inevitable, even natural, linear development path towards the formal market economy.

Grounded in this grand narrative of what constitutes 'progress', governments of post-Soviet nations have tended to concentrate exclusively on developing the formal economy, and have viewed informal work as, at best, playing a supporting role and, at worst, deleterious to development and something to be formalised. The whole thrust of economic policy is focused upon how to facilitate the 'transition' to a formal market economy (Kostera 1995; Parker 2002). The thesis of formalisation is therefore not just a theory seeking to reflect reality, but is what Butler (1990) calls a 'performative discourse' that seeks to shape lived practice, or what Hickel and Khan (2012: 205) term 'a regime in the truest sense of the term'. Yet despite the widespread acceptance of this formalisation thesis, recent years have seen a burgeoning literature contesting this discourse. The major reason is a widespread recognition that the informal economy is not some weak and disappearing realm, but strong, persistent and even growing in the contemporary global economy (ILO 2012; Loayza and Rigolini 2011; Schneider 2012; Williams 2004a, 2004b, 2005a). The outcome is the emergence of various theories which transcend the depiction of informal work as a remnant or residue of the past.

Structuralist theory: the informal economy as a by-product of the formal economy

One such perspective is that which portrays informal economies as expanding rather than dwindling and formal and informal work as inextricably intertwined rather than separate. In this discourse, informal work is growing due to the emergence of a deregulated, open world economy, which is encouraging a race-to-the-bottom in terms of labour standards (Amin *et al.* 2002; Castells and Portes 1989; Gallin 2001; Hudson 2005; Portes 1994). On the one hand, the growth of informal work, particularly informal waged employment, is seen to be a direct by-product of employers seeking to reduce costs by adopting informal work arrangements. This is reflected in the growth of sub-contracting to not only those employing off-the-books workers under degrading, low-paid and exploitative 'sweatshop-like' conditions, exemplified in the garment-manufacturing sector (Bender 2004; Espenshade 2004; Ross 2004), but also those working on a temporary self-employed basis. As Davis (2006: 186) puts it, what we are witnessing in contemporary capitalism is the re-emergence of 'primitive forms of exploitation that have been given new life by postmodern globalization'.

On the other hand, the growth of the informal economy more broadly defined to include unpaid work also results from the demise of Fordism and socialism (Amin *et al.* 2002; Hudson 2005). In the new post-Fordist era of flexible production, those of little use to capitalism are no longer maintained as a reserve army of labour and socially reproduced by the formal welfare state, but instead are off-loaded, resulting in their increasing reliance on the informal sphere as a survival strategy. In this reading, the informal sphere is thus extensive in marginalised populations where the formal economy is weak, since its role is to act as a substitute for the formal economy in its absence. It is a work practice undertaken by those involuntarily decanted into this sphere and conducted out of necessity in order to survive (Amin *et al.* 2002; Castells and Portes 1989).

Unlike the residue thesis where the formal and informal economies are temporally convened, this by-product thesis thus represents the informal economy as a core and integral component of contemporary capitalism. As Fernandez-Kelly (2006: 18) puts it, 'the informal economy is far from a vestige of earlier stages in economic development. Instead, informality is part and parcel of the processes of modernization.' Although rejecting the temporal sequencing of the residue thesis, however, the same normative hierarchical reading is maintained. The informal economy is depicted as possessing largely negative attributes and formalisation viewed as the route to progress, albeit more as a prescription of the required socially constructed trajectory of economic development rather than as an organic and immutable view of the direction of change. Exemplifying this by-product approach is the ILO (2012), which recognises that informal work is growing and inextricably intertwined with formal work; its 'decent work' campaign prescribes formalisation as the path to progress.

Neo-liberal theory: informal economies as an alternative to the formal economy

For others recognising the prevalence and growth of the informal sector, however, this hierarchical ordering that privileges the formal economy as the path to progress is replaced by a depiction of informalisation as the route to advancement. Akin to the residue discourse, the informal and formal economies are here often seen as separate and discrete, but unlike both the modernisation and structuralists perspectives, participation in informal work is depicted as possessing positive attributes and impacts and is viewed as conducted as a matter of choice rather than due to a lack of choice (Cooper and May 2012; Cross 2000; Gerxhani 2004; Sassen 2009). As Gerxhani (2004: 274) argues, for example, workers 'choose to participate in the informal economy because they find more autonomy, flexibility and freedom in this sector than in the formal one'.

The relationship between informal and formal work is thus read as substitutive, with one seen as a replacement for the other, and the difference between this school and structuralism is that participation in the informal economy is usually depicted as a choice rather than a necessity. For neo-liberals, informal work is not only seen more as a matter of choice than due to a lack of choice, but informal workers are depicted as heroes throwing off the shackles of a burdensome state, and informal work a rational economic path taken to escape over-regulation in the formal realm (Becker 2004; De Soto 1989, 2001; London and Hart 2004; Nwabuzor 2005; Small Business Council 2004). As Nwabuzor (2005: 126) asserts, 'Informality is a response to burdensome controls, and an attempt to circumvent them', or as Becker (2004: 10) puts it, 'informal work arrangements are a rational response by micro-entrepreneurs to over-regulation by government bureaucracies'. For De Soto (1989: 255), in consequence 'the real problem is not so much informality as formality'.

Informal work, usually depicted as own-account work conducted on a self-employed basis, therefore, is viewed as the people's 'spontaneous and creative response to the state's incapacity to satisfy the basic needs of the impoverished masses' (De Soto 1989: xiv–xv). It is a rational economic strategy pursued by entrepreneurs whose spirit is stifled by state-imposed institutional constraints and who voluntarily operate in the informal economy to avoid the costs, time and effort of formal registration (Cross and Morales 2007; De Soto 1989, 2001; Perry and Maloney 2007; Small Business Council 2004). Such work is consequently seen as the route to progress and an exemplar of how formal work, as well as the economy more generally, could be organised if it were deregulated. The solution, in consequence, is to liberate the labour market from intervention and the informal economy exemplifies how the formal sphere could be organised if it were deregulated. As Sauvy (1984: 274) explains, such work represents 'the oil in the wheels, the infinite adjustment mechanism' in the economy. It is the elastic in the system that allows a snug fit of supply to demand that is the aim of every economy. If left to operate unhampered by the state, then the informal sphere would provide this snug fit. At present, however, this cannot happen because, for example, the state through its formal welfare provision creates a 'dependency' culture, preventing populations from taking responsibility for their own livelihoods in the informal sphere. In this approach, in consequence, the informal economy represents a positive alternative to the regulated formal economy.

Post-structuralist theory: the diverse economies perspective

To contest the narrative that nations are universally pursuing a uniform and linear development path towards formal market economies, a corpus of post-development literature has emerged that has begun to re-read the trajectories of economic development of advanced 'market' economies (Byrne *et al.* 2001; Community Economies Collective 2001; Gibson-Graham 1996, 2003; Williams 2004b, 2005a), post-Soviet transition economies (e.g. Round *et al.* 2008; Smith

2004, 2010; Smith and Stenning 2006) and majority (third-)world countries (e.g. Escobar 1995, 2001; Esteva 1985; Latouche 1993; Sachs 1992). As Smith (2004: 14) succinctly explains, these commentators seek 'to liberate the non-capitalist from its secondary position in understandings ... and to reposition "capitalism"'. Viewing the advocacy of a move towards a formal market economy not as an abstraction seeking to reflect reality but as a performative discourse that is seeking to shape the world by making the reality conform to its image, this post-structuralist or post-development discourse asserts that accepting the thesis of the advent of formal market economies not only serves the vested interests of capitalism (by constructing market hegemony as a natural and inevitable future) but also results in a failure to contemplate the creation of alternatives. The net outcome is that the real world ends up conforming to the image. For post-structuralist commentators, therefore, there is a need to deconstruct the discourse of formalisation and marketisation and articulate alternative representations of the trajectory of economic development, not least by recognising and valuing the existence of economic practices beyond the formal market economy which shine a light on the possibility of constructing alternative futures beyond the hegemony of a formal market economy. As Samers (2005: 876) puts it, they seek to 'relinquish a vision of a largely unimaginable socialism as capitalism's opposite, and instead, recover and revalorise a multitude of non-capitalist practices and spaces that disrupt the assumption of a hegemonic capitalism'. In post-Soviet societies in particular, this demonstration that multifarious economic practices persist resonates with the broader transitology approaches of socio-cultural anthropologists (Burawoy and Verdery 1999; Hann 2006; Humphrey 2002).

To challenge the thesis of formal market hegemony, two broad strategies are used. On the one hand, and employing Derridean discourse analysis (Derrida 1967), the informal/formal and market/non-market binary hierarchies are challenged that endow the formal and market economies with positivity and the subordinate informal and non-market realms with negativity. To contest this, two approaches are used. First, attempts are made to revalue the subordinate term, such as by attaching a value to unpaid work (Goldschmidt-Clermond 1982; Luxton 1997). The problem, however, and as Derrida (1967) points out, is that revaluing the subordinate term in a binary hierarchy is difficult since it also tends to be closely associated with the subordinate terms in the other dualisms (e.g. non-market work is associated with reproduction, emotion, subjectivity, women and the non-economic, and market work with production, reason, objectivity, men and the economic). A second strategy is thus to blur the boundaries between the terms, highlighting similarities on both sides of the dualism so as to undermine the solidity and fixity of identity/presence, showing how the excluded other is so embedded within the primary identity that its distinctiveness is ultimately unsustainable. For example, the household is represented as also a site of production – of various goods and services – and the factory also as a place of reproduction (Gibson-Graham 2003). Pursuing either of these strategies can thus challenge the hierarchical binaries that pervade contemporary thought and have until now stifled recognition of the 'other' that is non-market work.

On the other hand, and alongside this Derridean approach, some post-structuralist writings follow the path laid by Foucault (1981) by seeking to deconstruct the formalisation and marketisation theses through: first, a critical analysis of the violence and injustices perpetrated by these theories or systems of meaning (what they exclude, prohibit and deny); and second, a genealogical analysis of the processes, continuities and discontinuities by which these discourses came to be formed. Exemplifying this is Escobar (1995), who reveals that prescribing the development pathway of formal market hegemony has violently 'subjected' individuals, regions and entire countries to the powers and agencies of the development apparatus. Rather than accept the vision of the 'good society' emanating from the west, Escobar's Foucauldian approach to development discourse opens the way towards 'unmaking' the third world by highlighting its constructedness and the possibility of alternative constructions (Escobar 2001). Importantly, his work points the way toward a repositioning of subjects outside a formalisation and marketisation discourse that produces subservience, victimhood and economic impotence.

Akin to Escobar, Gibson-Graham (1996) has re-read western economic development through a similar post-structuralist lens. For her/them (i.e. they are two authors writing as one), and adopting a similar Foucauldian approach, the use of the degree of formalisation and marketisation as a benchmark for 'development' and 'progress' and measuring countries against, results in a linear and unidimensional trajectory of economic development being imposed that represents non-western nations as backward, traditional, lagging and so forth and positions those western nations at the front with a closed future of ever greater formalisation and marketisation (see also Williams 2002, 2004b, 2005a; Williams and Windebank 2003). This, for them, is a representation of reality and discursive construction that reflects the power, and serves the interests, of capital. By representing the future as a natural and inevitable shift towards the formal market economy, one is engaged in the active constitution of economic possibility, shaping and constraining the actions of economic agents and policy makers.

By re-visioning post-Soviet economies as composed of a diversity of economic practices, the implications are two-fold. First, it suggests that there are other economic practices besides formal market economic practices. Second, by locating work beyond the formal market economy as existing in the here and now, one is engaged in the demonstrable construction and practice of alternatives to formalisation and marketism. This re-reading is thus not simply about bringing minority practices to light. It is about de-centring the formal market economy from its pivotal position in economic development and bringing to the fore the possibility of alternative economic practices and futures beyond the formal market economy. Until now, however, such a post-structuralist approach towards economic development has been seldom applied to post-Soviet spaces. Despite the dominance of the discourse that these so-called 'transition' economies are on a natural and inevitable pathway to a formal market economy, numerous small-scale qualitative case studies (as noted above, for example, Burrell 2011; Ghodsee 2011; Pavlovskaya 2004; Shevchenko 2009) have questioned either the dominance of the formal market economy or that the direction of economic development is towards formalisation and marketisation. Here, in consequence, this book further fills this lacuna.

Conclusions: re-figuring the economic in post-Soviet societies

As Chapter 2 showed, the recurring belief has been that post-Soviet economies have witnessed a process of both formalisation and marketisation since the fall of the Soviet bloc and thus that the post-Soviet world has been witnessing a process of transition towards a formal market economy. The outcome has been that one inevitable and immutable future for post-Soviet economies has been envisaged and economic policy has sought to enable this future to come to fruition by near enough entirely concentrating on the development of formal market economies. Indeed, Kostera (1995) has likened the massive intervention and investment to facilitate the emergence of the formal market economy to a religious crusade in which management educators and consultants have acted like missionaries transferring the cult of what Parker (2002) calls 'market managerialism' to the heathen masses. Yet as this book will reveal, the post-Soviet world has remained steadfastly grounded in a form of work organisation based on economic pluralism, and there appears to be no sign of this abating in the near future.

Not only is there little evidence of any widespread encroachment of the formal market economy in the post-Soviet world, but work beyond the formal market economy does not appear to be some traditional, stagnant, declining, backward, marginal sphere, but instead, if anything, is thriving, even growing. There is perhaps a need, in consequence, for those who have pursued market-led policy prescriptions with missionary zeal, and ignored developing other means of livelihood, to question whether this remains the appropriate way forward and whether all of one's eggs should be put into the basket of developing the formal market economy when considering the trajectory of economic development in the post-Soviet world.

The intention of this chapter has been to contest the myth that the advent of a hegemonic formal market economy is an inevitable and natural process and that no other options exist regarding the trajectory of economic development. On the issue of the inevitability of a formal market economy, this chapter has made it very clear that a future in which the formal market economy becomes hegemonic is not cast in stone. Indeed, to assert that the formal market economy is unavoidable is to fly in the face of the evidence. On the issue of whether the advent of a formal market economy is a natural process, meanwhile, this chapter has shown that the formal market sphere is not an autonomous sector that grows with little or no help. Rather, it has been energetically facilitated and sustained by a barrage of intervention.

Bearing this in mind, one has to wonder quite how widely and deeply the formal market economy would have penetrated post-Soviet spaces without such massive intervention and encouragement. If the formal market economy has only captured such a minor share of all economic activity even when governments have so actively intervened to encourage its growth, then one does wonder quite how expansive the formal market realm would have been if left to its own devices. Given this continuous and ongoing nurturing and support by government, it is thus obvious that the formal market economy is not an organic process. Once recognised, then the future trajectory of economic development becomes more open. Seeking to develop the formal market economy through controlled interventionism and paying little heed to the development of work beyond the formal market economy becomes clearly recognised as but one option available regarding the trajectory of economic development.

The result is to open up economic development to become an 'undefined, open-ended, heterogeneous transformative process' (Chowdhury 2007: 10). Rather than view post-Soviet spaces as lagging behind the west by reducing difference to backwardness, the aim of this book is to transcend the suppression and subjugation of 'another development' by opening up the future to other possibilities beyond a totalising formal market economy. Our project is to deconstruct the familiar notion of economic development as a transition to a formal market economy by revealing the fact that formal market economic practices are just one of a plurality of economic practices in post-Soviet spaces, thereby decentring the formal market economy and recovering alternative futures for economic development so as to disrupt dominant economic discourses about the future of post-Soviet economies as being towards a totalising formal market economy. However, we do not wish to replace one universal conceptualisation of the trajectory of economic development with another alternative universal.

Instead, we wish to argue in this book that not only is the informal and non-market economy persistent and even growing in many post-Soviet spaces (negating the formalisation and marketisation theses) but also that the role that they play in contemporary post-Soviet spaces is not always the same and that it varies according to both the type of informal work being considered and the population groups and places being evaluated. Some forms of informal work will be a by-product of formal employment in some places and among some populations groups, while others will act as complements and yet others as alternatives. Using Ukraine and Russia as case studies, the aim in the following chapters will be to start to tease out precisely the conditions under which different forms of informal work are a by-product, complement, alternative to the formal economy in general and formal market economy more particularly.

4 Beyond the formal–informal economy dualism

Unpacking the diverse economies of post-Soviet societies

Drawing inspiration from the burgeoning corpus of post-structuralist scholars, as discussed in the previous chapter, who have begun to question the narrative of the impending hegemony of the formal market economy in post-Soviet societies and beyond, this chapter seeks to further advance this emergent 'diverse economies' literature by constructing an analytical lens for representing the multiple labour practices in economies. Transcending the simplistic formal/informal economy dichotomy, this chapter seeks to conceptualise the multiple kinds of labour that exist in post-Soviet societies by adopting a 'total social organisation of labour' approach. As will be shown, this conceptualises a spectrum from formal-oriented to informal-oriented labour practices, which is cross-cut by another spectrum ranging from wholly monetised to wholly non-monetised labour practices. The resultant outcome is to provide an analytical lens for capturing the plurality of labour practices that exist in post-Soviet societies in a manner which shows how they all seamlessly merge into each other.

Having developed this conceptual framework for analysing diverse economies, the second section of this chapter then applies this to understanding the multifarious labour practices used in Ukraine and Russia. Presenting the overarching results of 600 interviews conducted across various populations in Ukraine and 313 interviews conducted in Moscow, the outcome will be to begin to reveal not only the shallow permeation of the formal market economy in Ukraine and Russia, which have been supposedly undergoing a 'transition' to formal market economies, but also the existence of diverse work cultures across different populations along with marked socio-spatial variations in the nature of individual labour practices. This sets the scene for the rest of the book, which unravels the lived experiences of transition in these post-Soviet societies.

Beyond the formal–informal economy dichotomy

To contest the notion of a formal/informal binary hierarchy, a diverse range of critical, post-colonial, post-development, post-structuralist and post-capitalist theorists (e.g. Chakrabarty 2000; Community Economies Collective 2001; Escobar 1995; Gibson-Graham 1996, 2006; Lee 2006; Leyshon *et al.* 2003; Williams and Round 2007) have begun to blur the boundaries between the two.

Following either Butler (1990) by highlighting the performativity of this normative separateness and/or the path laid by Derrida (1967) and Foucault (1977) of discourse analysis and deconstruction, these commentators have sought not so much to invert the normative hierarchy, but rather to highlight the similarities on both sides and to show how the formal and informal are not always composed of entirely different economic relations, values and motives (Chowdhury 2007; Escobar 2001; Gibson-Graham 2006; Gupta 1998; Lee 2006; Pollard *et al.* 2009; Smith and Stenning 2006; Williams 2005a; Williams and Zelizer 2005).

In consequence, there is now gathering pace a loose body of knowledge that is challenging the long-standing depiction of formal and informal labour as separate and unified spheres, as well as hostile worlds. The most common classificatory schema used in practice to demonstrate the need to recognise the differences and similarities on each side has been to retain a broad distinction between formal and informal labour, but to show how the informal side is not unified by breaking it down into three very different practices, namely: self-provisioning, which is where a household member engages in unpaid work for themselves or another member of their household; unpaid community labour, where a household member engages in unpaid work for somebody who lives outside of the household, and paid informal labour where paid work is conducted that is unregistered by, or hidden from, the state for tax, social security and/or labour law purposes (Leonard 1998; Pahl 1984; Slack 2007; Slack and Jensen 2010; Smith 2010; Smith and Stenning 2006; Wallace and Latcheva 2006; Williams 2005a, 2010a). The problem is that although this classification of labour practices unpacks some of the diversity in informal practices, it leaves intact formal labour as a unified whole and also the notion that the formal and informal are separate spheres composed of distinct economic relations, values and motives. This is similarly the case with other conceptual frameworks and analytical lenses. Gibson-Graham (2006), for example, differentiate transactions into three subcategories, namely market, alternative market (e.g. off-the-books, barter) and non-market (e.g. gift-giving, subsistence), and also labour practices again into three broad types, namely waged, alternative paid (e.g. cash-in-hand, reciprocal) and unpaid (e.g. family care, self-provisioning). Although these again unpack the informal labour side of the coin, they leave the formal side intact as a unified whole and continue to portray formal and informal as separate distinct spheres.

A total social organisation of labour approach

How, therefore, can the multiple kinds of labour that exist in economies be portrayed more in a manner that shows how the formal and informal are not separate, that the differences within formal and informal-oriented activities are as great as the variations between them, and that the economic relations, values and motives of formally oriented and informally oriented activities are not always different and hostile? Perhaps the most prominent and promising attempt so far is the 'total social organisation of labour' (TSOL) approach of Glucksmann (2005: 28), who reads 'the economy as a "multiplex" combination of modes, rather than as a dualism'. In this approach, and as Taylor (2004) shows, a continuum of labour practices according to their degree of formality is constructed and this continuum is then cross-cut by whether the labour is paid or unpaid (Glucksmann 1995, 2005). This analytical lens of the TSOL was originally used to elucidate the gendered connections between paid and unpaid work and has been widely applied (Acker 2006; Bradley 2007; Crompton 2006; Glucksmann 2000, 2009; McDowell 2005; Pettinger *et al.* 2005; Strangleman and Warren 2008). Much of the work has so far drawn attention to the 'multi-modal' character of contemporary capitalism and how terms like the 'dual economy' and the 'mixed economy' barely capture the complexity and variety of the forms of provision in existence. This concept, moreover, has been argued to be applicable at micro, meso or macro levels and to units at a range of scales, from the individual and household to a country or global region. One attempt to display this is the work conducted by Lyon and Glucksmann (2008) which compares the contribution of different modes of provision to elder care work in four countries (Italy, the Netherlands, Sweden and the UK), revealing how various forms of provision not only have different roles and significance in each country, but also interact in nationally distinctive ways.

In this chapter the intention is to apply this analytical lens of a TSOL to understanding how labour practices vary across post-Soviet spaces in general, and Russia and Ukraine more particularly. To map this, and as Figure 4.1 displays, a seamless range of labour practices is constructed, ranging first along a spectrum from relatively formal to more informal labour practices, and second, and cross-cutting this, along a further spectrum (rather than dualism) from wholly non-monetised, through gift exchange and in-kind labour, to wholly monetised labour practices. Hatched circles are deliberately used to display how, although various labour practices along these continua can be named, they are in effect part of a borderless continua of practices, rather than separate kinds of labour, which overlap and seamlessly merge into one another as one moves

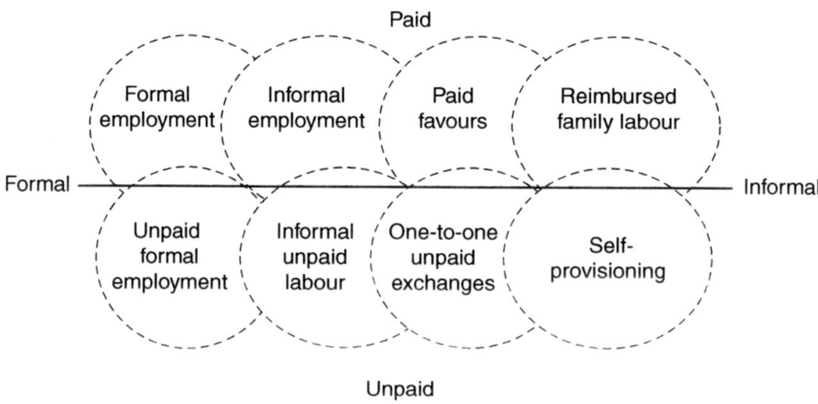

Figure 4.1 A typology of work practices: the total social organisation of labour.

along both the formal/informal spectrum of the x-axis as well as along the monetisation/non-monetisation spectrum of the y-axis. Here, therefore, and unlike previous frameworks, the borderless fluidity between different labour practices is captured and it is clearly shown how the multiple practices are not discrete but seamlessly entwined and conjoined.

The outcome is that eight broad, overlapping labour practices can be identified, each of which possess within them different varieties of labour and which merge at their borders with the other practices. First, there is formal paid labour or formal employment, defined as paid work registered by the state for tax, social security and labour law purposes. Within this formal sphere, three types of formal labour, namely in the private, public and third sectors, have been conventionally distinguished. However, given that private sector organisations are increasingly pursuing a triple bottom line, while public and third sector organisations are also pursuing profit (albeit in order to reinvest so as to achieve wider social and environmental objectives), an ongoing blurring of the boundaries of these three formal spheres is occurring. Paid formal employment as a whole, moreover, is not discrete and separate since it often merges with both unpaid formal employment and informal employment.

Informal employment is here defined as paid labour unregistered by or hidden from the state for tax, social security and labour law purposes (Williams 2009). Different varieties again exist, ranging from wholly undeclared labour where none of the payment is declared for tax, social, security and labour law purposes, to under-declared formal employment where formal employees receive an additional undeclared wage from their formal employer alongside their formal declared wage or the formal self-employed do not declare various portions of their earnings (Williams 2009). Conventionally, however, and adopting a formal–informal economy depiction of separate and hostile spheres, a job or labour contract was assumed to be either formal or informal, but not both. Nevertheless, under-declared formal employment clearly shows how labour can be concomitantly both formal and informal, meaning that the formal/informal divide is more blurred than previously considered in dualistic representations.

Formal employment not only overlaps with informal employment, but also formal unpaid labour. Again, various types exist. In the private and public sectors, formal unpaid labour can take the form of unpaid internships or one-week trials, and people do this expecting paid employment at the end. Sometimes, however, businesses fail to pay their formal employees for protracted periods (Shevchenko 2009), so it is not conducted as a matter of choice. It is in third sector organisations, nevertheless, that such labour is most extensive, and commonly termed 'formal volunteering', which refers to 'giving help through groups, clubs or organizations to benefit other people or the environment' (Low *et al.* 2008: 11). In some instances this can become 'off-the-radar' unpaid labour, when help is again provided through groups to benefit other people or the environment, but the formalities required by law have not all been fulfilled, such as when a children's football coach volunteers but without have undertaken the required police checks. One-to-one unpaid labour refers to labour provided on an individualised level to members of households other than one's own, such as kin living outside one's household, friends, neighbours and acquaintances. This again is of different kinds, ranging from individualised one-way giving (often termed 'informal volunteering') to two-way reciprocity. When reciprocity is involved, such unpaid endeavour often blurs into reimbursed favours since the reciprocity may take the form of either in-kind labour or gifts in lieu of payment. Indeed, whether one-to-one labour when reimbursed in-kind or with gifts (as well as when paid) is closer to informal employment or to paid favours depends on the economic relations, values and motives involved. Financial gain is usually more prominent when more distant social relations are involved, and redistributive and relationship-building purposes more prominent when conducted for and by closer social relations, thus displaying how informal employment and reimbursed favours represent a continuum of, rather than separate, labour practices.

Turning to labour practices within the family household, most is self-provisioning, which is defined as unpaid work conducted by household members for themselves or for other members of their household. Sometimes, nevertheless, family members are reimbursed for tasks conducted for and by other household members using either money, gifts or in-kind reciprocal labour. Monetary payment is nearly always reserved for inter- rather than intra-generational exchanges (e.g. from a parent to a child). When gifts and in-kind reciprocal labour are included, however, the divide between monetised and non-monetised labour becomes blurred. Indeed, it is perhaps rare in couple households that domestic tasks are today conducted wholly unpaid with no expectation of future reciprocity. Even unpaid housework, an activity often viewed as wholly non-monetised and non-exchanged, is often embedded in expectations of reciprocity in couple households. Moreover, what constitutes family and non-family is by no means always clear cut, and therefore differentiating family work (self-provisioning) from one-to-one community exchanges is sometimes difficult, since current acquaintances, friends and even neighbours might well be past or future family. In what now follows, this TSOL analytical lens which depicts a seamless spectrum from formal to informal oriented practices, cross-cut by a continuum from reimbursed to non-reimbursed practices, is now applied to understanding the 'economic' in both Russia and Ukraine.

Evaluating the diverse economies of Ukraine

Following the demise of the Soviet Union, many ex-socialist nations have witnessed severe difficulties in making the transition to a market economy. Ukraine, the second largest successor state of the former Soviet Union, is no exception. Unemployment and labour market insecurity became a reality overnight (see Cherneyshev 2006; Lehmann and Terrell 2006; Standing 2005). Indeed, official employment declined by about one-third between 1990 and 1999 (Cherneyshev 2006), and despite the euphoria in Ukraine surrounding the 'orange' revolution and a 'turn to the west', economic difficulties have been a persistent feature of post-socialism.

'Bribe taxes', administrative corruption and 'informal taxation' are rife in everyday life and represent significant barriers to both economic growth and the formalisation of economic practices (Hanson 2006; Round and Kosterina 2005). Indeed, in global surveys, Ukraine is often identified as one of the most corrupt nations in the world. The World Bank's 'Doing Business 2009' survey ranked Ukraine 145th of the 181 countries rated in terms of positive business climate, arguing that corruption and over-zealous bureaucracy stymies economic development (World Bank 2009). Ukraine was in 2009 ranked 180th out of 181 countries in terms of the ease of paying taxes (PricewaterhouseCooper 2009). A Transparency International (2005) survey, meanwhile, states that in Ukraine 82 per cent of respondents had recently paid a bribe to access services/goods to which they were entitled, the highest figure in the world. Although Anderson and Gray (2006) argue that the level of corruption is decreasing, they acknowledge there is still much work to be done.

It is perhaps little surprise, therefore, to find that when proxy indicators are used to measure the magnitude of informal employment, it is estimated to be equivalent to 47.3–53.7 per cent of GDP using physical input proxies (Schneider and Enste 2000) and 55–70 per cent using currency demand (Dzvinka 2002). Official Ukrainian government estimates, using indirect proxy methods, assert that some 55 per cent of Ukraine's GDP is produced in the informal economy (NCRU 2005). In 2005, furthermore, and according to official state figures, approximately ten million Ukrainians, around 20 per cent of the population, were receiving incomes below the state subsistence minimum level. As Round and Kosterina (2005) highlight, however, even this subsistence minimum figure has little relevance since it only allows for an extremely basic diet, for clothes to be replaced every 3–5 years and assumes that the 'market' runs efficiently (i.e. that benefits and subsidies can be accessed). The reality, as Rose (2005) identifies, is that 73 per cent of Ukrainians receive insufficient from their main income to buy what they need to survive. Until now, however, and beyond the New Democracies Barometer (NDB) surveys conducted between 1992 and 1998 (Wallace and Haerpfer 2002; Wallace and Latcheva 2006), no contemporary studies have analysed the coping practices people use to get by in Ukraine.

To evaluate market penetration in Ukraine and document the multiple labour practices in this society, therefore, a survey was undertaken in late 2005 and early 2006 comprising face-to-face interviews with 600 households on their livelihood practices in a diverse range of localities. Given that previous studies in Europe reveal significant disparities in the types of economic practice used between affluent and deprived as well as urban and rural populations (Leonard 1994; Renooy 1990; Williams 2005a), maximum variation sampling was employed to select four contrasting localities. First, in the capital of Kyiv, an affluent area was chosen, namely Pechers'k, heavily populated by government officials and the new business class, along with a deprived neighbourhood, Vynogradar, comprising dilapidated Soviet-era housing with high unemployment and widespread poverty. Continuing the process of maximum variation sampling, a deprived rural area near Vasyl'kiv was then chosen, which relied heavily on a nearby refrigerator-manufacturing plant for its employment until it closed nearly ten years ago, and since then has suffered high unemployment; and finally, a town on the Ukrainian/Slovakia border was selected, Užhgorod, which is the administrative centre of the Zakarpattia Oblast province and where a concern exists among its population that inflated prices due to cross-border trade mean they cannot afford many goods and services. This survey, therefore, is not based on a nationally representative sample, and care should be taken to avoid generalising the results to the national level. It does, however, avoid surveying only one locality-type, which might have a very specific configuration of work and imply that this is more widely applicable by examining a diverse range of locality types.

Within each locality, a spatially stratified sampling methodology was used to select households for interview (Kitchin and Tate 2001). In each locality, 150 interviews were conducted (600 in total). If there were 3,000 households in the area and 150 interviews were sought, then the researcher called at every twentieth household. If there was no response and/or the interviewer was refused an interview, then the twenty-first household was visited, then the nineteenth, twenty-second, eighteenth and so on. Table 4.1 provides an overview of the socio-economic profile of the respondents

To evaluate the labour practices supplied and used in Ukraine, structured face-to-face interviews were conducted. Besides gathering background data on gross household income, the employment status of household members, their employment histories, ages and gender, respondents were asked about the types of labour they used to secure their livelihood. Second, the labour practices that the household last used to complete 25 common domestic services were analysed; third, whether they had undertaken any of these 25 tasks for others during the past year using any of the ten labour practices; fourth, open-ended questions about each of the ten labour practices conducted and its relative importance to their household income; and fifth and finally, and using five-point Likert scaling, attitudinal questions concerning their ability to draw upon help from others and their views of the economy, politics, everyday life and their future prospects.

Beyond market hegemony: unravelling the plurality of labour practices in Ukraine

Table 4.2 reveals participation in the market to be not as extensive as sometimes assumed. Just 26 per cent of respondents had engaged in paid formal labour in the private sector during the previous 12 months. Relative to non-exchanged labour (which all respondents had conducted over the past year), one-to-one unpaid labour (which 62 per cent had conducted) and one-to-one paid community labour (44 per cent), participating in formal employment in the private sector appears confined to small pockets of the population with a similar participation rate to formal unpaid volunteering (25 per cent) and formal employment in the public and third sector (20 per cent). Participation rates in paid formal labour in the private sector display some marked socio-spatial variations from

Table 4.1 Socio-economic profile of respondents to Ukraine survey of livelihood practices, 2005–2006

	Number of respondents				
	Pechers'k	*Vynogradar*	*Vasyl'kiv*	*Užhgorod*	*Total*
	150	*150*	*150*	*150*	*600*
Age:					
0–16	0	1	0	0	0
16–25	9	21	10	30	18
26–35	29	26	25	11	23
36–45	28	26	24	24	25
46–55	21	12	19	23	19
56–65	3	9	11	6	7
>65	10	5	11	6	8
Gender:					
Men	67	49	57	39	53
Women	33	51	43	61	47
Household employment status:					
Multiple earner	65	55	51	61	58
Single earner	25	30	31	32	29
No earner: working age	2	5	3	2	3
No earner: retired	8	10	15	5	10
Work history of household:					
Continuous employment of all	60	48	62	48	55
Mostly all employed	21	27	19	22	22
Mostly all unemployed	16	15	7	19	14
Continuously unemployed	3	10	12	11	9
Gross household income:					
<600	9	11	23	9	13
600–1,399	29	28	66	39	41
1,400–2,199	25	26	8	28	22
2,200–2,999	15	13	2	11	10
3,000–3,800	10	12	0	5	7
>3,800	12	10	1	8	8

Source: Ukraine survey.

11 per cent among the lowest-income households to 34 per cent in the highest-income households. It is not just this labour practice, however, which varies socio-spatially. Participation rates in all ten labour practices (with the exception of one-to-one non-monetised exchange) are generally higher in affluent than deprived populations.

It does not necessarily follow that just because a labour practice is extensively used, households rely on it to secure their livelihood. Despite the relatively narrow participation rates in formal market labour, nearly one-third (32 per cent) of households chiefly depend on this labour practice to secure their livelihood. Over two-thirds (68 per cent) of households, therefore, primarily depend on

Table 4.2 Participation rates in labour practices in Ukraine: by locality and gross household income

	Monetised					*Non-monetised*				
	Formal job in private sector	*Formal job in public/ third sector*	*Informal employment*	*Paid favours*	*Paid family labour*	*Formal unpaid labour in private sector*	*Formal unpaid labour in public and third sector*	*Informal unpaid labour in groups*	*One-to-one unpaid labour*	*Self-provisioning*
All areas	26	20	10	44	4	4	25	1	62	100
By locality type:										
Affluent Kyiv	34	29	10	21	6	4	31	0	52	100
Deprived Kyiv	16	14	9	60	3	5	15	1	70	100
Deprived rural	18	16	9	63	2	3	19	2	73	100
Border town	29	26	12	30	4	4	33	1	54	100
By household income:										
<600	11	9	8	40	0	1	10	0	77	100
600–1,399	12	8	10	38	2	2	21	0	70	100
1,400–2,199	20	17	17	36	0	3	25	1	58	100
2,200–2,999	22	17	15	43	7	5	21	1	61	100
3,000–3,799	30	23	10	55	6	8	30	0	54	100
>3,800	34	26	16	61	8	4	40	0	52	99

Source: Ukraine survey.

practices other than private sector formal labour. Some 30 per cent chiefly rely on income from formal jobs in the public and third sector, 10 per cent on pensions/state benefits, 10 per cent on informal employment, 8 per cent on self-provisioning, 6 per cent on paid favours among close social relations and 4 per cent on unpaid one-to-one mutual aid.

Solely asking households about their primary livelihood practice, however, perhaps exaggerates the degree of reliance on the formal market economy. When also asked to name their second most important practice, just one in 25 households (4 per cent) depend entirely on the formal market economy and just one in ten households purely on formal income sources. The majority of households (96 per cent) either combine formal market labour with other practices (28 per cent) or else use some combination of labour practices that does not include formal market labour (68 per cent). To refer to Ukraine as a formal market economy, therefore, is a grave misnomer. Only one in 25 households define themselves as relying solely on the formal market economy to secure their livelihood. Instead, a plurality of labour practices is the norm. Households bundle together jobs in the formal sector, utilise the social welfare system, engage in subsistence production, and in community exchanges to secure their livelihood, as has been previously intimated in many other East-Central European countries (Smith and Stenning 2006; Wallace and Haerpfer 2002; Wallace and Latcheva 2006).

It is not just an examination of the labour practices supplied that highlights the diverse kinds of labour utilised in Ukraine. Evaluating the labour practices households last used to conduct 25 common domestic tasks, Table 4.3 finds that formal market labour was primarily last used in just 13 per cent of instances, displaying the limited commodification of domestic services in Ukraine. Indeed, only 25 per cent of domestic tasks involved any kind of paid labour; the remaining three-quarters used primarily unpaid labour, with some 71 per cent chiefly self-provisioning.

Nevertheless, there are differences across populations in both the permeation of formal market labour and the work cultures that prevail. As Table 4.3 reveals, higher-income households and those living in affluent localities more commonly use formal market labour to complete domestic tasks than lower-income households and those living in deprived areas. Indeed, the lowest-income households externalise to the formal market economy just 8 per cent of the 25 tasks surveyed compared with 44 per cent among the highest-income households. Similarly, while households in the affluent Kyiv district outsourced 20 per cent of the domestic tasks to formal market labour, this figure was just 6 per cent in the deprived rural area of Vasil'kiv.

The extent of outsourcing to formal market labour, however, is not the only difference in work cultures across populations. Populations use other labour practices to varying extents and also different combinations to secure their livelihood. Higher-income households and households in affluent areas, for example, use monetised labour practices to a greater extent than lower-income households and those in deprived areas who more heavily rely on community exchanges

Table 4.3 Labour practices used by households to conduct 25 everyday domestic services in Ukraine: by locality and gross household income

	Monetised					*Non-monetised*				
	Formal job in private sector	*Formal job in public/ third sector*	*Informal employment*	*Paid favours*	*Paid family labour*	*Formal unpaid labour in private sector*	*Formal unpaid labour in public and third sector*	*Informal unpaid labour in groups*	*One-to-one unpaid labour*	*Self-provisioning*
All areas	13	2	6	4	<1	0	<1	<1	4	71
By locality type:										
Affluent Kyiv	20	1	6	2	1	0	<1	<1	2	68
Deprived Kyiv	16	2	3	5	1	0	<1	<1	6	66
Deprived rural	6	2	4	6	<1	0	<1	<1	5	77
Border town	8	1	10	4	<1	0	<1	<1	3	73
By household income:										
<600	8	2	2	6	<1	0	1	<1	5	76
600–1,399	6	1	3	5	<1	0	<1	<1	4	79
1,400–2,199	11	2	5	4	<1	0	<1	<1	4	73
2,200–2,999	17	1	15	4	<1	0	<1	0	3	59
3,000–3,799	19	1	12	3	<1	0	0	0	1	63
>3,800	44	1	10	2	1	0	0	0	4	38

Source: Ukraine survey.

between closer social relations, both of the monetised and non-monetised variety, and non-exchanged labour. Socio-spatial variations exist not just in the extent of the permeation of the formal market economy and overall work cultures, but also in the nature of each labour practice in terms of its prevalence, the work relations and motives involved, and the extent to which such labour is concentrated at the overlap with other labour practices. To understand these socio-spatial variations, Part II of this book will evaluate each labour practice in turn. Before doing this, however, attention turns towards introducing a similar study of the diverse economies that prevail in the Russian global city of Moscow.

Evaluating the diverse economies in Moscow

To what extent has the formal market economy permeated the daily life of Muscovites? Do other labour practices persist, and if so, which kinds? And do the work cultures of Muscovites and the nature of individual labour practices vary socio-spatially? To answer these questions, the TSOL framework is here used to analyse evidence collected in 2005 and 2006 during 313 face-to-face interviews in Moscow, a global city of some 10.4 million inhabitants (Brooke 2006) where previous surveys reveal not only some marked cultural differences to the rest of Russia but also a long legacy of the use of work beyond formal employment (Brooke 2006; Caldwell 2004; Clarke 2002; Ledeneva 2006; Shevchenko 2009). This is also a global city that remains in transition to post-socialism, with the transformation being far from complete (Shevchenko 2009). As such, it is necessary to recognise that the forms of work organisation that prevail in different districts of Moscow are likely to be far from a steady-state.

As Clarke (2002) reveals in relation to Russia, moreover, during the Soviet period there were numerous services that no state enterprise provided and which were wholly delivered privately by individuals off-the-books, such as small construction and decorating jobs, repair of radios, televisions and washing machines, clothing repairs, care for the elderly and sick, private transport and private tuition. Indeed, until 1987, doing these odd jobs for pecuniary reward was illegal per se, despite citizens having no other way of obtaining such services. The outcome was a heavy reliance on informality in the so-called ‘second economy’ (Ledeneva 1998). Informal employment in the contemporary era, in consequence, has a different historical legacy for the population of Moscow in particular, and the ex-Soviet bloc more generally, compared with western economies and much of the third world. Furthermore, it is important to understand the context in which household employment decisions are made, especially Russian labour market legislation and the tax and benefits regimes. Superficially, taxation is extremely straightforward, with a uniform rate of 13 per cent on personal income and a corporation tax level of 20 per cent. In practice, however, it is more complex. As Round *et al.* (2008) outline, many formal employees receive two wages from their formal employer, one formal and the other in cash at the end of the month. This allows employers to evade payroll taxes and state pension contributions, and makes wage payments very uncertain for employees as they have no guarantee that their unofficial wage will be paid. If it is not, they have no recompense because if they complain to the state, they will be open to accusations of tax evasion on previously paid informal payments. Labour legislation is also extremely problematic in Russia. Although myriad labour regulations exist to protect workers, few are adhered to in practice (see Round *et al.* 2008). As Clarke (2002) displays, many people rely on contact networks to obtain employment, as opposed to applying for posts in open competition, and in some instances bribes are required to obtain employment (Round *et al.* 2008). In sum, great care is needed not to extrapolate the findings from this survey to either Russia more generally, post-socialist societies or other regions of the world. Instead, the intention here is solely to use this study of Moscow to begin to highlight how the TSOL varies across locality types within this global city so as to draw attention to the intra-urban variations in the TSOL, which can then be tested to see if they are also valid elsewhere.

Given that previous studies in Moscow (Pavlovskaya 2004; Shevchenko 2009), Russia (Clarke 2002; Kim 2002), East-Central Europe (Wallace and Haerpfer 2002; Wallace and Latcheva 2006; Williams 2005b) and western nations (Leonard 1998; Renooy 1990; Williams 2010a) identify significant variations in participation in formal and informal labour across affluent and deprived populations, the decision was taken to use maximum variation sampling to select three contrasting districts of Moscow to survey. First, an affluent region in the west of Moscow, namely Krylatskoe, was chosen; second, one of the most deprived regions located in the southeast of Moscow; and third and finally, a mixed region to the west of the Moscow region, about 25 km out from the Moscow ring road (which is the Moscow city border), namely Leshkovo, where 'new Russians' live in large expensive houses alongside benefit-dependent pensioners and the 'working poor'.

In each region a spatially stratified sampling methodology was used to select households for interview (Kitchin and Tate 2001). If there were some 1,000 households in the region and 100 interviews were sought, the researcher called at every tenth household. If there was no response and/or an interview was refused, then the eleventh household was visited, then the ninth, twelfth, eighth and so on. This provided a spatially stratified sample of each region. In total, 313 face-to-face interviews were conducted in the three regions. The response rate for generating interviews at the original households was 15 per cent, 41 per cent when the households on either side are included and 68 per cent when the two households on either side are included. Although this survey is, of course, not representative of Moscow as a whole, it nevertheless unravels the multifarious kinds of labour being used in contrasting regions in this city and how work cultures and the nature of individual labour practices vary socio-spatially.

Table 4.4 outlines the socio-demographic profile of the participants in each of the three regions. This reveals that in the affluent region, the residents have lived there for much shorter periods than in the deprived and mixed region, the number of people in households is greater and there are more couple households, the average age is lower and the total gross household income is significantly higher.

Table 4.4 Socio-demographic profile of participants in Moscow survey: by locality type

Percentage of respondents	*Affluent oblast: Krylatskoe (n = 125)*	*Deprived oblast: in southeast (n = 100)*	*Mixed oblast: Leshkovo (n = 88)*	*All (n = 313)*
Number of years lived in area:				
0–5	7	1	3	4
6–10	17	3	5	9
11–15	35	7	7	18
16–20	26	3	8	13
21–25	7	6	3	5
26–30	0	10	6	5
31–35	4	43	2	16
36+	4	27	66	30
Number of people in household:				
1	28	47	48	40
2	24	11	36	23
3	28	21	10	21
4	10	9	3	8
5	9	10	1	7
6+	1	2	2	1
Adult gender composition of household:				
Female only	28	52	51	42
Male only	7	6	8	7
Male and female	65	42	41	51
Age of respondent:				
16–25	14	4	2	8
26–35	10	5	3	7
36–45	14	9	6	10
46–55	10	9	10	10
56–65	4	12	18	11
>65	48	61	61	54
Work history of household:				
Continuous employment of all	14	22	23	19
Mostly all employed	21	20	14	19
Mostly all unemployed	11	7	6	8
Continuously unemployed	12	7	3	8
Pension since post-socialist time	42	44	54	46
Total gross household income (R):				
<3,000	5	20	2	8
3,001–7,000	18	28	38	27
7,001–11,000	10	26	9	14
11,001–15,000	9	6	10	8
15,001–19,000	12	10	11	11
>19,000	46	10	30	32

Source: Moscow survey.

Similarly, although the deprived and mixed regions are similar in terms of the number of people in households, the gender composition of households, age profile of respondents and the work history of households, those in the mixed oblast have lived there longer than in the deprived oblast and the total gross household income in the mixed area reflects the polarised nature of household income levels, while the deprived oblast reflects the lower overall income levels. It is important to note, however, that not everybody in the relatively affluent oblast is on a higher income and not everybody in the deprived oblast on a lower income.

To evaluate the plethora of labour practices used, previous studies indicate that respondents find it difficult to recall when various kinds of labour were used or supplied when open-ended, relatively unstructured interviews are employed (e.g. Leonard 1994; Pahl 1984; Williams 2004a). At the outset, therefore, the decision was taken to use structured interviews. Besides gathering background data on gross household income, the employment status of household members, their employment histories, ages and gender, first, respondents were asked about the forms of work they primarily and secondarily relied on to secure a livelihood, second, the sources of labour the household last used to complete 25 common domestic services so that comparative data was available across regions on the different labour practices used for the same set of tasks, third, whether they had undertaken any of these 25 tasks for others during the past year and, if so, what labour practice had been used. Fourth, open-ended questions were asked about any other work conducted using each of the eight labour practices; and fifth and finally, using five-point Likert scaling, attitudinal questions concerning their ability to draw upon help from others and their views of the economy, politics, everyday life and their future prospects.

The 25 common domestic services examined covered house maintenance (outdoor painting; indoor painting; wallpapering; mending a broken window; and maintenance of appliances), home improvement (putting in double glazing; plumbing; improving a kitchen; improving a bathroom), housework (routine housework; cleaning windows inside; doing the shopping; washing clothes; cooking meals; washing dishes; hairdressing; household administration), making and repairing goods (making or repairing clothes; making or repairing curtains; making or repairing tools; making or repairing furniture) and caring activities (daytime baby-sitting; night-time baby-sitting; tutoring).

Mapping the plurality of labour practices in Moscow

Table 4.5 reports the labour practices used to conduct a set of 25 common tasks across different regions and household income levels. The reason for using a set of 25 common everyday tasks was to allow comparative data to be gathered on the labour practices used for the same set of tasks. The finding is that participation in the formal paid labour market is not extensive in Moscow. Of course, this has to be seen in the context of the relatively large number of retired people interviewed. Nevertheless, only one-third (37 per cent) of respondents had engaged in formal paid employment over the past year even though 46 per cent

Table 4.5 Participation rates in labour practices in Moscow: by locality and gross household income

	Monetised				*Non-monetised*			
	Formal job	*Informal employment*	*Paid favours*	*Paid family labour*	*Formal unpaid labour*	*Informal unpaid labour in groups*	*One-to-one unpaid labour*	*Self-provisioning*
All areas	37	24	65	5	31	1	63	100
By locality type:								
Deprived	25	20	48	1	20	2	72	100
Mixed	30	23	68	4	28	1	70	100
Affluent	54	30	75	7	39	0	52	100
By household income:								
Lowest quartile	23	20	41	1	18	2	72	100
Lower quartile	31	22	63	3	33	3	65	100
Upper quartile	41	28	74	5	35	1	60	100
Highest quartile	57	26	82	11	38	0	55	100

Source: Moscow survey.

of participants were of working age, meaning that one-fifth of working-age respondents has not engaged in formal paid employment during the past year. Relative to self-provisioning (which everybody had undertaken over the past year), unpaid one-to-one labour (which 63 per cent had conducted) and paid favours (65 per cent), participation in the formal labour market is thus confined to small pockets of the Muscovite population.

Nevertheless, participation rates vary socio-spatially. Engagement in formal paid employment ranges from 25 per cent in the deprived district, through 40 per cent in the mixed district, to 54 per cent in the affluent district, with greater proportions of the working-age population not engaging in formal employment in the deprived than affluent district (36 per cent compared with 7 per cent). Similarly, participation in formal employment was just 25 per cent among those adults living in the lowest-income quartile of households, but 31 per cent in the lower middle-income quartile, 41 per cent in the upper middle-income quartile and 57 per cent in the highest-income quartile. However, it is not just engagement in formal paid employment which varies socio-spatially. Participation rates in all eight labour practices (with the exception of unpaid one-to-one labour and off-the-radar unpaid labour in organisations) are higher in the affluent compared with deprived populations. In Moscow, therefore, there appear to be relatively 'work busy' populations engaged in a wide range of labour practices, especially market-oriented and monetised practices, and relatively 'work deprived' populations engaged in a narrower range of practices.

The socio-spatial variations in the penetration of capitalism and the differences in the organisation of labour can also be seen when one examines the practices that households in different districts use to get by in everyday life. Evaluating the source of labour last used to conduct 25 common domestic service tasks, as Table 4.6 reveals, the finding is that there is a relatively shallow permeation of daily life by formal labour. Formal labour, for instance, was last used in just 7 per cent of instances to get these common domestic tasks completed. Indeed, only 26 per cent of domestic tasks even involved paid labour; the remaining three-quarters were last conducted by unpaid labour, with some two-thirds (67 per cent) conducted on a self-provisioning basis.

Nevertheless, there are differences across populations in both the permeation of formal labour and their overarching work cultures. As Table 4.6 reveals, people living in the affluent district more commonly use formal labour in particular, and paid labour in general, than those in the deprived district. The vast majority of outsourcing of domestic tasks among the Moscow households surveyed, however, is to paid informal labour rather than to the formal economy. The degree to which households externalise to the monetised and formal sphere is not the only difference in work cultures across populations. Other labour practices are also used to differing extents and in varying combinations. Those living in deprived districts more heavily rely upon self-provisioning and unpaid one-to-one labour. So, too, do those households in the lowest- and lower middle-income quartile compared with more affluent households, who rely more on paid favours, informal employment and formal labour.

Table 4.6 Labour practices used by households to conduct everyday domestic services in Moscow: by locality and gross household income

	Monetised						*Non-monetised*						
	Formal job in private sector	*Formal job in public/ third sector*	*Informal employment*	*Paid favours*	*Paid family labour*	*All paid*	*Formal unpaid labour in private sector*	*Formal unpaid labour in public and third sector*	*Informal unpaid labour in groups*	*One-to-one unpaid labour*	*Self-provisioning*	*All unpaid*	X^2
All areas	7	<1	12	7	<1	26	<1	<1	<1	7	67	74	–
By locality type:													
Deprived	4	<1	7	4	<1	15	<1	1	<1	7	78	85	185.23
Mixed	4	<1	12	8	<1	24	<1	<1	<1	9	67	76	31.46
Affluent	10	<1	13	9	1	32	<1	<1	<1	6	62	68	53.26
By household income:													
Lowest quartile	2	0	4	4	<1	10	<1	<1	<1	11	79	90	132.21
Lower quartile	4	0	9	6	<1	19	<1	<1	<1	7	74	81	72.61
Upper quartile	8	<1	14	8	<1	30	<1	<1	<1	6	64	70	29.68
Highest quartile	14	<1	21	10	2	45	<1	<1	<1	4	51	55	143.92

Source: Moscow survey

Note
$X^2 > 23.589$ in all cases, leading us to reject H_0, within a 99.5 per cent confidence interval, that there are no household income or spatial variations in the sources of labour used to complete the 25 everyday domestic services.=

The overarching finding, however, is not simply that relatively affluent populations are more likely to engage in formal and paid labour practices while deprived populations are more likely to engage in informal and unpaid labour practices. This is only a partial representation of the socio-spatial variations in the organisation of labour. Rather, there seems to exist a spectrum ranging from relatively affluent 'work busy' populations who engage in a multitude of labour practices (as shown by their higher participation rates in most sources of labour) to relatively disadvantaged 'work deprived' populations who conduct a much narrower range of practices. Socio-spatial variations prevail not just in the penetration of formalisation and the range of and type of labour practices conducted, but also in the nature of each labour practice used in terms of the work relations and motives involved. To understand these socio-spatial variations in individual labour practices, each will be evaluated in Part II of this book.

Conclusions

To start to question the narrative of the impending hegemony of the formal market economy in post-Soviet societies, this chapter has sought to further advance the emergent 'diverse economies' literature by developing an analytical lens for representing the multiple labour practices in economies. Moving beyond the simplistic formal–informal economy dichotomy, this chapter has conceptualised the multiple kinds of labour that exist in post-Soviet societies by adopting a 'total social organisation of labour' approach. This conceptualises a spectrum from formal-oriented to informal-oriented labour practices, which is cross-cut by another spectrum ranging from wholly monetised to wholly non-monetised labour practices. The resultant outcome is to provide an analytical lens for capturing the plurality of labour practices that exist in post-Soviet societies in a manner which shows how they all seamlessly merge into each other.

Having developed this typology, this has then been used to provide an overarching understanding of the multifarious labour practices used in Ukraine and Russia. Analysing the results of 600 interviews conducted across various populations in Ukraine and 313 interviews conducted in Moscow, this has first shown the shallow permeation of the formal market economy in Ukraine and Russia that have been supposedly undergoing a 'transition' to formal market economies. It has also revealed the existence of diverse work cultures across different populations, along with marked socio-spatial variations in the nature of individual labour practices. To begin to develop a deeper understanding of these socio-spatial variations in individual labour practices, attention turns in the following chapters to evaluating each of the eight forms of labour that are used to secure a livelihood in post-Soviet societies.

Part II

The lived experience of transition

5 The role of the informal in the formal sphere

Introduction

In a full-blown formal market economy, most goods and services would be produced, sold and distributed in the formal marketplace. This would mean that the vast majority of people would be in formal jobs since, to earn money to purchase the goods and services they need, they would have to earn money in the formal economy to purchase them. In this chapter, therefore, we first evaluate employment participation rates in post-Soviet/socialist economies to show the share of the population engaged in formal employment. This will reveal not only the small proportion of the population that directly participates in the formal market economy, but also how there are increasingly blurred edges between the private, public and third sectors, given that private sector organisations are increasingly pursuing a triple bottom line, while public and third sector organisations are also pursuing profit (albeit in order to reinvest so as to achieve wider social and environmental objectives).

Second, we then show that a large proportion of those apparently engaged in formal employment both in the formal market economy and the public and third sectors are in fact often not engaged in formal employment in its pure form, but rather quasi-formal employment; it appears to be formal employment but is not quite. Put another way, we will reveal that a large number of formal employees working for formal employers with formal work contracts actually receive two wages, an official declared wage and an unofficial undeclared ('envelope') wage. In the third section, we then extend the analysis of the illegitimate nature of formal employment beyond the issue of envelope wages to evaluate the extent and character of workplace crime in these post-Soviet societies, from cradle to grave. This will analyse how informality pervades formal provision in kindergartens, schools, universities, entry to the labour market and healthcare. The concluding section then argues that not only is the formal economy in general, and formal market economy in particular, a much smaller proportion of the whole economy than has been popularly assumed, but even those people counted as being engaged in formal employment are often engaged simultaneously in illicit practices. The outcome will be to highlight not only the shallow and uneven permeation of formal employment in contemporary post-Soviet spaces, but also how the formal market economy often blurs into more illicit work practices.

Participation in formal employment in post-Soviet/socialist economies

In 2010 in Central and Southeastern Europe and the Commonwealth of Independent States (CIS), the employment participation rate among the working-age population was 59.2 per cent. This means that four in every ten people of working age in the post-Soviet/socialist world were not participating in the formal economy. As Table 5.1 displays, moreover, there are significant cross-national variations. Even in Kazakhstan, the country with the highest employment participation rate, one in four people of working age do not participate in the formal economy. In Moldova, meanwhile, just 46.4 per cent of the working-age population are in formal jobs, meaning that the majority of the working-age population do not participate in the formal economy.

Table 5.1 Labour force participation rate (15–64 years old), 2010 in post-Soviet/socialist societies

Country	*Percentage of working-age population in formal jobs*
Kazakhstan	77.4
Estonia	74.0
Latvia	73.7
Russian Federation	72.9
Slovenia	71.2
Lithuania	70.7
Kyrgyzstan	69.9
Czech Republic	69.7
Tajikistan	68.7
Slovakia	68.7
Georgia	67.7
Ukraine	67.2
Bulgaria	67.0
Albania	66.5
Poland	65.6
Croatia	64.5
FYR Macedonia	64.4
Uzbekistan	63.9
Romania	63.8
Armenia	63.7
Turkmenistan	63.6
Serbia and Montenegro	63.5
Hungary	62.3
Bosnia and Herzegovina	54.5
Moldova, Republic of	46.4

Source: ILO Key Indicators of the Labour Market (KILM), http://kilm.ilo.org/kilmnet.

It is not only participation in the formal economy that is relatively shallow in post-Soviet societies. Contrary to the perception that there has been a shift towards formal market economies in post-Soviet societies, this is not borne out by the evidence on participation rates in formal jobs in the private sector. In the 313 households surveyed in Moscow, only 37 per cent of the surveyed population had participated in the year prior to the survey in paid formal labour registered by the state for tax, social security and/or labour law purposes and just 22 per cent in formal labour in the private sector, although participation rates are higher in affluent than deprived populations (see Table 4.5). Similarly, in the 600 households surveyed in Ukraine, just 56 per cent had participated in the year prior to the survey in paid formal labour and just 26 per cent in formal labour in the private sector. Despite all of the hyperbole about the shift towards a formal market economy, therefore, less than one-quarter of the surveyed population in Ukraine and the Russian city of Moscow work in this sphere.

Indeed, even these figures on participation rates in private sector formal employment possibly exaggerate the incursion of the formal market economy in its 'pure' profit-motivated form. This is because even those participating in employment in the private sector cannot increasingly be seen as engaged in purely capitalist modes of production, if by that one means the production and exchange of goods and services for monetary exchange in order to make a profit. This is because many private sector businesses in post-Soviet societies are increasingly pursuing a 'triple bottom line' in the sense that profit is not their sole motive and they are instead also pursuing social and environmental goals, as displayed by the widespread adoption of corporate social responsibility (CSR) into their visions and missions. Over the past decade or so, firms in both Russia and Ukraine have been increasingly turning their attention to not only pursuing profit, but also striving to respond to the environmental and social needs of their respective communities and societies (Basharina 2008; Crotty and Rodgers 2012; Kuznetsova and Kuznetsov 1999; Koleva *et al.* 2010; Kolot 2012; Kurinko 2011; Kuznetsov and Kuznetsova 2003; McCarthy and Puffer 2003, 2008).

The result is that there is a blurring of the private, public and third sectors within the formal economy in post-Soviet societies. Private sector organisations are increasingly pursuing a triple bottom line, while public and third sector organisations are also pursuing profit (albeit in order to reinvest so as to achieve wider social and environmental objectives), resulting in a blurring of the boundaries between these three spheres of the formal economy. To identify a separate purely profit-motivated formal market economy, therefore, separate from the public and not-for-profit sectors, is an increasingly difficult task. Formal paid employment as a whole, moreover, is not discrete and separate from the informal economy since it is often infused with informality in post-Soviet states. As will now be revealed, much of what appears superficially to be formal sector employment is not quite as formal as it first appears when one delves deeper into the employment contracts that many formal employees have with formal employers in post-Soviet societies.

The illusion of formalisation: the prevalence of quasi-formal employment

A long-standing and recurrent assumption has been that formal jobs are entirely separate from informal jobs. Jobs are widely depicted as either formal or informal. Reflecting the formal/informal economy dualism, the idea that a job might be simultaneously both formal and informal has been rarely considered. Since the turn of the millennium, however, this dichotomous portrayal of jobs as either formal or informal has started to be contested. A small but burgeoning literature focusing on post-Soviet spaces has begun to reveal that formal employers sometimes pay their formal employees both an official declared salary as well as an additional undeclared salary, or what is termed an 'envelope wage', which is hidden from, or unregistered by, the state for tax and social security purposes. Such studies of envelope wages have been undertaken in Estonia (Meriküll and Staehr 2010), Latvia (OECD 2003; Meriküll and Staehr 2010; Sedlenieks 2003; Žabko and Rajevska 2007), Lithuania (Karpuskiene 2007; Meriküll and Staehr 2010; Woolfson 2007), Romania (Neef 2002), Russia (Williams and Round 2007) and Ukraine (Round *et al.* 2008; Williams 2007).

The principal rationale for formal employers paying an envelope wage to their formal employees is so that they can evade their full social insurance and tax liabilities by paying a portion of their formal employees' salaries as an envelope wage. Nevertheless, although this is the main reason for using this illicit wage arrangement, it is not the only one. It is also a useful tool for formal employers when seeking to make a formal employee redundant. By refusing to pay their envelope wage, formal employers can encourage those formal employees they no longer wish to retain to voluntarily leave their formal job, thereby enabling the employer to evade social costs in the form of redundancy pay (Hazans 2005; Round *et al.* 2008).

Why, therefore, are envelope wages more common in some post-Soviet/socialist societies than others? In order to explain this, two alternative explanations can be adopted. On the one hand, and from a neo-liberal economic perspective, it might be argued that such illicit wage payments are a product of high taxes, over-regulation and state interference in the free market. From this viewpoint, therefore, such illicit wage payments would be more prevalent in countries with higher taxes and levels of state intervention in work and welfare systems, and are a response to over-regulation (Becker 2004; De Soto 1989, 2001; London and Hart 2004; Nwabuzor 2005; Small Business Council 2004). As Becker (2004: 10) puts it, 'informal work arrangements are a rational response ... to over-regulation by government bureaucracies'. To resolve the problem of envelope wages, therefore, tax reductions, deregulation and minimal state intervention would be pursued.

On the other hand, and from a social democratic structuralist perspective, it could be argued that these illicit wage payments by employers are a product of the lack of regulation of labour markets and inadequate levels of labour market intervention and social protection. For structuralists, in consequence, the contemporary mode of production is one where businesses are employing informal modes of organising and organisation so as to achieve flexible production, profit and cost reduction (Castells and Portes 1989; Davis 2006; Gallin 2001; Sassen 1996; Slavnic 2010). Viewed through this lens, envelope wages are one manifestation of how this is being achieved. Besides sub-contracting various stages in the production process to the informal economy, formal employers are also achieving flexible work arrangements, profit and cost reduction by paying formal employees some of their wage as an undeclared envelope wage. Those in receipt of such envelope wages are thus seen as unfortunate and unwilling pawns who out of necessity are forced into this illegitimate wage practice (Ahmad 2008; Gaetz and O'Grady 2002; Ghezzi 2010). Envelope wages therefore arise in this perspective due to the lack of regulation in the economy, and greater regulation is required to resolve this problem. As such, this illicit wage practice would be less prevalent in post-Soviet/socialist countries with higher levels of state intervention in work and welfare systems.

To evaluate these competing views, the prevalence of this wage practice will be analysed in more neo-liberal post-Soviet/socialist regimes with lower levels of state intervention and in more 'welfare capitalist' post-Soviet/socialist economies where there is greater intervention in work and welfare in order to evaluate two hypotheses:

1. Envelope wage payments are more popular in countries with higher tax rates.
2. Envelope wage payments are more popular in countries with greater levels of state intervention in the economy and welfare provision.

To do this, we here report the 2007 Eurobarometer survey which examines the prevalence of envelope wage arrangements in the ten East-Central European member states belonging to the European Union (TNS Infratest *et al.* 2006; European Commission 2007). Some 10,171 face-to-face interviews were conducted in these ten East-Central European economies, namely Bulgaria, Czech Republic, Estonia, Hungary, Latvia, Lithuania, Poland, Slovakia, Slovenia and Romania.

This face-to-face interview first asked those who reported that they were formal employees:

> Sometimes employers prefer to pay all or part of the regular salary or the remuneration for extra work or overtime hours cash-in-hand and without declaring it to tax or social security authorities. Did your employer pay you all or part of your income in the last 12 months in this way?

Second, in order to comprehend the nature of envelope wage payments, they were asked:

> Was this income part of the remuneration for your regular work, was it payments for overtime, or both?

Third, they were asked to estimate the percentage of their gross yearly income from their main job received as an undeclared envelope wage; fourth, they were asked whether they were happy to receive a portion of their salary as an envelope wage. Here, and in order to answer the research questions above, data on cross-national variations in tax rates, levels of social protection and the degree of state redistribution via social transfers are integrated into this dataset on envelope wages.

The extent of quasi-formal employment in post-Soviet/socialist societies

Of the 10,171 face-to-face interviews conducted in these ten East-Central European economies, 4,164 participants reported that they had formal jobs. Of these 4,164 formal employees, one in eight (482 employees in total) had received an envelope wage from their formal employer over the past 12 months. If extrapolated to the population of these ten countries as a whole, this intimates that, scaled up, some eight million employees in these East-Central European countries receive envelope wages. The prevalence of this illicit wage arrangement, however, is not evenly distributed across these East-Central European nations. As Figure 5.1 displays, there are marked cross-national variations, ranging from 23 per cent of formal employees in Romania reporting that they receive an envelope wage to just 3 per cent of formal employees in the Czech Republic.

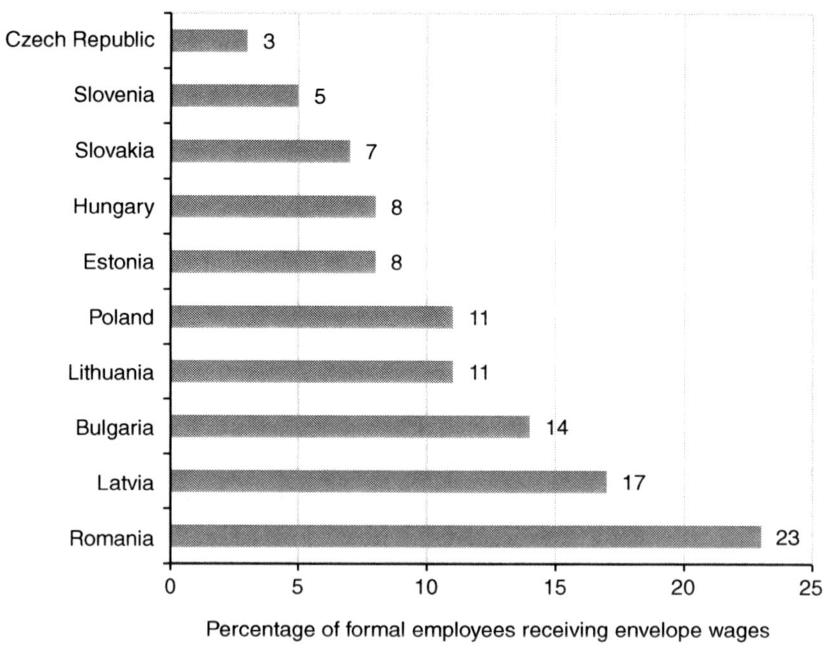

Figure 5.1 Prevalence of envelope wages in East-Central Europe.

Nor is the nature of these envelope wage arrangements the same in all ten countries. As Table 5.2 reveals, across all ten countries, those paid envelope wages receive 38 per cent of their total wage illicitly, but this ranges from 86 per cent in Romania to 14 per cent in the Czech Republic. There are also variations in whether formal employees are paid an envelope wage for their regular work and/or for overtime conducted. In Romania, Poland, Latvia and Lithuania, for example, the vast majority of employees receive envelope wages for their regular work and/or both regular work and overtime, while in countries such as the Czech Republic, Hungary and Slovenia, nearly half of the recipients of envelope wages receive them for overtime or extra work conducted.

On the one hand, therefore, there are a group of East-Central European countries in which this envelope wage practice is extensive, paid to employees more for their regular hours, and it amounts to, on average, around one half of formal employees' wages (i.e. Bulgaria, Latvia, Lithuania, Poland and Romania). On the other hand, there are a group of East-Central European countries where envelope wages are less common, paid more for overtime or extra work and amount on average to just one-fifth of employees' gross wage (i.e. Czech Republic, Slovenia, Slovakia, Hungary and Estonia). How, therefore, can these cross-national variations be explained? Are envelope wages more common in 'welfare capitalist' societies in which there is greater interference in the economy and welfare? Or is it more common in neo-liberal regimes where intervention in work and welfare is much lower? To evaluate this, first, the relationship between envelope wages and tax rates, and second, between state intervention and envelope wages, will be evaluated. This will allow conclusions to be reached on the validity of the neo-liberal and structuralist explanations regarding whether envelope wages are correlated with over- or under-regulation.

Relationship between national tax rates and quasi-formal employment

The neo-liberal perspective argues that envelope wages are a direct result of high tax rates and that the consequent remedy is to reduce taxes in order to decrease their prevalence. To evaluate this, first we here examine the relationship between envelope wages and the implicit tax rates (ITR) on employed labour in these ten East-Central European member states of the European Union (Eurostat 2011). This, in effect, is a summary measure of the average effective tax burden on labour income. It is the total of all direct and indirect taxes and employees' and employers' social contributions levied on employee income divided by the total compensation of employees. Direct taxes on labour income cover the revenue from personal income tax, while indirect taxes on labour income are taxes such as payroll taxes paid by the employer. Employers' contributions to social security (including imputed social contributions) and to private pensions and related schemes are also included. The compensation of employees is the total declared remuneration, in cash or in kind, payable by an employer to an employee. It is thus the gross (declared) wage from employment before any charges are withheld (Eurostat 2007).

Table 5.2 Characteristics of envelope wage arrangements in East-Central Europe

Country	*No. of formal employees surveyed*	*Percentage of gross income received as envelope wages (median)*	*Envelope wage paid for:*			
			Regular work (%)	*Overtime/extra work (%)*	*Both regular and overtime work (%)*	*Refusal or don't know (%)*
East-Central Europe	4,164	38	41	20	36	3
Romania	452	86	49	9	41	2
Poland	286	49	35	17	48	0
Latvia	492	46	44	18	36	1
Lithuania	423	43	42	11	47	0
Bulgaria	415	30	48	16	34	2
Estonia	399	19	38	17	31	14
Slovakia	506	17	45	39	16	0
Hungary	333	15	25	46	25	4
Slovenia	357	15	12	41	29	18
Czech Republic	501	14	14	50	36	0

Source: Eurobarometer survey of undeclared work, 2007.

Figure 5.2 graphically displays the relationship between the cross-national variations in the prevalence of envelope wages and the variations in implicit tax rates on labour (i.e. the average effective tax burden on labour income) across these East-Central European countries. Using Spearman's rank correlation coefficient (r_s), the finding is that there is a strong significant correlation between the cross-national variations in the average effective tax burden on labour income and cross-national variations in the prevalence of envelope wages across East-Central Europe (r_s=–0.872**). Indeed, 63 per cent of the variance in the prevalence of envelope wages is correlated with the variance in implicit tax rates (R^2=0.6295). However, the direction of the correlation is not in the direction suggested by neo-liberal thought. The prevalence of envelope wages does not rise with increases in the effective tax burden on employed labour. Instead, quite the opposite is the case. Consequently, the neo-liberal representation that envelope wages directly result from high taxes, and that the remedy is to therefore pursue tax decreases, is refuted.

In consequence, envelope wages are significantly correlated with the effective tax burden on employed labour but not in the way neo-liberals assert. Instead, the finding is that as the effective tax burden on employed labour increases, the prevalence of envelope wages declines. Nations with higher ITRs on labour income witness lower levels of envelope wage payments. To begin to better understand this, we now turn to examining the relationship between envelope wages and different work and welfare regimes.

Relationship between state intervention and quasi-formal employment

Is it the case that nations with greater levels of state interference have higher levels of envelope wages, as neo-liberals assert? Or is it that nations with greater state intervention have lower levels of envelope wages, as the structuralist perspective asserts? To answer these questions, the correlation between the cross-national variations in the prevalence of envelope wages and the cross-national variations in, first, the extent of state labour market interventions as a proportion of GDP, second, the level of social protection expenditure as

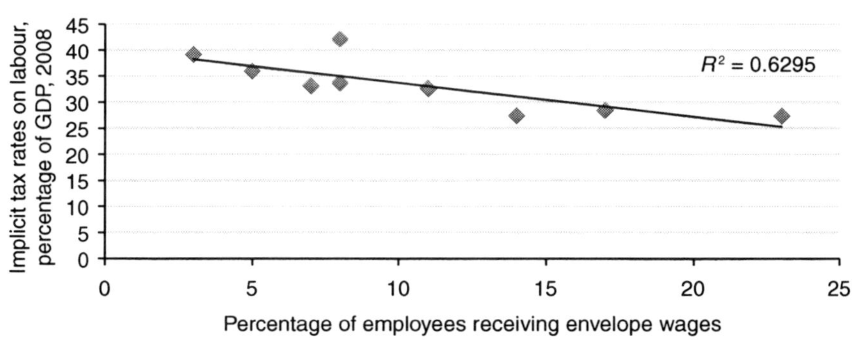

Figure 5.2 Relationship between implicit tax rates on labour and envelope wages.

a proportion of GDP and, third, the impact of state redistribution, will be analysed.

To evaluate whether greater intervention in the labour market is correlated with an increase or decrease in the prevalence of envelope wages, a bivariate analysis is conducted of the cross-national variations in the prevalence of envelope wages and the cross-national variations in the level of spending on labour market interventions to correct disequilibria, explicitly targeted at groups of the population with difficulties in the labour market, such as those who are unemployed, in employment but at risk of involuntary job loss, and inactive persons currently excluded from the labour force but who would like to join the labour market but are somehow disadvantaged (Eurostat 2011). As Figure 5.3 displays, there is no significant correlation between the cross-national variations in the proportion of GDP spent on labour market policy measures and the cross-national variations in the prevalence of envelope wages (r_s=–0.012), with 6 per cent of the variance in the prevalence of envelope wage payments correlated with the variance in the proportion spent on labour market interventions (R^2=0.0592). Therefore, there is no support for the neo-liberal explanation for the cross-national variations in envelope wages. Neither, however, is there any support for the structuralist perspective that there is a significant correlation between higher levels of state labour market policy expenditure and reductions in this illicit wage arrangement.

Examining the relationship between cross-national variations in the prevalence of envelope wages and the degree of intervention in welfare, as measured by the proportion of GDP spent on social protection benefits, excluding old-age benefits (European Commission 2011: table 3), stronger correlations can be identified. As Figure 5.4 displays, there is a very strong statistically significant correlation (r_s=0.832**), with 49 per cent of the variance in the prevalence of envelope wages correlated with the variance in the proportion spent on social protection (R^2=0.491). However, it is not in the direction intimated by neo-liberal thought. Post-Soviet/socialist countries where a higher proportion of GDP

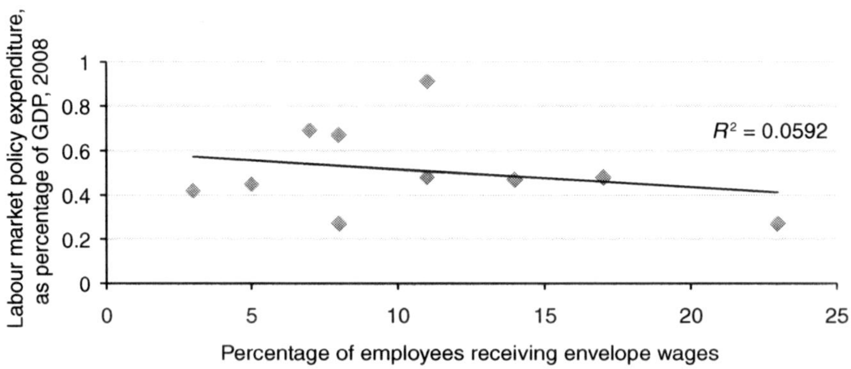

Figure 5.3 Relationship between labour market policy spending and envelope wages.

is spent on social protection have a lower incidence of envelope wage payments. Consequently, a higher level of state intervention in the form of social protection is correlated with a decrease in envelope wage payments, as suggested by the structuralist perspective.

This correlation between greater state intervention and a decrease in the prevalence of envelope wages is further reinforced when the redistributive impacts of state intervention are evaluated. Examining the reduction in percentage points of poverty before and after social transfers, with poverty defined as the proportion of people with an income below 60 per cent of the national median income (European Commission 2011: table 3), Figure 5.5 shows that member states where social transfers have a greater impact on reducing poverty have lower proportions of formal employees receiving envelope wages, not larger numbers as neo-liberals intimate. This is a very strong statistically significant correlation ($r_s = -0.817^{**}$, $R^2 = 0.5195$).

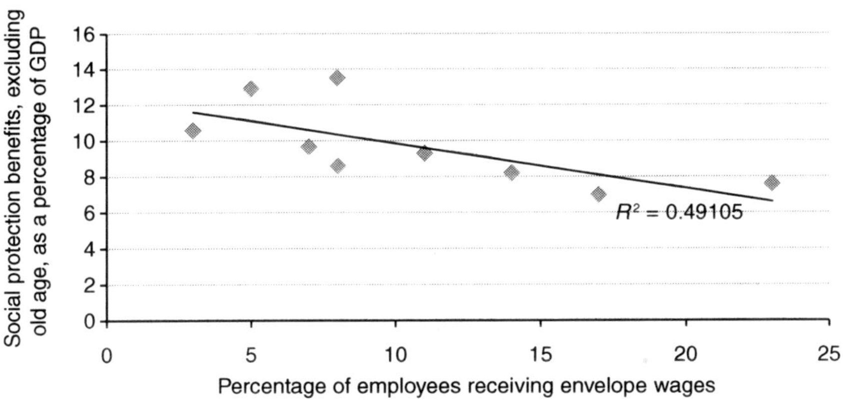

Figure 5.4 Relationship between social protection benefits and envelope wages.

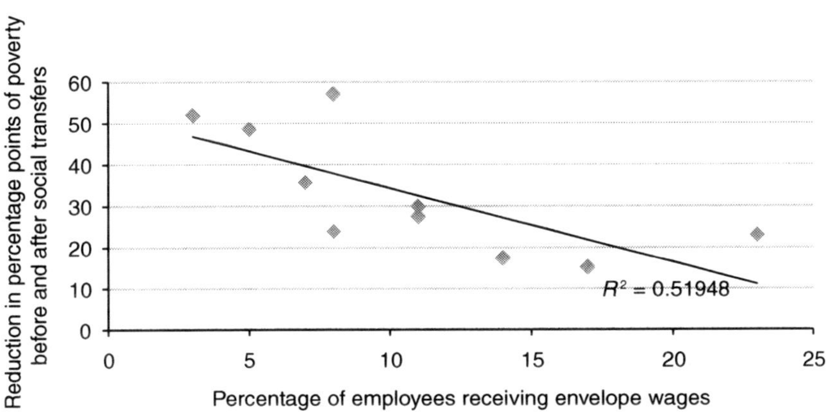

Figure 5.5 Relationship between impacts of state redistribution and envelope wages.

In sum, no evidence has been found to support the neo-liberal view that envelope wages arise due to high taxes. Neither has any evidence been found to support the neo-liberal view that greater levels of state interference lead to higher levels of this illicit wage arrangement. Instead, the finding is that greater state intervention in the form of social protection and redistribution is significantly correlated with a reduction, rather than increase, in the prevalence of envelope wages. These findings thus raise grave doubts about whether deregulation, tax reductions and minimal state intervention is the way forward by showing that the problem appears to be not one of over-regulation, but rather under-regulation.

Until now, however, little attention has been paid to how envelope wage arrangements are experienced on the ground by employees and employers. It is to this that attention now turns.

Lived experiences of quasi-formal employment

Are those receiving envelope wages happy to do so? Given that they potentially receive higher wages than if employers had to deduct the tax and social insurance contributions, one might believe that employees would be content with this arrangement. However, Table 5.3 reveals that just two in five (39 per cent) employees receiving envelope wages are happy to do so. A third (33 per cent) would prefer full declaration and the remaining 28 per cent are either undecided or refused to answer. Their attitude, nevertheless, largely depends on whether such payments are for regular hours worked or for overtime. Contentment was highest among those receiving such wages for extra work or overtime hours; 55 per cent are happy with this arrangement. Employees receiving envelope wages for their regular work, or for both their regular work and overtime hours, are less happy and would prefer full declaration.

Employees' attitudes towards envelope wages, moreover, also vary across different population groups. Men, younger age groups, those earning lower formal wages and working low hours are more content receiving an envelope wage than other groups. However, this is largely because these groups are most likely to receive envelope wages for overtime or extra work rather than for their regular hours.

During the fieldwork in both Ukraine and Moscow, further understanding of this lack of contentment with envelope wage payments was sought. In major part, the finding is that it is because when their official declared wage is lower than their actual wage, it prevents them accessing their full entitlement to social security and pension payments and constrains their ability to get credit, loans and mortgages (Williams 2007; Williams and Round 2007). Indeed, this dissatisfaction with receiving envelope wages, especially for regular work, clearly signals that the decision to pay envelope wages is not reached cooperatively and amicably between the employer and employee. It appears to be largely imposed on employees by employers. Many employees would prefer to receive their regular salary (as well as overtime payments) on a declared basis, but their employer obliges them to receive a portion as an envelope wage. Indeed, in the

Table 5.3 Attitude towards envelope wages in East-Central Europe: by population group

	Happy with this	*Prefer full declaration*	*It depends*	*Don't know/refuse*
All	39	33	17	11
By type of envelope wage:				
Part of remuneration for regular work	37	31	18	14
Overtime, extra work	55	25	14	6
Both regular and overtime work	33	38	18	11
Gender:				
Man	43	32	14	11
Woman	30	34	23	13
Age:				
15–24	53	26	15	6
25–39	39	35	16	10
40–54	34	34	18	14
55+	33	30	11	26
Occupation:				
Managers	29	35	19	17
Other white-collar workers	50	21	15	14
Manual workers	38	36	17	9
Gross formal job income/month:				
<€500	42	35	16	7
€500–1,000	34	38	14	14
€1001–2,000	31	25	22	22
€2001–3,000	0	67	33	0
€3,001+	0	0	0	
Hours/week in formal job:				
<10	75	13	0	12
10–20	36	36	9	19
21–30	33	33	8	26
31–40	39	33	16	12
41+	38	33	19	10

600 face-to-face interviews conducted in Ukraine, the finding was that 30 per cent of formal employees were paid envelope wages by their employer. Although sometimes this cash-in-hand element was received for overtime, most of the time it was not. They were receiving a proportion of their regular salary in this manner. Very few employees were happy with this arrangement as receiving part of their wages in this manner affected their social security and pension entitlements as well as their ability to apply for visas to travel abroad and get credit, since their official wage was lower than their actual wage. Although such a practice is common in Ukraine, the formal procedures of various institutions such as banks do not take it into account formally when making decisions on loans (even if informally they do so). As one respondent seeking a mortgage recounted, the bank informed him that he would need seven guarantors due to his 'low' wages. Getting seven people together was not a problem for him, but as he stated:

> All my work colleagues had pieces of paper with them that said they earn only US$400 per month which was not enough for the bank. However, all seven had SUV vehicles parked outside of the building – we had to take the bank manager outside to show them to him and say 'this is what we really earn' – in the end they agreed to give me the loan.

Similarly, the 313 face-to-face interviews conducted in Moscow also revealed the widespread prevalence of envelope wage payments; nearly one-third (30 per cent) of the formal employees interviewed received envelope wages amounting to, on average, 40 per cent of their total wage. Indeed, 35 per cent of men and 25 per cent of women in formal jobs receive envelope wages. There was no difference between women and men, however, in terms of the proportion of their total wage paid as an envelope wage, which is largely not for overtime, but part of their regular salary. This is not just the case for the 'budjetniki', including doctors, the police, teachers, nurses and so on who earn 4,000–10,000 roubles (£80–300) per month, but across the income spectrum. Few receiving this envelope wage, however, see this as beneficial. Nor is it a chosen practice. Nearly all employees receiving it asserted that it was imposed on them by their formal employer. The extensiveness of this labour practice, therefore, reveals that the formal economy is infused with informality in Moscow. Many formal employees in Moscow are in jobs that are at the formal–informal border.

Given that envelope wages have significant implications for pension entitlements and social protection, some two-thirds receiving envelope wages were opposed to receiving such 'tax-free' wages precisely for this reason. As one man in his mid-forties working in the home improvement sector stated, 'Due to my low "official" wage, none of the banks wanted to lend me the amount I wanted for my mortgage. I told them about my envelope wages but they didn't include it. It's crazy.'

On the whole, however, banks are perhaps correct not to do so. One-quarter (25 per cent) of the participants interviewed receiving envelope wages had experienced difficulties in receiving this wage. As a woman in her late twenties, who had worked as a manager in a large Russian pharmaceutical company, explained:

> They said that my formal salary would be 5,000 roubles a month but the real wage would be up to US$2,000.... At the end of the month they paid me my formal 5,000 roubles and said that I would get all the 'additional money' the next month ... but the next month nothing changed. I got my formal salary again and a promise that the next month the company would compensate my efforts and I would get 'my off-the-books additional income for 3 months'. By that time I had talked to other people who worked there. They said that they never got what they were promised. Something like once every 4 months, the company would pay them about US$500 as additional income with promises to pay the rest next time. The more the company

> owes a worker, the more the pressure they put on them. They have developed a system of fines and look for tiny little mistakes in the work (like somebody coming back from their lunch break one minute late) and then fine them US$50. So in the end the company does not owe anything and the worker feels grateful for the additional US$500 once every 4 months. I did not have any fines so I just left.

Again, there are no differences between women and men in witnessing such difficulties. It is important to realise, however, that three-quarters received their envelope wages without problems. As a woman in her mid-forties stated,

> I write computer programs for a well-known company.... My formal salary is 6,000 roubles (£120) a month, but my real income is about 30,000 roubles (£600) a month. I have never had any problems with my envelope wage. The company pays it regularly.

In sum, envelope wages are a popular practice in post-Soviet/socialist societies. Some one in eight formal employees receive an envelope wage, and this on average amounts to 38 per cent of their wage packet. The result is that even if 59 per cent of the working-age population are engaged in formal employment in post-Soviet/socialist societies, some one in eight of these are in quasi-formal jobs. This not only blurs the divide between formal and informal jobs, but also means that the proportion in purely formal employment is even lower than previously assumed. This, however, is not the only way in which the formal economy is infused with informality. Here, attention turns towards the extent and character of workplace crime in post-Soviet societies.

Crime and corruption in the formal economy: informal payments from cradle to grave

As the above discussion of quasi-formal employment has shown, formal employment is often infused with informality. In this section we extend this discussion of how the formal economy in post-Soviet countries is permeated by informality by examining how crime and corruption is witnessed in dealings with the formal economy from cradle to grave. One of the abiding features of crime and corruption in post-Soviet spaces is its closeness to everyday life. Informal payments are expected from, or on behalf of, all ages and sectors of society, from the registration of births, to accessing free kindergarten places, entering university, securing employment and healthcare through to securing a well-sited burial plot. While such payments 'grease the wheels' of the system and provide incomes to low-paid workers, they are also opportunistic and predatory actions, engendering a culture of informality throughout the society and lead to a system where those paying come to see such payments as an 'investment' which will be earned back at some point in the future. To see this, we commence this section by looking at the prevalence of informal payments surrounding kindergartens, followed by schools, universities, entry to the graduate labour market and the realm of healthcare services, thus displaying the permeation of the formal economy by informality from cradle to grave.

The informal economies of kindergartens

Whereas the Soviet system provided preschool education, this is no longer the case. As Zdravomyslova (2010) makes explicit, since the collapse of the Soviet welfare system, in Russia whilst nursery schools remain, there is not enough space available for existing demand. The federal government states that regional authorities should provide free entrance to kindergarten for all children. Yet the shortage of places sees fierce competition for places at kindergartens. Whilst such places are officially 'free', in practice this is rarely the case. They are often now either not financed by the state budget at all or only part financed. As such, parents are required to pay. Alongside 'state-run' nurseries there has been witnessed the rapid growth of wholly commercial nursery schools, especially in Moscow and Russia's large urban centres.

The gap between the formal state provision of childcare and the increasing demand for places has inevitably led to strains on the system and the manifestation of informal payments as a means to facilitate gaining a place in a nursery school. Gradkova (2010: 181) discusses how the majority of her respondents had to make informal payments to ensure a space for their child 'ranging from a hundred to several thousand dollars'. As well as direct informal payments, parents are often asked for gifts for the school to ensure admittance (Oberemko 2006).

Once within the kindergarten, the requests for payment do not stop. These can include items for the children, such as books and/or furniture, and direct gifts to the teachers (Gradkova 2010). As one of our interviewees in Moscow asserted:

> The payments we have to make to the kindergarten are non-stop. There is always something that needs fixing or replacing. We also have to spend time making repairs or clearing the snow in the winter. It would be interesting to know where the money that the government provides for these services goes.... Of course we cannot say anything as we want the best treatment for our child and we just give in to every request.

Clearly not all households can afford such payments, leaving an increasing number of children without childcare places, with Gradkova (2010) estimating that 27.5 per cent of children in urban areas cannot attend preschool because of the lack of places. A lack of a place puts enormous pressure on the household as school does not start until the child is 6–7 years old. One response, which was observed in both affluent and deprived areas, was for several households to share childcare, creating informal kindergartens:

> Several people in our circle got talking about how finding a place at kindergarten was so difficult so we decided to share child care. I like looking after

> kids so during the day I look after the children of four of my friends. Obviously I cannot go to work but my friends give me money from their salary and give me materials for the children's activities.

When asked if they would ever formalise the practice, they stated,

> Of course not! The reason we do this is to escape all of the payments we are supposed to make. If we made it formal then we would have to pay bribes to get the licences and we would have to pay tax. It is much better to keep everything small and out of sight.

While this is clearly a satisfactory arrangement for those concerned with high levels of trust involved, these households are making payments or spending time on services which should be free at entry and then low cost each month, putting further pressure on household budgets.

Informality in the formal school system

Such informal payments for formal sector provision do not end when the child enters school. Although entrance to state schools is free, interviewees discussed how informal payments were solicited from institutions with a high demand for places (Osipian 2011). Although the majority of this concerns corruption around university entrance exam schemes (considered further below), bribes are still a regular occurrence within the secondary education system. Interviewees with school children all discussed the biggest problem with informal payments was the regular requests for 'help' from the school. As an interviewee in Kyiv reported:

> Every time we have a parents meeting we are told we need to make another payment for something that is wrong at the school. Last time we had to also bring toilet paper for the school as the head said they could no longer 'afford' it. No one can complain as you don't want your child to have difficulty at school

Indeed, she then asserts that in Russia's regions, parents annually pay between 3,000 and 20,000 roubles per year to their children's schools. As an interviewee in Kyiv reported,

> Every time we have a parents meeting we are told we need to make another payment for something that is wrong at the school. Last time we had to also bring toilet paper for the school as the head said they could no longer 'afford' it. No one can complain as you don't want your child to have difficulty at school.

Nikitina (2009) lists some of the payments that parents are expected to make, including mops, toilet paper, flooring, new windows, projectors, payments for security guards, among many others. She discusses how the sum collected from the parents is much higher than the actual cost and that when one respondent asked for a receipt, her child was sent to a 'remedial' class. Parents are also expected to provide free labour throughout the school year. This might include the painting and repair of the school during the summer vacation to the clearing of snow during the winter. Without doubt, post-Soviet schools suffer from serious underfunding, but there is clearly the misappropriation of funds for such activities at some point in the chain.

According to the media monitoring and analysis service, public.ru, there is a price list within certain schools of payments to pass exams with good grades. For example, they state that in the Republic of Dagestan it will cost you from 500 roubles to be allowed to take your mobile phone into an exam to 10,000 roubles for the teacher to help with the exam (public.ru). The situation is exacerbated by the very low salaries of teachers in post-Soviet states. In 2012 the average salary for a secondary school teacher in Russia was 12,000 roubles per month, less than two times higher than the subsistence minimum figure. As Patico (2002) remarks, gift-giving to teachers is therefore a very common practice in Russia, and although similar practices exist everywhere, it is perhaps at a much higher level in post-Soviet states. On set days such as 'teachers day', 1 September (the first day of the school year) and on birthdays, it is expected that students present gifts such as flowers and chocolates. While these are welcomed by the teachers, often they are recycled as gifts, to save money, or resold to provide an income. On 1 September, when students take flowers to the teachers, flower sellers discussed with the authors how after school, many teachers sell the majority of the flowers back to the sellers for 50 per cent of their original cost. Parents, aware of the low salaries, discussed how they now purchase supermarket gift vouchers as gifts in order to supplement teachers' income. Teachers also undertake informal work to bolster their salaries. This includes tutoring for the university entrance exam, giving private lessons after school hours, or indeed holding other cash-in-hand positions outside of teaching.

The giving of private lessons is a revealing example of the scale, and internal power, of informal practices. The authors during their fieldwork interviewed numerous teachers and became friends with some. At first glance, their informal practices seem lucrative as it was not uncommon for teachers to be informally teaching groups of 8–10 students, each paying US$5 per hour, two to three times per week. Two teachers in Moscow, for example, discussed how they quadrupled their income by providing extra English lessons in the school they work at, after formal teaching hours, to the children of 'rich Russians'. However, many feel trapped by the process and wish to discontinue. Given the income it generates, this seemed surprising until they discussed that to do this work they have to pay cash to their bosses to be 'allowed' to undertake such work. In one instance, the school director was threatening to report them to the tax police if they stopped giving informal lessons. Common to the theme running throughout this book, the teachers discussed that without their informal incomes they would not be able to afford to teach. However, they all note that such practices are extremely stressful and that they wish for their lives to be more formal. This is similarly the case for those who must provide such payments, since finding this money from already tight household budgets is often very difficult. Indeed, this is perhaps why Rotkirch and Kesseli (2012: 146) assert that 'Two children puts you in the zone of social misery'. Not only is the cost of everyday goods to feed and clothe two children very difficult to find for most, but informal payments need to be made as they progress through childhood.

Informality in the university system

As with all the discussions presented in this book, we are not here suggesting in this analysis of corruption and informality in the university system that the practices are taking place within every university or by everyone employed within them. However, from interviews with graduates and students in Ukraine and Moscow, it is clear that informal payments and corruption are very serious issues. Nor is such corruption confined to Ukraine and Moscow. It is common across numerous post-Soviet states (Heyneman 2007, 2010; Karakhanyan *et al.* 2011; Osipian 2010, 2011, 2012; Petrov and Temple 2004). Indeed, Forbes Russia (2012) recently reported in a country-wide survey on corruption in Russia that the higher education sector was seen as the third most corrupt state sector (46 per cent of respondents), exceeded only by the traffic police (52 per cent) and preschool education (51 per cent). As Burova and Ozmidova (2012) eloquently state, in Russia '[t]he corruption that exists in higher education is like a drop of water that reflects the situation in society as a whole', with 50 per cent of students encountering it. Agranovich (2008) similarly states that 50 per cent of students believe that the only way to enter university is through paying a bribe, while Osipian (2012) states that over 30 per cent of Ukrainian students pay bribes to enter higher education and, above this, others take advantage of personal connections. As Heyneman *et al.* (2008) discuss, other forms of informal payments range from the Ministry of Education demanding payments from rectors for institutional accreditation to professors delaying the approval of a student's thesis until a 'fee' is paid. Corruption, however, is not just limited to those within the system; as Osipian (2011) points out, there is a thriving market for simply purchasing postgraduate degrees in post-Soviet states.

Within post-Soviet states, a university degree is a prerequisite for the vast majority of jobs. As one interviewee in Ukraine commented, 'you need a degree to get a job just picking up the telephone'. Therefore, there is intense competition for the best universities and courses in countries such as Ukraine, entrance to which is governed by competitive entrance exams. Students discussed how they were asked for bribes outright for a place or were told if they paid for tuition in how to do well in the exams, entrance would be guaranteed. Attending these sessions was, of course, optional after paying. One quite ingenious scheme was related by a senior academic whereby a 'price' would be given to pass the entrance exam and most students would pay it. Making the payment made no difference to the chances of success as a certain percentage would be accepted onto the course anyway. Those who did make the payment and were rejected were simply told that something had gone wrong and their money was returned. The academics then kept the money from the people who thought they had paid a bribe and thus made a significant sum for doing nothing. Nevertheless, sometimes such payments did help. As one Ukrainian student said, after refusing to make an informal payment for entrance to the city's most prestigious university,

> I got the highest score out of all the applicants for my English language exams. Yet I did not get a place. Why? Because I scored zero in my Ukrainian language exam. How can this be, I wonder, as I am fluent in Ukrainian? [said in an extremely mocking tone]

The same process happened when applying for the second-ranked university; she was only accepted without making a payment into what is considered to be the third best. Another interviewee discussed how they failed to enter their chosen course for six years as they refused to make the requested payment:

> I totally refuse to pay bribes. My father was very high up during the Soviet period and he kept telling me that he could help me get in. But I did not want that. I wanted my degree to be only from my abilities. If I paid bribes or used connections how would I know my degree was worth anything?

Such examples highlight that the best students are not allocated to the best courses and institutions, which both impacts on their future careers and decreases the country's human capital. Osipian (2012) discusses that the most popular courses in Kyiv require a bribe of between US$10,000 and US$15,000 to enter, ensuring that only the richest sections of society can access them and thus the opportunities that arise for the graduates. Within Ukraine, students are classed as either 'budget' or 'contract'. The former are those for whom tuition and a stipend are paid by the university and the latter have a set yearly payment for course fees. This is obviously an area where corruption is possible. With regards to the budget places, informal payments can be made to access them, meaning that it is often the richest students who have these places. As one student stated:

> Look at all the people on the budget in my course. They are all from rich families whose parents can afford to influence the correct people. They don't need the money the stipend gives them but it is all to do with power. They can alter the system, so they do it.

Grishina and Korchinsky (2006) note one course where out of 120 budget places, 96 were allocated prior to the entrance exams, inferring that these places were bought by bribes and via connections.

Once in the university system, payments are sometimes requested to pass exams or obtain good grades. The propensity for one-to-one oral examinations facilitates this, where a payment can be requested for the desired grade, as the following student discusses:

> We have such a crazy system here in Ukraine. When we have to get a *zachot* our professor will tell us to queue outside his office, for example, at ten o'clock in the morning. We all stand there, you know, half pretending with each other that we are worried about the exam. Yet, you know [laughing], we all know that we will simply give him some money and pass this exam. It works like that. It's kind of like a big show, we are pretending that we have a real exam and the lecturer pretends to be examining us.

This is obviously not the case for every exam, and among interviewees there was a feeling that it tended to be older or younger less established members of staff who undertook such practices, whereas established 'middle-aged' academics, it is believed, can supplement their income through lecturing in numerous universities, grants or entrepreneurial activities, thus reducing the need to earn informal incomes. However, the majority of interviewees said they had encountered such practices at some point in their degree and had to comply with them:

> We don't have a choice. We either pay our lecturers and pass our exams or we risk getting thrown out. It does not matter what we know and whether we want to learn or not. It simply matters about money. What can we do? If we don't pay and leave university, then what? In our country, a person with no qualifications has no future, no chance for progression.

The payment is often small, which is why there is more a resigned acceptance to the practice rather than widespread anger. However, over the course of a year it accumulates to a significant sum for the recipient. If the student does not want to take the exam, interviewees discussed how it would be common knowledge that there was a member of staff who could be approached, who in turn would approach the module leader. For example, in one university a member of the sports department plays this role. The payment would be made to them and they would then share it with the corresponding academic. This person also possessed knowledge about on what modules such practices were possible and which members of staff should never be approached over informal payments. On occasions, money payments would not be requested but a service provided to the university would be performed instead. For example, in one university those who had failed exams were asked to paint the university's interior over the summer in order to 'pass' the retake exams without actually having to sit them. The money allocated to pay for the painting would then be split between those running this 'scheme'.

The majority of students have to undertake part-time, or in some cases approaching full-time, work in order to support themselves during their university course. Numerous students discussed how one form of income was writing coursework assignments for richer students. While there are regular anti-corruption drives in the higher education sector within many faculties, frameworks for checking the validity of marks is very weak. Second marking, for example, is virtually non-existent and although some universities discourage oral examinations to reduce the possibility of informal payments, it is often not fully enforced. Frequently there is no, or little, moderation of module marks and a system of external examiners to moderate marks is not used. It would appear, although caution is taken when making this statement, that paying to pass exams is less prevalent in more prestigious universities, potentially because of the relatively higher salaries paid to staff.

In Ukraine an independent external assessment (IEA) scheme was recently introduced in an attempt to remove the entry process from universities, but this has also become mired in complaints about corruption. However, as is usual with corrupt practices, new ways to circumnavigate anti-corruption legislation were quickly found. For example, names were added to lists and entrants were given the status of winners of school competitions (who are exempt from the entrance exams) to ensure their entrance. Several loopholes therefore still remain in the entrance process, allowing corrupt practices to remain or to flourish. Notably, in the first couple of years after the IEA's introduction there were reports in the media in Ukraine that some of the exam questions had been leaked. More significantly, a small change in the education system, introduced by the minister of education, Tabachnyk, has facilitated new, subtle forms of corrupt practices to develop within the entrance system. While Tabachnyk has kept the external testing system for higher education entrants, a system of school certificates accounting for around 25 per cent of each student's higher education entrance mark has been re-introduced. Since this re-introduction, numerous reports have appeared in Ukraine's media highlighting the knock-on effect of corrupt practices in Ukraine's secondary schools.

Simultaneously, other new varieties of corrupt practices have developed. In the past couple of years increasing numbers have been exploiting small loopholes in Ukraine's education legislation in which large amounts of benefits are given to children from village schools, disabled children and to others enjoying social privileges. Seemingly, the numbers of such entrants into Ukraine's HEIs has risen sharply since the introduction of the IEA system, with enterprising families forging medical certificates for their child or transferring their child to a village school before their official graduation. It is not just in the university system, however, that such corruption and informality is found.

Finding employment through connections

There is a small but growing literature on the informal practices employed by organisations in post-Soviet states. This has explored the use of connections to develop businesses (McCarthy *et al.* 2012), the demand for payments to access free healthcare (Aarva *et al.* 2009), crony capitalism (Sharafutdinova 2011), the links between big business and the state (Lane 2011) and the extent of organised crime (Holmes 2008). What has been less investigated so far are the informal practices that employers utilise in relation to recruitment and their employees.

To address this lacuna, this section starts by looking at the 'closed' nature of Russia's labour market, concentrating on the graduate labour market (which is much wider than in western European economies), therefore continuing to explore the lived experiences of students as they leave university. Given the type of employment under discussion, we do not here engage in any depth with the processes for positions as manual labourers, where personal connections play a less significant role when finding employment (Walker 2010, 2011). Similar to previous research on entry into the labour market, we will here argue that such entry is relatively closed and that personal connections are key to obtaining decent employment (Demidova and Signorelli 2012; Gerber and Mayorova 2010; Gimpelson *et al.* 2010; Kapelyushnikov *et al.* 2012; Vishnevskaya and Kapelyushnikov 2007; Yakubovich 2005). In the following section, we then expand on this body of knowledge by detailing the informal practices that 'applicants' without wide-ranging personal connections must endure when trying to obtain employment. Though many might believe that the use of personal connections is not a 'criminal act', it can be argued that it goes against labour legislation and at best is demonstrative of the informal nature of the 'formal' labour market. As many commentators assert, the form that the Russian labour market model currently takes is a mixture of very inflexible formal legislation and the informal practices that are employed to get around them (Gimpelson *et al.* 2010; Kapelyushnikov 2011; Kapelyushnikov *et al.* 2012), many of which are fairly easy to label as criminal. The section then concludes by briefly exploring some of the practices employers use to ensure maximum profit from their workforce.

As Gerber and Mayorova (2010: 896) note, 'The labor market got more personal in the course of Russia's market transition. The prominence of personal networks as a method of successful job search grew.' This is a two-way relationship as employers become, according to Mayorova (2008: 9), 'social capitalists', taking advantage of their connections to secure employees as well as employees using their networks to obtain work. The use of connections to obtain work is not a new occurrence and nor is it unique to post-Soviet spaces. As the seminal work of Granovetter (1973, 1983) demonstrates, workers in mature economies often draw upon their strong and weak ties when looking for work. However, what is clear is that it is a much more common tactic in transition economies. Clarke (2002: 492) discusses, for example, that in his study of 90 managers in Russia, only one had applied directly for their position, with the rest relying to differing extents on their networks. This, he argues, has led to a 'closure' of the Russian labour market as 'in the past, connections were used primarily as a means of getting a better job. Now it is becoming increasingly necessary to have connections to get any job at all.'

As Mayorova (2008) notes, this enables employers to have greater trust in their employees and for informality to increase as the trust relation means that it is easier to negotiate outside of formal labour regulations. Therefore, an extremely flexible system develops to the advantage of employers (Kapelyushnikov *et al.* 2012), which is markedly different from central and western European models

(Gimpelson *et al.* 2010). One interviewee, a lawyer in Ukraine, described how his father's connections ensured his smooth entry into the labour market:

> When I left university, I was already assured a job as a lawyer, the profession I had studied in. My father helped me with this. He has a construction company. They build small shopping centres around the city and across the whole of Ukraine. With this he has numerous meetings with lawyers of one company. He asked a favour of the boss ... and he agreed. As soon as I completed my diploma, I began to work in the office as a legal junior.

Among interviewees with prestigious formal employment, this story was repeated many times. This is not to say that the interviewees did not deserve the posts they held, or that they are not talented within them, but there is a definite 'closure' within such spheres. This perpetuates informal relationships both within and between firms. However, there can be negative outcomes of such relationships when employees are foisted upon them by those who are owed favours or in lieu of making an informal payment to obtain a service or contract. Granovetter's weak ties are also very much in evidence, especially among lower-income posts. Managers will ask their staff if they can recommend anyone for vacant positions; this saves times as there is no need to advertise or interview widely and it provides an obligation to work hard as they need to repay the trust of the person who recommended them. Thus, it is clear that having a good social network is key to obtaining employment in post-Soviet spaces. While this is not corruption per se, it does lead to a misallocation of resources as it is not necessarily the most suitable person who fill the posts via this method. It also raises levels of informality as often whole negotiations will take place 'off the record', thus increasing the chances of informal payments being agreed. Furthermore, and central to the theme of this book, such informal frameworks perpetuate themselves and allow corruption to flourish, and in the instance discussed here sometimes produce positive outcomes, but mostly the end result is far from constructive, especially for those without the connections needed to break into the labour market.

Entering and surviving a 'closed' labour market

Many of the interviewees without connections had experienced difficulties above and beyond the usual of identifying and applying for opportunities when trying to obtain full-time employment. These difficulties had involved being asked for bribes to secure a job, dismissal after a very short period of time, the misuse of internships and an overall lack of job security. It is clear from the interviews that there are serious problems across the whole of the post-Soviet labour market, ranging from 'prestigious' roles through to the burgeoning service sector. Indeed, given the service sector's rapid post-Soviet expansion and the higher proportion of women in this sector, a strong dose of gender inequality can be observed, reflecting the patriarchal power structures within these societies. As Turbine and Riach (2012: 182) note, although the state professes gender equality in access to employment, 'women are still marginalized through the systems, processes and social beliefs that underpin the post-Soviet labour market'. This links back to the point made above that while there are wide-ranging employment laws, the general culture of informality often renders them obsolete.

Furthermore, as Klimova and Ross (2012) note, while labour market participation has risen for women, the inequality in access to 'good' jobs has widened. Interviewees discussed how they felt that some of the interviews they had undertaken were exploitative. Many talked about how they had been asked to continue the interview at a restaurant or sauna, with the implications of accepting/declining made very clear. As one said,

> After the first interview, which I thought had gone really well, someone from the company called me and suggested that the second interview should take place at a sauna near their offices in the evening. It was clear what he really meant by this. It is so frustrating to be treated in this way when all I am trying to do is get a steady job.

Many also discussed how they had been asked outright to pay a bribe to be given a job. As with the informal payments within the university sector, these payments were not, on average, particularly large, but for the recurrent recipient, when they are combined, it provides a worthwhile tax-free income. While interviewees often refused to make such payments, some discussed how they calculated whether it would be in their long-term interest to make the payment. Sometimes this was proven correct, but in other instances it brought only further problems. It was not uncommon to hear that once the bribe was paid, the worker who had paid it was dismissed soon afterwards. This was more common in the service sector; the following example is not untypical:

> After passing the interviews I was told that to get the job I would have to make a large payment to the boss. I went home and thought about this situation and decided to pay the bribe as the job seemed great.... I started work and was really enjoying it when I was abruptly told that my appearance wasn't right and that I was rude to the customers.... I was upset of course and soon found out that several other women had received similar treatment. We met up and soon realized we had been taken for a ride. We had all paid upfront and then worked for four months, essentially paying off our 'payment' before we were dismissed.

By using such processes, enterprises are securing themselves a free labour supply as any salaries that are paid out are covered by the initial informal payment. Similar to this are cases where significant bribes were requested in order for new employees to be provided with tax code numbers or for all of their workplace registrations to be completed. Again, interviewees discussed how they had to make calculations about whether it was worthwhile to make such payments.

Even when entrants managed to gain a foothold in the labour market, the stresses still continue. Although there is extensive employment legislation designed to protect workers, it is in many cases extremely difficult to uphold. As Gimpelson *et al.* (2009: 24) note, while comprehensive labour legislation was inherited in Russia from the Soviet Union, the weakness of state institutions means that 'interventions are inefficient and non-random'. The use of the term 'non-random' is telling as there is a widespread belief that the courts operate in a way that protects business and those with power and there is little consideration for individual employees. For example, Turbine and Riach (2012) write at length about the prevalence of dismissal due to pregnancy in Russia and the near impossibility of successfully taking guilty parties to court. It is similarly the case in Ukraine. Interviewees virtually unanimously believe that if they had a problem in the workplace, there was no one they could turn to for outside help, arguing that no one would take their problem seriously, and hiring legal assistance is beyond the means of the majority. As one interviewee said:

> You know, you work hard, earn some money but your boss is watching over the situation like a wolf. He waits for his moment and pounces. You have no choice, no defence. What was I to do, complain and try and take him to court – there is no official documentation of our 'agreement'. It is his word against mine. He is a big boss and I am nobody, who do you think the court here will listen to?

Another interviewee discussed how even though he sought legal advice, it was of little use as he was told that it was pointless taking his case to court as the enterprise was able to arrange for a certain judge to hear cases against them and that they always went in their favour.

Given that it is so difficult for those without connections to find work and to maintain it over the initial few months, there are very high levels of anger among this group. The 'closure' of the labour market means they are unable to employ their skills and education, they have to move between employment on a regular basis, thus stymieing their career progression, and they have little belief that the situation will improve. Only 30 per cent of the survey respondents were optimistic about the future economic and social development of Ukraine, with the figure falling to 24 per cent among the 16–25-year-old age group. In Russia in 2010, nationwide surveys revealed that only 51 per cent of people were satisfied at work and that 86 per cent had recently become more afraid of losing their employment. Given the difficulties of finding and sustaining work, it is no surprise that large numbers have withdrawn fully from the formal labour market in order to gain more control of their work and to escape the pressures of predatory employers (Roberts 2001).

Often, and with varying degrees of success, they would set themselves up as micro-entrepreneurs, as discussed later, and become involved, for example, in shuttle trading, informal selling and/or cash-in-hand work. This, therefore, is a tactic employed to bypass the strategies of those with power in post-Soviet societies. Given that many of the interviewees had experienced the need to make informal payments to pass through the higher education system, this second negative experience of trying to gain entry to the labour market has significant impacts on their attitudes towards post-Soviet society. As Roberts *et al.* (2000: 135) state:

> Most of the young people we interviewed seemed to feel that they were growing up in times where nothing was stable.... Few believed that they lived in a 'just world' where riches normally followed effort and poverty was a fair punishment for sloth.... The young people knew full well, often from bitter personal experience, that, in the short term at any rate, educational backgrounds and qualifications would not count.

This lack of belief legitimises informal work practices as they are seen as a more 'just' alternative to the 'formal' labour market. Notions of social justice were a common theme in interviews. Many were extremely keen for Ukraine to join the European Union, not for the benefits that this would bring to the country, but because the subsequent freedom of movement would enable them to work in more mature economies without the constant spectre of corruption (for other examples of similar sentiments towards outward migration among young people in post-Soviet contexts, see Dafflon 2009; Mojić 2012; Roberts and Pollock 2011).

Interviewing postgraduate students at a prestigious university in Moscow, whose qualifications *should* offer relatively easy entry into the labour market, similar feelings were regularly articulated. This is perhaps somewhat surprising, given the opportunities available in Moscow, but again the issue of stability was central:

> I have had enough part-time and summer jobs to know that nothing is certain even in big corporations. I know I could get a well paid job here [in Moscow] but even then it is still stressful as you don't know what is going to happen tomorrow, next week or the month after. Amongst my friends who are already working you hear so many bad stories about their experiences from their bosses. Although you can earn a lot of money in Moscow I want to work in Europe as it would be much less stressful.

Even positions in multinational companies are not seen as particularly 'safe', though they potentially provide a path to the international labour market. When asked what they considered the 'safest' employment in Russia, the vast majority (80 per cent) replied that positions in public administration would be the most stable as 'people there look after their own'. These are particularly worrying sentiments as if such highly qualified students wish their future to be elsewhere because of the informality in the Russian labour market, then their abilities will be lost from the nation's future development (see Dafflon 2009, for a country-wide discussion of this issue). Furthermore, and this is an extremely important point, as informality becomes normalised and institutionalised, then its perpetuation becomes ever more entrenched.

When trust was gained with young interviewees in Ukraine, they were asked if they would take bribes if they were in a position to do so in the future. In the context of their anger and disillusionment with their country's education and labour market, a majority (55 per cent) said they would do so. They rationalised this in a number of ways. First, they argued that there is a need to 'earn back' the investments they have made in their education; second, as work is so insecure there is a need to gain as much income as possible in the shortest time; and third, there is a sense that if it is such a norm then why should they act differently, especially in relation to the actions of the state. In other words, if the state is acting informally, then why should individuals act any differently? Finally, and of great relevance to debates on anti-corruption measures, several participants discussed how, in order to integrate into a workplace, you have to adopt its culture. Therefore, for example, if informal payments are the norm within a workplace and you do not participate, you become the exception and will be viewed with suspicion, leading ultimately to exclusion.

Informality in the formal healthcare system

It is not solely in the realms of education and entry into the graduate labour market, however, that one witnesses the permeation of informality. It is also the case with regard to the healthcare system. With male life expectancy in Russia at just over 60, the lowest in the global North, there has been a great deal of research into the problems surrounding the country's health and the state of its healthcare system. While the percentage of GDP spent on healthcare in Russia, 5.2 per cent against an EU average of 9 per cent (Popovich *et al.* 2011), is relatively small, the number of healthcare professionals and hospital beds per capita appears impressive (OECD 2012). However, studies have revealed that there is too high a percentage of low-level trained staff (Rivkin-Fish 2011), issues with adopting the latest approaches and diagnostic methodologies (Rechel *et al.* 2011), the centralisation of the system and limited access to information (Popovich *et al.* 2011) and access problems (Fotaki 2009).

There has also been a growing concern that although free access to healthcare is a constitutional right (Popovich *et al.* 2011), informal payments for supposedly free healthcare are rampant. Many households have to make informal payments in order to see a doctor of their choice, to speed up access or to be referred to specialists (Fotaki 2009). As Kuhlbrandt *et al.* (2012) note, those receiving medical care constantly worry that they will have to make large payments to receive treatment. This was reinforced in our household survey. Of the 199 respondents entitled to free medicines, 120 (60 per cent) stated that they had encountered difficulties in obtaining them and in many instances had made an informal payment to do so. Only 9 per cent of respondents believed it was easy to obtain 'free' healthcare. Popovich *et al.* (2011: 87) state that in 2009, the latest figures available, 38.5 per cent of the population had 'paid under the table for treatment while inpatients' and 28.6 per cent had done similar for outpatient care. Fotaki's (2009) study found even higher figures, with 80.9 per cent of respondents making informal payments, which can have a dramatic impact on the budgets of lower income households.

It is little surprise, therefore, that many households forego the medicines they need. As one senior citizen asserted:

> I need a lot of medicines, but when we don't have enough money it is very hard to buy them all even though they are meant to be 'free'. Over the summer it is easier as we sell some products from our dacha but over the winter it is very hard. Sometimes I am in so much pain from my ulcers but I have to chose between buying medicines or having enough food to eat.

Sometimes a lack of money can have more serious consequences. After one focus group in Ukraine, a young woman approached the authors and said she wanted to talk to us in private. As the conversation progressed she became visibly upset and although it was offered to end the conversation, she said she wanted to continue as she 'wanted people to know what things are like here':

> My father had a heart attack at the dacha. We knew it was too far for the ambulance to come in time so we managed to get him into the car and drove to the nearest hospital. When we arrived mom ran into the hospital to get help and some administrator, or something, came out. He asked us straight out how much money we had to pay for the treatment. We told him we had very little money and he simply replied that they could not help. My dad died in the car park.

While this might seem an extreme example, an interviewee in Moscow discussed how exactly the same thing happened to her father, suggesting that these are not isolated incidents. Furthermore, even when in hospital often informal payments are required for medicines, and family members or friends must provide care. An interviewee in Moscow discussed the treatment of her mother in 2012:

> She was in hospital for a broken shoulder but the conditions were so bad she got an infection and almost died. The nurses were very little help and I had to almost live at the hospital. I had to change and wash my mother and clean her bedclothes. We had to take all the food she needed with us and we had to pay for almost all of her medicines.

Similar stories were told to the authors on many occasions (see also Fotaki 2009). Interviewees discussed how they believed giving an informal payment to medical personal would speed up access to treatment and would enable them to see the best doctors. This is important as, with most areas of post-Soviet life, the healthcare system is bureaucratic. One interviewee told of how she had to obtain six stamps on a request for a walking stick, necessitating queuing in six different locations across Moscow. A letter to *Argumenty i Fakty* newspaper aptly reflected the situation (Kiseleva 2004: 17):

> My mother is 95 years old. She is an invalid but she does not have the official documents on disability [needed to claim disability benefits]. She is not strong enough to wait in the numerous queues in the hospital to take the medical tests needed to prove her disability.

As one interviewee noted, 'one has to be well to be able to obtain disability benefits'.

Conclusions

In sum, this chapter has revealed that despite all of the hyperbole about the hegemony of the formal market economy, just 59.2 per cent of the working-age population is employed in the formal economy. This means that four in every ten people of working age in the post-Soviet world were not participating in the formal economy. Even this, however, is an exaggeration of the reach of formalisation in post-Soviet societies. Many of those who are in formal employment are in jobs infused with informality.

Envelope wages are a popular practice in post-Soviet societies. Some one in eight formal employees receive an envelope wage and this on average amounts to 38 per cent of their wage packet. The result is that even if 59 per cent of the working-age population is engaged in formal employment, some one in eight is in a quasi-formal job. This not only blurs the divide between formal and informal jobs, but also means that the proportion in purely formal employment is even lower than previously assumed. This, however, is not the only way in which the formal economy is infused with informality. As the case studies of kindergartens, schools, the university system, entry into the graduate labour market and healthcare provision reveal, the formal economy in post-Soviet societies remains riddled with crime, informality and corruption. In doing so, this chapter has revealed that it is impossible to view the formal and informal economies as separate and discrete spheres. Informality is an inherent feature of the formal economy in post-Soviet societies.

6 Informal employment

Introduction

Informal employment is here defined as paid labour unregistered by or hidden from the state for tax, social security and labour law purposes (European Commission 2007). Akin to the other eight labour practices considered in this book, different varieties exist, ranging from waged informal employment where employees are employed on an undeclared basis by formal or informal businesses to informal self-employment which can be conducted by own-account workers who work either wholly or partially off-the-books.

In this chapter, the intention is to evaluate the prevalence and nature of informal employment in post-Soviet/socialist spaces. To achieve this, first, a brief review is undertaken of the different methods of measuring informal employment and the varying estimates produced by such methods of the magnitude of informal employment in post-Soviet/socialist societies. Second, and so as to provide a richer and more textured understanding of how informal employment is embedded in daily life in post-Soviet societies, empirical evidence from Ukraine is reported, followed in the third section by evidence from Moscow. This will reveal not only the multifarious forms of informal employment in post-Soviet societies, but also how informal employment is not a distinct category but merges into the other forms of labour considered in other chapters. At the outset, however, it is necessary to be clear what is being discussed in this chapter. Despite being variously referred to by 45 adjectives, such as 'cash-in-hand', 'informal', 'black', 'underground', 'hidden' and 'shadow' and 12 nouns including work, employment, economy and sector (Williams 2004a), there is a strong consensus regarding the types of endeavour included and excluded when discussing this form of work. Informal employment is widely accepted as involving only the production and sale of goods and services that are licit in all respects besides the fact that they are unregistered by or hidden from the state for tax, benefit and/or labour law purposes (European Commission 1998; Feige 1999; Portes 1994; Renooy *et al.* 2004; Thomas 1992; Williams 2006a; Williams and Windebank 1998). When the goods and services provided are illicit (e.g. drug-trafficking), such endeavour is excluded, as are non-cash exchanges and subsistence production that is not exchanged. Blurred edges, nevertheless, do remain.

As shown in the previous chapter, informal employment overlaps with formal employment since formal employees often receive undeclared wages from their formal employer. In this chapter, however, this is excluded since it was discussed in the previous chapter. There are also blurred edges between informal employment and paid favours (discussed in Chapter 7) since informal self-employment merges with paid favours, depending on the economic relations involved and the motives of the participants.

Participation in informal employment in post-Soviet/socialist societies

Different measurement methods produce different estimates of the prevalence of informal employment in post-Soviet societies. Here, we briefly review the measurement methods used and their estimates of its size. To do this the indirect measurement methods will be reviewed, followed by the more direct survey methods.

Indirect methods for measuring informal employment

Indirect methods seek evidence of informal employment in macroeconomic data collected and/or constructed for other purposes. These indirect methods have been of three broad types. First, there are those seeking statistical traces of informal employment in non-monetary indicators. The most common methods using such non-monetary surrogate indicators are, first, those that seek traces in formal labour force statistics (e.g. Alden 1982; Crnkovic-Pozaic 1999; Del Boca and Forte 1982; Hellberger and Schwarze 1986), second, those that use very small enterprises as a proxy (e.g. ILO 2002a; Portes and Sassen-Koob 1987; Sassen and Smith 1992; US General Accounting Office 1989) and, third, those that use electricity demand as a surrogate (e.g. Friedman *et al.* 2000; Kaufmann and Kaliberda 1996; Lacko 1999). Second, there are methods that employ monetary proxy indicators to estimate the magnitude of informal employment. Three principal proxies have been used: large denomination notes (Bartlett 1998; Carter 1984; Freud 1979; Henry 1976; Matthews 1982); the cash–deposit ratio (e.g. Atkins 1999; Caridi and Passerini 2001; Cocco and Santos 1984; Matthews 1983; Matthews and Rastogi 1985; Meadows and Pihera 1981; Santos 1983; Tanzi 1980); and the total quantity of money transactions (Feige 1979, 1990; Isachsen *et al.* 1982), although a multiple indicators, multiple causes (MIMIC) approach has emerged that has perhaps become the most commonly used indirect method for measuring the magnitude of informal employment (Bajada and Schneider 2003; Chatterjee *et al.* 2002; Giles 1999a, 1999b; Giles and Tedds 2002; Schneider 2001, 2011; Schneider and Enste 2002). Third, there are those methods analysing discrepancies between income and expenditure levels either at the aggregate national level (Apel 1994; Hansson 1982; Langfelt 1989; Paglin 1994; Park 1979; Tengblad 1994), or through detailed microeconomic studies of different types of individuals or households (Dilnot and Morris 1981; Macafee

1980; O'Higgins 1981), premised on the assumption that even if the informally employed can conceal their incomes, they cannot hide their expenditures.

Given that there are already many in-depth critical reviews of the advantages and disadvantages of all these different indirect measurement methods (Bajada 2002; Feige and Ott 1999; OECD 2002; Schneider and Enste 2002; Williams 2004a, 2006b), we will not repeat the findings. Suffice it to say that despite each and every method suffering from some serious shortcomings, there has emerged a consensus that while direct survey methods (considered below) should be used to understand the nature of informal employment in terms of the types of informal work that take place, who does it and their motives, indirect methods can produce overall estimates of the relative magnitude of informal employment in different places (European Commission 2007; OECD 2011; Williams 2006b). Indeed, for well over a decade now, the MIMIC approach, despite recognition of its shortcomings, has become the standard means of estimating the magnitude of informal employment in different countries. This views the causes (and indicators) of informal employment as: the burden of direct and indirect taxation, both actual and perceived; the burden of regulation; and tax morality (citizens' attitudes towards paying taxes). Figure 6.1 reports the estimated magnitude of informal employment in post-Soviet/socialist societies using this MIMIC measurement method (Schneider 2012). Here we report the results for 2007, when we conducted our fieldwork in Russia and Ukraine. This reveals that the magnitude

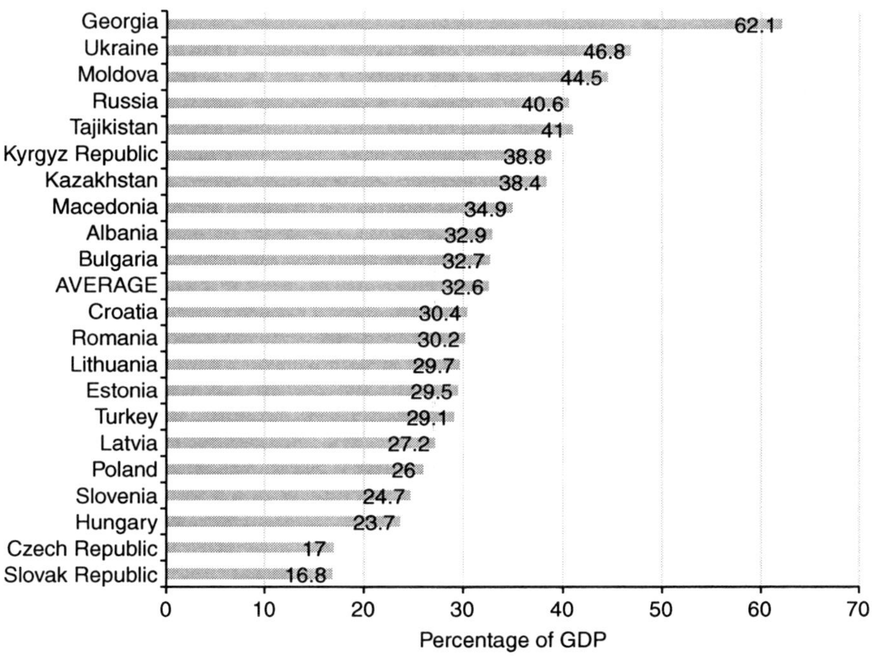

Figure 6.1 Informal employment as a percentage of GDP, 2007: by country (source: derived from Schneider 2012: Table 1.1).

of informal employment in post-Soviet/socialist economies was on average equivalent to 32.6 per cent of GDP, although its magnitude varied from the equivalent of 16.8 per cent of GDP in Slovenia to 62.1 per cent in Georgia at this time. It also importantly reveals that Ukraine and Russia were, in 2007, among the countries with the highest levels of informal employment in the post-Soviet/socialist world, with informal employment estimated to be equivalent to 46.8 per cent of GDP in Ukraine and 40.6 per cent of GDP in Russia.

This MIMIC measurement method also provides data on whether informal employment is growing or declining relative to the formal economy over time. Figure 6.2 reports the results for post-Soviet/socialist economies. It reveals that besides a slight rise between 2008 and 2009, when the economic crisis started to hit hard, there has been an ongoing decline in informal employment in these post-Soviet/socialist societies between 2003 and 2012. During the current economic crisis, therefore, informal employment according to this measurement method has been declining as a proportion of GDP in those post-Soviet/socialist economies for which such longitudinal data is available.

However, caution is urged when considering these results. It is not only possible to challenge all of the supposed causes (and indicators) used by this approach, but there is also little recognition in this approach that it is not these factors per se but, rather, how they combine with a multitude of others factors

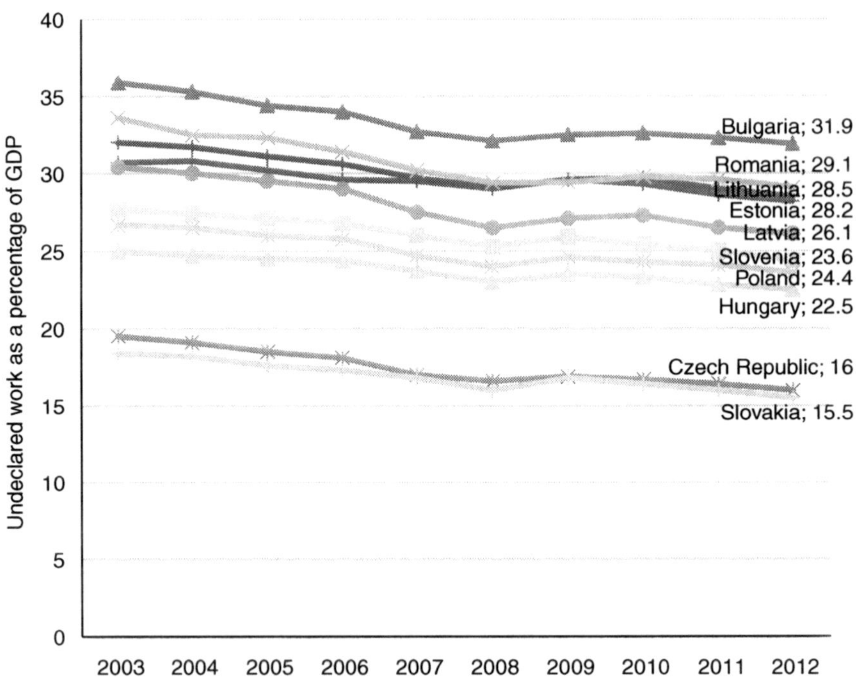

Figure 6.2 Informal employment as a percentage of GDP, 2003–2012 (source: derived from Schneider 2012: Table 1.1).

that produces high or low levels of informal employment. It is also important to recognise that to understand the role of informal economies in post-Soviet/socialist economies, it is not so much the magnitude of informal employment that needs to be understood, but rather how the informal employment is being used in everyday livelihood practices and by whom and for what reasons. To seek understanding of these issues that provide us with a more textured comprehension of the role of informal economies in the post-Soviet/socialist world, it is the direct survey methods that are a more useful tool.

Direct survey methods

Rather than use proxy indicators to evaluate the magnitude and/or character of informal employment, a parallel stream of research has conducted direct surveys of informal employment using both mail shots as well as various interview methods (e.g. Boren 2003; Burawoy and Verdery 1999; Meurs 2002; Pavlovskaya 2004; Smith 2002a, 2002b, 2004, 2010; Smith and Stenning 2006). Most of these have been studies of single nations and small-scale qualitative surveys. Although these are useful, as will be seen below, for unpacking rich and textured understandings of the nature of informal employment, they have been less useful for getting a feel for the cross-national variations in the magnitude of informal employment. One exception is the 2007 Eurobarometer survey which measures the participation rates in informal employment using the same questionnaire survey method across a range of post-Soviet/socialist countries. Table 6.1 reports the results. This displays that participation rates range from 15 per cent in Latvia and 11 per cent in Estonia to 4 per cent in Romania. This does not mean, however, that the undeclared economy (i.e. informal employment and paid favours) is necessarily more extensive in those nations with higher participation rates. As can be seen, in nations such as Romania, the average hours worked in the undeclared economy is higher as is the average income earned from such work. In consequence, although a smaller share of the population engage in the undeclared economy in some countries, they work for more hours than those in countries with higher participation rates where the undeclared economy appears to be composed of smaller-scale and piecemeal activities such as baby-sitting and odd-jobs.

So, too, does the configuration of informal employment vary across nations. As displayed in Table 6.1, marked variations exist in the proportion which is waged employment, self-employment and paid favours for closer social relations. For the moment, paid favours will be excluded from the analysis since this will be treated separately in Chapter 7. In this chapter the focus is upon the ratio of informal waged employment to informal self-employment. Examining Table 6.1, it becomes apparent that this ratio significantly varies across countries. In Bulgaria, for instance, nearly twice as much informal waged employment takes place as informal self-employment, while in Slovakia the opposite is the case: participation in informal self-employment is nearly twice as likely as participation in informal waged employment. It is important to be aware, therefore, that

Table 6.1 Prevalence and configuration of the undeclared economy in East-Central European countries

Country	*Percentage engaged in undeclared work in last 12 months*	*Average total hours of undeclared work in last 12 months*	*Mean annual undeclared income/capita (€)*	*Mean annual undeclared income/undeclared worker (€)*	*Percentage of undeclared work that is:*			
					Waged work	*Paid favours*	*Self-employment*	*Other/don't know/refusal*
Latvia	15	390	602	4,015	18	41	32	9
Estonia	11	182	305	2,772	20	41	35	4
Czech Republic	7	157	88	1,252	23	66	3	8
Hungary	7	296	87	1,244	33	39	24	4
Lithuania	7	347	369	5,275	15	43	42	–
Slovakia	6	198	112	2,245	16	53	28	3
Poland	5	359	84	1,686	26	32	31	11
Bulgaria	5	649	240	4,802	50	22	28	–
Slovenia	5	97	45	752	15	66	13	6
Romania	4	266	449	11,234	12	57	19	12

Source: Eurobarometer survey on undeclared work, 2007.

informal employment is often very differently configured in different post-Soviet/socialist societies.

Here, therefore, and to provide a richer and more textured understanding of the role of informal employment in the livelihoods of those living in post-Soviet/socialist societies, we begin to unpack the more qualitative meanings of informal employment to those engaged in it in terms of the role of such work to those engaged in it. To do this, we report the findings of our fieldwork using a direct survey method conducted in Ukraine and in the Russian city of Moscow.

Prevalence and nature of informal employment in Ukraine

Asking the 600 respondents about the form of work most important for their standard of living, along with what the second most important is, one in six (16.4 per cent) households report that they rely primarily on informal employment for their livelihood. A further quarter, citing some other form of work as their principal source of livelihood, moreover assert that informal employment is the second most important contributor. In total, therefore, 40 per cent of Ukraine households cite informal employment as either the principal or secondary contributor to their living standard. To depict informal employment as a residual and weak realm is thus a misnomer in Ukraine.

Who, therefore, relies on informal employment for their livelihood? Evaluating the structuralist view discussed in Chapter 3 that it is marginalised populations excluded from the formal economy, the finding is that just 13 per cent of households with nobody in formal employment cited informal employment as their primary strategy, but 24 per cent of households with one formal wage earner and 14 per cent of households with multiple formal wage earners. Indeed, of all households chiefly relying on informal employment for their livelihood, just 6 per cent were households with nobody in formal employment (12 per cent of all households surveyed), 51 per cent were multiple-earner households (58 per cent of households surveyed) and 43 per cent single-earner households (29 per cent). Analysing whether it is nevertheless the jobless in these households who engage in informal employment, the finding is that in multiple-earner households, it is in 96 per cent of cases those with formal jobs who engage in informal employment, while in single-earner households it is in 70 per cent of cases the formal wage worker who also undertakes the informal employment. Therefore, informal employment is not confined to those excluded from the formal labour market as suggested by structuralist accounts of the informal economy.

Do people operate in this sphere, therefore, due to their exclusion from the formal economy (as structuralists assert) or because they are voluntarily exiting the formal realm either because of the problems associated with working legitimately (as neo-liberals assert) or for rationales more grounded in social and redistributive motivations (as post-structuralists assert)? To evaluate this, first, the rationales of consumers will be evaluated, and second, the rationales of suppliers. Examining the reasons consumers gave for using informal employment, as Table 6.2 displays, some 38 per cent of off-the-books transactions were sourced because they had no choice but to do so, and a further 22 per cent included this issue in their explanation. For many, therefore, informal employment was used in preference to the formal economy. For neo-liberals this explanation covers problems associated with sourcing formal goods and services, including the availability, quality and speed of formal service provision. For example, it might be stated that formal businesses often do not turn up to give quotes for work and/or fail to turn up to do the work and even if they do turn up, tend to only partially complete the work and then move to another job until harried to return and finish the work. In this study, some 24 per cent of off-the-books transactions were conducted purely for this reason and a further 26 per cent included this issue in their rationale. Meanwhile, post-structuralists assert that participation is also out of choice, but explain this in terms of social or redistributive rationales. The finding is that some 10 per cent of informal labour was used due to either a desire to help someone who is in need of money and/or as a favour among friends, colleagues and acquaintances. A further 13 per cent included this issue in their explanation. In reality, of course, such social/redistributive explanations are often embedded in economic rationales in that the reason that a neighbour or friend is being asked to do a task is to redistribute money to them in a way that does not appear to be 'charity'.

Consumers' rationales, nevertheless, vary across populations. Indeed, while 'exclusion' drivers are more commonly cited among low-income households and those living in deprived neighbourhoods, 'exit' drivers, particularly regarding poor formal provision, are more frequently cited among high-earners and those in affluent and rural areas. Social/redistributive rationales, meanwhile, are more frequently the chief rationale among higher-income households and affluent urban areas. The result is that participation in informal employment for low-income groups and those in deprived areas is more a result of exclusion, while engagement among high-income groups and those living in affluent areas is more due to voluntary exit. In consequence, different explanations are relevant to different groups.

Turning to suppliers' rationales, Table 6.3 again divides rationales according to whether the primary reason cited is exclusion (e.g. because they could not find a regular job, the employer insisted on them being paid off-the-books or because there is no alternative) or whether it is more a decision to exit, and if so, whether this is because of the problems of working legitimately or whether it is more for social/redistributive rationales. The finding is that 30 per cent of informal employment is explained purely in terms of exclusion from the formal economy, 48 per cent solely due to a desire to voluntarily exit the formal economy, as argued by neo-liberal and post-structuralist commentators, and 22 per cent for a mix of both exit and exclusion rationales. Breaking down the decision to voluntarily exit the formal economy, 35 per cent of all informal employment was to avoid the costs, time and effort of formal registration and in preference to formal employment and 13 per cent for social and/or redistributive reasons, such as a desire to help someone who is in need of help who would otherwise be unable to afford to get the work completed.

Table 6.2 Consumers' motives for using informal labour in Ukraine: by population group

	No choice/ exclusion	*Poor formal provision alone*	*Social rationales alone*	*Mixture of no choice and poor formal provision*	*Mixture of no choice and social rationales*	*Mixture of poor formal provision and social rationales*	*Mixture of all three rationales*
All	38	24	10	15	2	6	5
Gross formal income/month:							
Lowest quartile	46	25	8	17	0	2	2
Lower quartile	38	20	9	13	0	10	10
Upper quartile	35	23	10	12	3	9	8
Highest quartile	30	30	15	15	2	4	4
Locality type:							
Affluent Kiev	30	29	16	10	0	9	6
Deprived Kiev	45	20	7	16	2	5	5
Deprived rural	42	30	7	15	2	3	1
Mixed urban	33	21	11	13	4	7	9

Source: Ukraine survey.

Table 6.3 Suppliers' primary motives for participation in informal employment in Ukraine: by socio-economic group and location

	Factors related to desire to exit formal economy:		*Factors related to exclusion from formal economy*	*Both exit and exclusion factors*
	Problems of working legitimately	*Social/ redistributive rationales*		
All	35	13	30	22
Gross formal income/month:				
Lowest quartile	30	10	38	22
Lower quartile	35	13	32	20
Upper quartile	34	14	31	21
Highest quartile	41	17	17	25
Locality type:				
Affluent Kiev	42	18	11	29
Deprived Kiev	29	9	37	25
Deprived rural	40	11	33	16
Mixed urban	31	13	27	29

Source: Ukraine survey.

Again, however, the rationales vary across population groups and areas. Voluntarism, and therefore the neo-liberal and post-structuralist explanations, is more commonly cited by informal workers living in higher-income areas, rural areas and affluent localities. The structuralist assertion that participation is more the result of exclusion from the legitimate realm, meanwhile, is more common among low-income households, and those living in urban and deprived areas. It is not just across different socio-economic and spatial populations, however, that there are variations in the reasons for participating in informal employment.

Do the reasons vary, however, according to whether it is informal self-employment or waged informal employment that is being conducted? This survey finds that of all informal employment undertaken, 38 per cent is informal self-employment and the remaining 62 per cent is waged informal employment. Examining the reasons for participating in each of these different types of informal employment, Table 6.4 reveals that those studying informal employment from the perspective of exclusion are more likely to find what they seek in waged employment; some 55 per cent is conducted for factors related to exclusion and 20 per cent for rationales associated with both exit and exclusion, compared with just 20 per cent and 23 per cent, respectively, of informal self-employment. Similarly, the desire to exit the formal economy is greater in own-account work. Neo-liberals depicting participation more as a voluntary decision to exit the formal economy so as to avoid the costs, time and effort of formal registration, therefore, have been correct to focus upon informal self-employment (55 per cent of self-employment is conducted for this reason), while post-structuralists depicting engagement to be a choice conducted for

Table 6.4 Relationship between type of informal employment and reasons for participation in Ukraine

Percentage of informal labourers explaining their participation in terms of:	*All types*	*Type of informal employment:*	
		Self-employed for other private persons, households or businesses	*Salaried employees for firms or businesses*
Desire to exit formal economy	48	57	25
• due to problems with the formal realm	35	55	22
• for social/redistributive reasons	13	2	3
Exclusion from formal economy	30	20	55
Both exit and exclusion factors	22	23	20

Source: Ukraine survey.

social/redistributive rationales have been correct to focus upon own-account work embedded within closer social networks of familial and community solidarity (46 per cent is conducted for such reasons).

It is important to be aware, however, that even if there is a close relationship between these different varieties of informal employment and the contrasting explanations, it is far from the case that all work in each category can be explained purely in terms of simply either exclusion or exit. To see this, each variety of informal employment is briefly reviewed in turn.

Informal waged employment in Ukraine

Examining waged informal employment, one finds considerable support for the structuralist representation of informal employment as conducted under 'sweatshop-like' conditions, as becoming an inherent part of employment practices in capitalism, as possessing largely negative attributes and impacts, and as conducted out of necessity rather than choice (e.g. Bender 2004; Castree *et al.* 2004; Espenshade 2004; Hapke 2004; A. Ross 2004; R. Ross 2004), especially in the garment manufacturing sector (e.g. Bender 2004; Espenshade 2004; Hapke 2004; Ram *et al.* 2002a, 2002b; R. Ross 2004). Although informal employees were identified working in wholly off-the-books businesses under 'sweatshop-like' conditions, such as in clothing manufacturers, mostly out of necessity, these employees represent only one segment of all informal waged employees in Ukraine. Waged informal employment takes many forms, as Clarke (2002) has identified in Russia. Some 20 per cent of waged informal employees work for wholly informal businesses, with the remaining 80 per cent working for legitimate businesses on an informal basis. Such work, moreover, is sometimes full-time (30 per cent of such work) but more often part-time, temporary or occasional.

Neither are they all in the lowest-income groups. Some 53 per cent of informal employees were in the lowest quartile of households by total gross household income, 30 per cent in the second quartile, 15 per cent in the third quartile and just 2 per cent in the highest income quartile. Examples of the work they undertake are multifarious. However, they were clustered in the construction and consumer service sectors in jobs such as labourers on building sites, taxi drivers, market stall workers, and waiters and cooks. Moreover, 55 per cent of informal waged workers say that they work in this realm due to their exclusion from the formal realm, 25 per cent for reasons related to a desire to exit the formal economy and 20 per cent for a mixture of both exclusion and exit factors (see Table 6.4). For example, respondents commonly asserted that 'I did it because no other work was available', 'I did it to earn much needed extra cash' and 'I do it because I need the money.' Although other reasons prevailed, such as to help out the owner of the business (e.g. 'he needed staff so I helped him out; he is an acquaintance'), most is conducted out of economic necessity and/or because they had no other choice. On the whole, in consequence, informal waged employment is more likely to be a product of exclusion than other forms of informal employment.

Informal self-employment in Ukraine

The 600 face-to-face interviews revealed a high level of self-employment in Ukraine. Some 331 individuals living in these households had engaged in some form of self-employed activity in the past three years. Of these, just 33 (10 per cent) stated that this activity was wholly legitimate and that they had registered this activity with the state, had been in possession of the required licences and had conducted all their transactions on a formal basis. The remaining 298 (90 per cent) operated wholly or partially in the informal economy. Some 39 per cent had a licence to trade and/or the person was registered as self-employed, but a portion of their activity was conducted in the informal economy, while 51 per cent operated on a wholly unregistered basis with no licence to trade and conducted all of their activity in the informal economy (see Table 6.5).

Are there variations between men and women who are informally self-employed in terms of the portion that trade off-the-books and the type of off-the-books business that they operate? The finding is that although similar proportions of women and men who are self-employed trade off-the-books, men are more likely to operate registered enterprises and to conduct a portion of their

Table 6.5 Share of self-employed working wholly or partially informally in Ukraine

	All	*Men*	*Women*
Number	331	161	170
Percentage operating informally	90	89	91
Percentage wholly legitimate	10	11	9
Percentage registered but conducting share of trade off-the-books	39	46	31
Percentage not registered	51	43	60

Source: Ukraine survey.

transactions off-the-books, while women are more likely to operate unregistered enterprises and to trade wholly off-the-books. Examples of such wholly informal businesses operated by women include: a childcare business operated from home by a grandmother responsible for providing the daytime care for her preschool grandchild; a home-based catering business which undertook work for both domestic and commercial customers; a business making curtains and other soft furnishings; an enterprise making and repairing clothes; a pensioner who supplemented her state pension by selling cigarettes at a train station, and an illegal street vendor who sold flowers which she grows on her dacha just outside a market. All were unregistered enterprises trading wholly in the informal economy.

Who, therefore, engages in such informal self-employment? Some 55 per cent are in formal employment, operating their business alongside their formal waged work as an 'on-the side' activity, and the remaining 45 per cent are a mixture of various categories of people registered as non-employed, including the 'economically inactive' such as housewives and others unregistered as engaging in any form of employment, pensioners and people claiming unemployment benefit. This reinforces the wider finding elsewhere that those starting-up enterprises often tend to be people in waged employment and that it is only later in the development of the enterprise that they might become fully self-employed and to leave their waged employment (e.g. Reynolds *et al.* 2002). As a study in Russia has displayed, 26.5 per cent of the newly self-employed work on an informal basis as a second job at the outset, displaying how the informal sphere is an incubator for new self-employed businesses (Guariglia and Kim 2006).

Of those engaged in such self-employed activity that currently also engage in waged employment, about 80 per cent use the skills, tools and/or networks directly related to their employment and/or employment-place in their informal self-employment. For example, those working as plumbers in their formal occupation tend to operate plumbing enterprises 'on the side' and others tend to use contacts from their employment-place in order to find work for their informal enterprise. An example would be university teachers who offer university entrance examination candidates tuition on an informal basis in order to help them pass their entrance examinations. The remaining one-fifth of those in waged formal employment operating an informal enterprise do so in fields that arose out of what Stebbins (2004) refers to as some 'serious leisure' such as a hobby or interest that leads them to set up enterprises selling goods produced or services resulting from it. This included those who had learned some skill by pursuing some hobby or interest (e.g. painting, carpentry) and had then decided to establish an enterprise based on this skill. This Ukraine survey reveals that nine out of ten starting up a self-employed enterprise in the last three years had chosen to work on an informal basis, and some two-thirds had still not even registered their enterprises and were working wholly off-the-books. For most of these informal self-employed, the formal economy was seen as possessing largely negative attributes and impacts due to the existence of corrupt state officials and their lack of belief that taxes would be used for the social good, while the informal economy was perceived as a positive alternative that gave them free rein and was largely entered out of choice rather than necessity. Looking at this group of informal workers and type of work, there is thus superficially strong support for the representation of the informal economy as an alternative economy and sphere of resistance, as has been previously identified elsewhere (De Soto 1989; Williams 2006b).

This, however, depends on the group of informal self-employed considered. This is because the informal self-employed are clustered at the two ends of the income spectrum. In the lowest quartile of households surveyed in terms of gross income, one finds clustered 35 per cent of the informal self-employed in Ukraine, while in the highest quartile of households one finds 41 per cent of all informal self-employed. Those informal self-employed in the lowest quartile largely do not have a formal job (85 per cent of them) and engage in own-account work as a survival strategy. This is mostly poorly paid work, such as selling flowers outside street markets, cigarettes outside stations or providing routine domestic services. Indeed, the vast majority of respondents asserted that they would prefer a 'normal' formal job so as to minimise their risks of being cheated, robbed and to be able to have paid leave, but did not have the opportunity to do so. Instead, they had to rely on largely piecemeal informal own-account work. As such, these necessity-oriented informal self-employed adhere to the by-product depiction of the informal employed as those off-loaded by capitalism forced to eke out a living in this sphere as a last resort. Those informal self-employed in the highest quartile in terms of gross household income, however, usually engage in relatively well-paid informal self-employment, which in nearly half (45 per cent) of all such cases directly arises out of opportunities from their formal employment or self-employment. This includes not only university teachers who provide preparation for the university entrance examinations and school teachers who provide after-school additional lessons for pupils, but also software engineers providing informal services for the clients of the business where they are formally employed, and self-employed plumbers, electricians and builders conducting a portion or all of their business informally. Nearly all asserted that they worked informally so as to avoid the 'bribe taxes', administrative corruption and 'informal taxation' rife in Ukrainian public life (Hanson 2006; Round and Kosterina 2005; Wallace and Latcheva 2006). 'Katrina', who runs a catering business, reflects the opinion of many of these higher-income own-account informal workers interviewed when she states:

> I would like to have my own 'legit' business. I would be very proud.... People would look at me differently ... but it is very difficult ... our 'chinnovniki' [government officials] want money, money and more money but I cannot afford to do that.... It is a shame because it has always been my dream to be a 'khozyaika' [enterprise owner], but it isn't to be.

She wanted to go 'legit' but currently could not see how this could be achieved because public officials would demand cash payments from her for the required licences and to remain in business.

For most of the higher-income self-employed, it was perceived to be far too difficult to legitimise their operations. A self-employed taxi driver in his fifties neatly summed up the feeling of most of these respondents when he stated:

> I have never thought about getting a licence because it is a very complicated bureaucratic process. I just do not have time and the nerve to stand in lines for days and weeks. It is amazing; if the state wants taxes why does it not organise things so that all the procedures to get a licence go quickly and without bribes? I have the impression that if a person wants to pay taxes out of his/her informal income in this country, they have to be obsessed by this idea and fight for their rights to do it with the state itself.

Most of the higher-income self-employed running wholly illegitimate businesses, moreover, saw nothing wrong in doing so. For them, it was the state and its officials who were corrupt and they who were in the right. They saw themselves as entrepreneurs and part of the burgeoning 'capitalist' culture in Ukraine, but operating informally due to the corruption, bribery and bureaucracy inherent in the 'old' system that they were helping replace. Many were also very willing to pay taxes but refused to do so while the income went into what they believed to be the pockets of state officials rather than being used for the public good. The motives of such respondents, therefore, very much reflect the thesis that depicts informal employment as a chosen alternative to a harmful formal economy that is putting a brake on economic development and growth.

In sum, the informal self-employment identified in Ukraine is not a complement to the formal economy since it is not simply reinforcing the disparities produced in the formal economy, but neither is it purely either a by-product or alternative to the formal economy. Although lower-income informal own-account workers reinforce the by-product thesis of marginalised groups engaged out of necessity in this work, higher-income own-account workers reflect the view that it is a chosen alternative to a failing bribe-ridden and corrupt formal economy. For the vast majority of the informal self-employed, nevertheless, such informal self-employment is central to their livelihood.

It is not an aim of the above arguments to over-romanticise the observed informal practices as alternatives to formal market processes. However, their widespread existence questions the stories of the formal market economy's successful creation that the state and outside actors such as the EU promulgate. Simply put, Ukraine's formal market economy could not function without the informal, as such activities enable individuals to perform their formal roles. For example, if a teacher could not earn money informally they would have to leave the profession, as their formal income is not enough to live on. If senior citizens refused to engage in informal practices, then the state would be forced to confront questions on why pensions are so low and how corruption is allowed to impinge on the everyday of this group to such a large extent. This disengagement with the informal is obviously not going to occur as people need to operate in this manner in order to survive; thus, as Mitchell (2003) points out, the discourse of the dominance of the formal market economy remains unchallenged at a state level. Therefore, it can be argued that for many their informal practices are created as a result of exploitation. This is not explicit – for example, working in sweat-shop conditions – but a more subtle outcome of low wages and pensions. For many of a working age, their informal work has to take place in addition to their formal obligations, and obviously a great deal of time is devoted to work. This has serious implications for the household and for society in general as the following interviewees discuss:

> During the ten years of the old government [the first two post-Soviet governments] people were hoping for better a life. But instead it became harder and harder. Everyone is now very stressed, be it about their children, the ecology or whether there will be another financial catastrophe. Even when having fun with friends it is not like it used to be as everyone is so stressed. Everyone is too busy 'under-working' so we can't meet at the week-ends. Everyone has a lot of problems.

Many interviewees noted that they often experience feelings of humiliation at having to undertake so much extra work. As one interviewee said, also reinforcing the above point on the time factor of such tactics:

> If you only work on one job the wage is not enough even to exist on. So we [the majority of workers] are forced to look for jobs on the side. It is like this! We have to go from extra work to extra work. This is how an ordinary worker lives, our wages are minimal. We have no privileges, only humiliation.

For senior citizens, while they have more time to undertake informal practices, these are often physically demanding and offer little long-term security. Most interviewees stated that it is extremely difficult to save considerable sums of money, and those engaged with domestic production can often only generate enough income to see them through the coming winter.

Yet many people take great pride in their informal practices. Many of the practices are extremely ingenious and would contribute greatly to the formal economy if the barriers to entry were lowered. The social capital which facilitates these processes also provides a security far beyond the economic. Many interviewees discussed how their social networks are built on deep levels of trust and thus individuals know that in a time of crisis they have people to turn to. As Lefebvre (2006: 171) argues '[d]aily life has served as a refuge from the tragic, and still does: above all else, people seek, and find, security there'. An extension of this is the importance of the spaces within which the processes take place. De Certeau (1988) talks at length, in an urban context, about how such networks, and use of space, extend the 'living room' of the household into the everyday spaces that surround them. For example, a small plot of land used for subsistence production might be seen as 'backwards' by the state, a brake on the development of the 'market', but it can be of crucial importance to those who use it, not just for the food it produces but for the spaces of resistance it provides to externally introduced marginalisation.

Furthermore, as De Certeau (1988: 108) says, in relation to how individuals use their neighbourhood and the networks within it, '"I feel good here": the well-being under-expressed in the language it appears in like a fleeting glimmer is a spatial practice.' Such sentiments clearly exist in the spaces that the above informal practices take place in and, to paraphrase de Certeau, many people further believe that 'I can survive here.' Thus, schemes which seek a geographical fix by encouraging the movement of economically marginalised groups to regions with lower living costs are doomed to failure as coping tactics are deeply entwined within the spaces they are taking place within (for an example of a failure of a scheme to move people out of the climatically inhospitable Russian north, see Round 2006). Therefore, the spaces informal practices take place across can be simultaneously sites of formal/informal processes, strategies/tactics, exploitation/resistance with the boundaries between them often blurred. With the state unwilling to engage with such complexity, preferring to reduce informal processes to a means of 'cheating the state', it is extremely difficult for them to develop policies which could truly impact positively on the everyday lives of Ukraine's economically marginalised.

Prevalence and nature of informal employment in Moscow

Asking the 313 participants in the survey in Moscow what work is most important for securing their livelihood, along with what is second most important, the finding is that one in three (32 per cent) primarily rely on informal employment for their livelihood and a further one in nine (11 per cent) assert that informal employment is the second most important contributor. Some 43 per cent thus cite this sphere as either the principal or secondary means of securing a livelihood. As such, informal employment is again not a residue or leftover. It is a core livelihood practice, as previously identified elsewhere in post-Soviet societies (Wallace and Haerpfer 2002; Wallace and Latcheva 2006). Who undertakes such practices? Only 25 per cent of working-age households with nobody in formal employment cited informal employment as their primary strategy, but 40 per cent of households with one formal wage earner and 35 per cent of households with multiple declared wage earners. Indeed, of all households chiefly relying on informal employment, just 20 per cent had nobody in formal employment (22 per cent of all households surveyed), 25 per cent were multiple-earner households (35 per cent of households surveyed) and 55 per cent single-earner households (43 per cent). To portray informal employment as used by marginalised Muscovites excluded from the formal labour market is therefore erroneous.

There are, however, some major differences across the districts studied in terms of the dependence of the populations on informal employment. In the affluent west Moscow district of Krylatskoe and the deprived district in south-east Moscow, around one-quarter of households relied on informal employment as their primary means of livelihood (28 per cent and 24 per cent, respectively). In the mixed area of Leshkovo, however, where the affluent and 'working poor'/ state benefit-dependent live alongside each other, reliance on informal employment was higher with just under half (47 per cent) of households chiefly depending on such employment for their livelihood. In this district, such work is largely undertaken by lower-income groups who supply the rich Russians living alongside them with gardening services, baby-sitting, domestic cleaning and home repair and maintenance. This reinforces the finding of previous studies in western nations that higher levels of informal employment exist in districts with a mix of higher- and lower-income groups (Portes 1994; Williams and Windebank 1998). In consequence, informal employment is not some marginal sphere of minor importance to a limited range of households but, rather, is an important practice for a large proportion of the Moscow population, and this applies across all of the districts studied. Indeed, this centrality of informal employment becomes even more apparent when analysing the sources of labour households use to complete a range of common domestic service tasks. Analysing the source of labour last used by households to undertake common domestic tasks, the finding is that overall, 18.2 per cent were last completed using informal employment, and just 6.9 per cent using formal labour. In other words, in the domestic services sector, nearly three times more tasks are conducted using informal employment than are undertaken using formal labour.

In what spheres is informal employment rife? Analysing the tasks in which the use of informal employment is most commonly used (see Table 6.6), the finding is that these are plumbing (which in 75.2 per cent of cases was last completed using off-the-books labour), bathroom refurbishment (72.9 per cent), appliance maintenance (66.2 per cent), floor laying (57.0 per cent), glazing (56.8 per cent), kitchen refurbishment (56.3 per cent), indoor painting (45.6 per cent), wallpapering (40.2 per cent), double-glazing installation (31.6 per cent), tutoring (31.3 per cent) and hairdressing (22.2 per cent). Analysing the ratios of informal to formal labour for each task, moreover, the magnitude of informal relative to formal labour can be evaluated for different tasks. Both washing dishes and domestic appliance repair are never conducted on a formal basis (the former displaying the total absence of formally employed domestic workers), while informal employment is 12 times the size of the formal economy in the sphere of plumbing, ten times the size in the realm of indoor painting, 7.7 times in the realm of glazing and 7.6 times for wallpapering.

It is also important to see how the gender divisions in the informal labour market reflect and reinforce the gender divisions of domestic labour. As Table 6.6 reveals, the tasks which women are most likely to conduct as informal employment mirror the tasks for which they are deemed to have responsibility when conducted as self-provisioning. Therefore, and akin to the formal labour market, the informal labour market mirrors the gender divisions found in the unpaid domestic realm.

Why, therefore, do people engage in informal employment in Moscow? To evaluate this, first, consumers' rationales are evaluated and, second, suppliers'

Table 6.6 Comparison of the gender divisions of informal employment and unpaid domestic work in Moscow: by task ($n = 313$)

	Percentage of households last sourcing task on an off-the-books basis	*Percentage of informal employment conducted by women*	*Percentage of unpaid domestic work conducted by:*		
			Man alone	*Woman alone*	*Shared*
House maintenance:					
Indoor painting	43	10	61	19	20
Wallpapering	40	16	37	24	39
Mend window	57	11	71	21	8
Maintain appliances	66	15	58	33	9
Lay floor covering	57	10	61	17	22
Home improvement:					
Double glazing	30	0	100	0	0
Plumbing	75	0	37	26	37
Put in bathroom	55	0	100	0	0
Refurbish kitchen	73	10	29	42	29
Routine housework:					
Do housework	2	100	8	87	5
Clean windows	4	100	9	84	7
Do the shopping	2	100	8	85	7
Wash clothes/sheets	3	100	8	89	3
Cook meals	1	100	8	89	3
Wash dishes	1	100	8	88	4
Hairdressing	22	100	12	88	0
Administration	0	0	17	49	3
Making and repairing goods:					
Repair clothes	0	0	10	90	0
Repair furniture	3	60	3	97	0
Make curtains	3	80	7	93	0
Repair tools	11	10	100	0	0
Caring:					
Baby-sitting (day)	5	90	2	96	2
Baby-sitting (night)	5	90	2	94	4
Tutoring children	31	50	0	100	0
Tending sick	19	100	10	80	10

Source: Moscow survey.

rationales. Examining consumers' rationales, and as Table 6.7 displays, some 40 per cent of informal employment is used due to their lack of choice and/or exclusion from the formal economy, and a further 21 per cent included this issue in their explanation. Other consumers, however, use informal employment in preference to formal labour. Neo-liberals assert that this is because of the problems associated with sourcing declared goods and services, including the availability, quality and speed of the provision of legitimate goods and services. In this Moscow survey, some 26 per cent of informal employment was sourced purely

Table 6.7 Consumers' motives for using informal employment in Moscow: by income level and location

	No choice/exclusion	*Poor formal provision alone*	*Social rationales alone*	*Mixture of no choice and poor formal provision*	*Mixture of no choice and social rationales*	*Mixture of poor formal provision and social rationales*	*Mixture of all three rationales*
All	40	26	8	15	2	5	4
Gross declared income/month:							
Lowest quartile	46	26	5	14	1	4	4
Lower quartile	44	22	7	13	2	7	5
Upper quartile	36	26	11	15	3	6	3
Highest quartile	27	30	14	17	2	5	5
Locality type:							
Affluent	32	33	12	12	1	6	4
Deprived	46	21	5	15	3	5	5
Mixed	45	26	5	17	1	5	3

Source: Moscow survey.

for this reason and a further 24 per cent included this issue in their rationale. Post-structuralists, meanwhile, again assert that consumers use informal employment in preference to the formal economy, but explain this in terms of social or redistributive rationales. Some 8 per cent of informal employment was primarily to help someone and/or as a favour among friends, colleagues and acquaintances. A further 11 per cent included this issue in their explanation.

Consumers' rationales, nevertheless, vary across populations. While 'exclusion' is more commonly cited among low-income households and those living in deprived neighbourhoods, 'exit' factors, particularly regarding poor formal provision, are more frequently cited among high-earners and those in affluent and rural areas. Social/redistributive rationales, meanwhile, are more frequently the chief rationale among higher-income households and affluent urban areas. Participation in informal employment for low-income groups and those in deprived areas is therefore more a result of exclusion, while it is more due to voluntary exit among high-income groups and those living in affluent areas. In consequence, different explanations are relevant to different groups.

Turning to suppliers' rationales, Table 6.8 again differentiates those engaging in informal employment according to whether it is primarily due to their exclusion from the formal economy (e.g. because they could not find a regular job, the employer insisted on them being paid off-the-books or because there is no alternative) or a decision to exit the formal economy, and if so, whether this is due to problems faced working legitimately or for social/redistributive rationales. The finding is that 27 per cent of informal employment is explained purely in terms of exclusion from the formal economy, 50 per cent solely due to a desire to voluntarily exit the declared sphere, as argued by neo-liberal and post-structuralist

Table 6.8 Suppliers' primary motives for participation in informal employment in Moscow: by income level and location

	Factors related to desire to exit formal realm:		*Factors related to exclusion from formal employment*	*Both exit and exclusion factors*
	Problems of working legitimately	*Social/ redistributive rationales*		
All	38	12	27	23
Gross formal income/month:				
Lowest quartile	28	9	42	21
Lower quartile	36	12	35	17
Upper quartile	35	13	32	20
Highest quartile	43	18	20	19
Locality type:				
Affluent	45	17	10	28
Deprived	25	8	40	27
Mixed	33	12	25	30

Source: Moscow survey.

commentators, and 23 per cent for a mix of both exit and exclusion rationales. Breaking down the decision to voluntarily exit the formal economy, 38 per cent of all informal employment was to avoid the costs, time and effort of formal registration and/or in preference to formal economy, and 12 per cent for social and/or redistributive reasons, such as a desire to help someone who is in need of help who would otherwise be unable to afford to get the work completed.

Again, however, the rationales vary across population groups and areas. Voluntarism, and therefore the neo-liberal and post-structuralist explanations, is more commonly cited by those engaged in informal employment living in higher-income households, rural and affluent localities. Exclusion from the formal economy, meanwhile, is more common among low-income households and those living in urban and deprived areas. It is not just across different socio-economic and spatial populations, however, that variations exist in the reasons for participating in informal employment.

Breaking down informal employment into its component parts, the overarching finding is that 78 per cent is informal self-employment and the remaining 22 per cent is waged informal employment. The suggestion, therefore, is that in stark contrast to Ukraine, the vast majority of informal employment in Moscow is informal self-employment. Examining the reasons for participating in each of these different types, Table 6.9 reveals that some 51 per cent of waged informal employment is conducted for factors related to exclusion and 26 per cent for rationales associated with both exit and exclusion. Similarly, the desire to exit the legitimate realm is greater in own-account work, with those depicting participation more as a voluntary decision to exit the formal economy so as to avoid the costs, time and effort of formal registration, finding what they seek in informal self-employment (52 per cent of such endeavour is conducted for this reason).

Table 6.9 Relationship between type of informal employment and reasons for participation in Moscow

Percentage of informally employed explaining their participation in terms of:	*All types*	*Type of informal employment:*	
		Self-employed for other private persons, households or businesses	*Salaried employees for firms or businesses*
Factors related to desire to exit formal economy	50	56	23
• due to problems with the formal realm	38	52	21
• for social/redistributive reasons	12	4	2
Factors related to exclusion from formal economy	27	20	51
Both exit and exclusion factors	23	24	26

Source: Moscow survey.

It is important to be aware, however, that even if there is a close relationship between these different varieties of informal employment and the contrasting explanations, it is far from the case that all work in each category can be explained exclusively in terms of either exclusion or exit. To see this, each variety of informal employment is briefly reviewed in turn.

Informal waged employment in Moscow

In Moscow, 30 per cent of all informal waged employment is in wholly off-the-books enterprises. The majority (80 per cent) is in legitimate organisations. Moreover, although nearly two-thirds (60 per cent) of informal waged employment is conducted by men, women are more likely to work in informal waged employment for formal enterprises rather than for wholly informal enterprises; some 90 per cent of women in informal waged employment work in formal enterprises and 10 per cent for wholly informal enterprises. Meanwhile, just 75 per cent of men in waged informal employment work in formal enterprises and 25 per cent in wholly informal enterprises. This gender segmentation of the organisations in which men and women undertake informal waged employment is reflected in the type of work they undertake. Of all informal waged employment, 32 per cent is full-time work and mostly carried out by men in wholly informal enterprises on a temporary or occasional basis, while 68 per cent is part-time employment and conducted more by women on a regular basis. Informal waged employees are not just employed by businesses, but also by affluent Russian families ('new Russians') in the personal services sector. These informal employees are often senior citizens working as cleaners, baby-sitters, cooks and gardeners. In Moscow, the official average salary is 15,000 roubles (£300) per month, which is about what is required to get by. Although war veteran pensioners receive 10,000–15,000 roubles, all other pensioners receive 3,000–4,000 roubles (£60–80), which is slightly higher than elsewhere due to a supplement being paid by the Moscow government. This is insufficient for most to get by, so informal employment is sought. Participants spoke of exploitative working conditions in this personal services sector, including beatings and mistreatment by employers and failures to pay, mirroring the conditions for domestic servants elsewhere in the world (Cox 2006). It needs to be recognised, nevertheless, that this is but one segment of those engaged in waged informal employment, albeit one that portrays well the poor working conditions that can occur in this sphere.

Examining why people engage in waged informal employment, those engaged in such work are more likely to do so for reasons of exclusion (63 per cent) or for reasons of both exit and exclusion (23 per cent). Just 14 per cent do so for exit reasons. This is reflected in the fact that 70 per cent do not have formal jobs and such informal waged work is what Pfau-Effinger (2009) terms a 'poverty-escape' type in that it is their main source of income and largely done out of necessity. When conducted as what she terms the 'moonlighting' type, that is, on a temporary or part-time basis as a way of earning some additional income by those in formal jobs, then it is more often conducted primarily out of choice.

Informal self-employment in Moscow

In the 313 households interviewed comprising 702 adults, 102 engaged in self-employment. Of these, just 4 per cent had registered their business, although even these all conducted a portion of their trade informally. The remaining 96 per cent had not registered their enterprise, did not have a licence to trade on a self-employed basis and conducted all their transactions off-the-books. The only conclusion that can be reached, therefore, albeit from a small sample, is that the vast bulk of the self-employed in Moscow are not even on the radar of the state. Who, therefore, are these self-employed? The finding, akin to Ukraine, is that they are polarised at the two ends of the income spectrum. Some 56 per cent of the informal self-employed surveyed live in the highest quartile of households by gross household income and 30 per cent in the lowest income quartile. At both ends of the income spectrum, moreover, households heavily rely on the income from this informal self-employment as a means of livelihood. Just under two-thirds (61 per cent) of the informal self-employed living in the highest-income households assert that this is their primary source of livelihood, as do 68 per cent of those who have started up enterprises who live in the lowest-income households. For most informal self-employed, therefore, this is their prime source of income.

This, however, is where the similarities between higher- and lower-income households end. The type of informal self-employment conducted is very different. Those living in higher-income households often have a formal job and use their formal job to engage in relatively well-paid informal self-employment. An example is a husband and wife who are both school teachers and earn through their formal jobs about 6,000 roubles a month each. They then provide supplementary lessons on an off-the-books self-employed basis. Between them, they have four groups of ten children who each pay 200 roubles for a 1.5 hour lesson. Each gives three informal lessons per week, so they earn 24,000 roubles per week additional income. However, it is not just professional people using their formal employment to engage in informal self-employment. Often people keep their low-paid formal jobs because of the informal earnings they can make. An example is a 52-year-old cleaner at a meat processing plant who has a formal salary of 3,000 roubles per month. Each day, she collects up some 20 kg of 'waste' meat which is supposed to be thrown away, and has an agreement with the butchers that they will leave out good pieces for which she pays them 400 roubles per day. She sells the meat to a butcher at the market for 50 roubles per kilogram (1,000 roubles per day), who in turn sells it to customers for 220 roubles per kilogram. She therefore makes 600 roubles per day, or 12,000 per month, to supplement her 3,000 roubles formal salary.

Those in lower-income households, in stark contrast, often do not have a formal job that they can use to engage in informal self-employment. Instead, they are confined to lower-paid forms of informal self-employment. Indeed, all respondents interviewed in these households who engaged in informal self-employment asserted that they would prefer a 'normal' formal job so as to minimise their risks of being cheated, robbed and to be able to have paid leave, but did not have the opportunity to do so. Instead, they had to rely on piecemeal informal self-employment in order to raise sufficient income to survive. Examples are a pensioner who supplements her state pension of 2,200 roubles/month by selling cigarettes at a train station, an illegal street vendor who sells flowers which she grows on her dacha just outside a market, and a security guard at the block of flats where he himself lives who is paid by the formally employed security guard 10 per cent of his salary to provide 24-hour cover for him. On the whole, however, most informal self-employed are not officially classified as unemployed. Some 60 per cent have a formal job and operate their business alongside their formal waged work as an 'on-the-side' business venture. Most of these are concentrated in the higher-income brackets and depend on the income from their nascent enterprise as their prime source of income due to the relatively low level of earnings from their formal employment. The remaining 40 per cent are a mixture of various categories of people registered as non-employed, including the 'economically inactive' such as housewives and others unregistered as engaging in any form of employment, pensioners and people claiming unemployment benefit. These tend to be concentrated in the lowest household income bracket and to earn less from their informal self-employment.

Turning to the rationales for informal self-employment, meanwhile, similar findings are identified to Ukraine. Those in the lower-income populations are more likely to engage in informal self-employment out of necessity and those in higher-income populations more out of choice. Typical responses of the 45 per cent asserting that they primarily engaged in informal self-employment out of necessity so as to generate sufficient income to live or survive were 'you cannot survive on state benefits, it doesn't even pay for your food'; 'if I hadn't, I wouldn't have enough money to be able to survive'; 'it was my only option'; and 'I had no choice. I wanted to buy things like clothes for my children and food.' Popular responses by the 25 per cent asserting that it was to increase their income, meanwhile, were 'my official earnings are not enough to pay for anything else other than our housing and food bills' and 'I needed extra to be able to buy more than just the necessities.' Unlike in other nations where necessity entrepreneurs might pursue such ventures due to a lack of formal employment opportunities, however, this was not the case in Moscow. Instead, the necessity to pursue such a venture is often borne out of the fact that the income provided by their formal employment or state benefits was inadequate to meet their daily needs. Akin to Ukraine, meanwhile, those doing so more out of choice often engage in informal self-employment either to avoid the costs, time and effort of formal registration, or for social and redistributive reasons.

In transition to the formal economy?

Do the informal self-employed view themselves as in transition to the formal economy? On the whole, less than 5 per cent regard themselves as likely to make the transition to becoming registered enterprises declaring their income for tax and social insurance purposes. The first reason for this is a lack of trust in the state to use taxes for purposes of public benefit. An example is a woman who runs a kindergarten from home. Responsible for a young preschool child, she looks after five other children whose parents pay 3,000 roubles per month for each child, meaning she earns 15,000 roubles a month, the official average Moscow salary. As she puts it,

> I raise my granddaughter [her daughter had died giving birth], and raise her in good company. I thought about getting a licence at the very beginning. I would not be allowed. It is necessary to have special educational qualifications to apply for such a licence. Of course, you can always 'buy' a licence but I do not think I should do it. What for? My group is very small and I earn just enough to make a living.... Also, I think that paying 13 per cent tax out of my small income would be unfair. Besides, I am not even sure that the state is able to use our taxes properly. They did not pay for the health care to save my daughter.

This lack of trust in the state to use taxes to provide public services was the most common rationale given in 66 per cent of cases by these self-employed for not registering their business. The second most common reason, stated by 60 per cent, was the difficulties encountered when attempting to register a business and pay taxes. A self-employed decorator/builder neatly summed up the attitude of many we interviewed:

> Why become formal? It is too much hassle and my business is very small and it will never grow that much bigger. The whole operation is cash in hand – suppliers want paying in cash and customers want the price as cheap as possible. If I need extra labour I have plenty of people I can call and pay cash for a few days' work. There is just no logic to formalising as if I did I would have to pay a lot of tax and spends days filling out paperwork. It is better just to keep small, earn a decent income and keep out of view from the authorities.

In this Moscow survey, in sum, informal employment is a work practice widely used as a primary tactic for securing a livelihood. There are, nevertheless, differences in the reasons for engaging in such a practice according to both the type of informal employment conducted and the situation of the household. Those engaged in waged informal employment are more likely to do so out of necessity, while those engaged in informal self-employment are more likely to do so out of choice. On the whole, moreover, lower-income populations tend to engage in informal employment more out of necessity and higher-income populations out of choice. Such generalisations, however, should be treated with caution since there are many variations both within each population group and across each type of informal employment.

Conclusions

This chapter has revealed that informal employment in post-Soviet/socialist economies is not some small residue that is steadily disappearing from view. According to one popular indirect measurement method, its magnitude is equivalent to 32.6 per cent of GDP across post-Soviet/socialist economies and although it has declined slightly over the last few years relative to the formal economy, it remains a sizeable feature across all post-Soviet/socialist societies. Indeed, examining the results of the surveys conducted in Ukraine and Moscow, this chapter has revealed that informal employment plays a central role in the livelihood practices of a large proportion of households. Indeed, some 40 per cent of Ukrainian households cite informal employment as either the

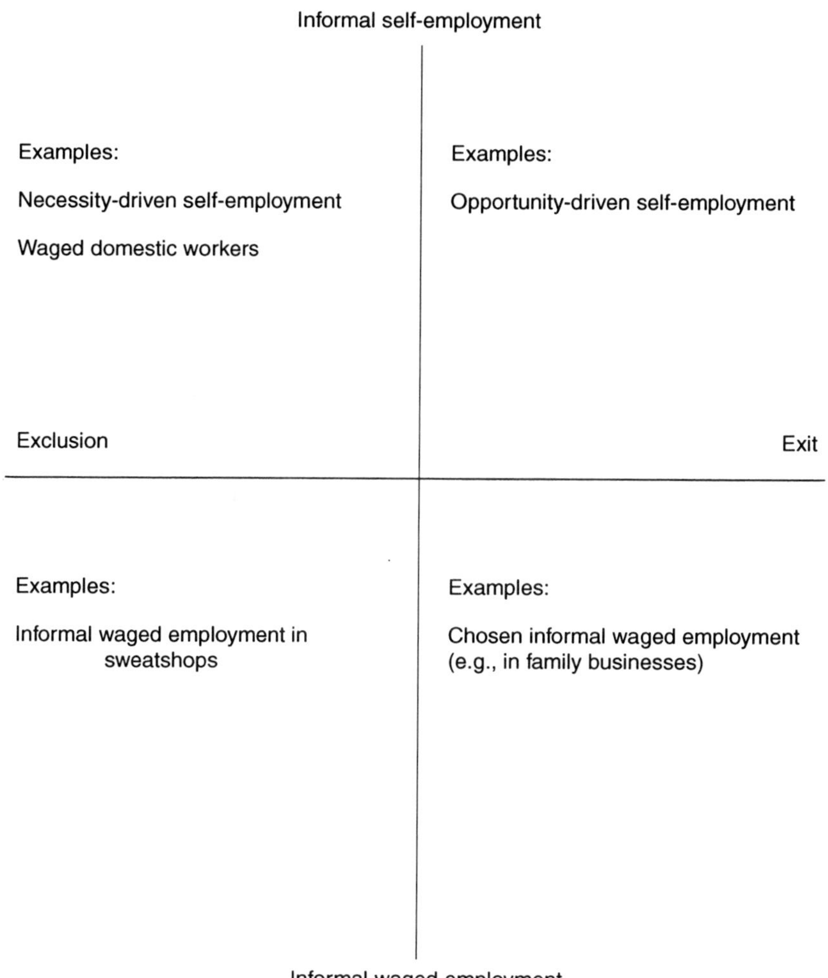

Figure 6.3 Typology of the multifarious nature of informal employment.

principal or secondary contributor to their living standard and 43 per cent in Moscow.

Examining their reasons for engaging in informal employment, moreover, in Ukraine, 30 per cent of informal employment is explained purely in terms of exclusion from the formal economy, 35 per cent purely to avoid the costs, time and effort of formal registration and in preference to formal employment, and 13 per cent purely for social and/or redistributive reasons, with the remaining 22 per cent a mix of these rationales. Similar levels of reliance on informal employment and diversity in the rationales among those engaged in informal employment was identified in Moscow. Despite this heavy reliance on informal employment in both countries and similar rationales being expressed for engaging in this work, the configuration of informal employment differs markedly across the two countries. The finding is that in Moscow, 78 per cent is informal self-employment and 22 per cent is waged informal employment. In Ukraine, in contrast, 38 per cent is informal self-employment and 62 per cent waged informal employment. Yet despite this, the rationales for engagement in each type of informal employment and by each population group are markedly similar in both countries. Voluntarism, and therefore the neo-liberal and post-structuralist explanations, is more commonly cited by those engaged in informal self-employment and those living in higher-income households, rural and affluent localities. Exclusion from the formal economy, meanwhile, is more commonly cited among those engaged in waged informal employment and among low-income households, and those living in urban and deprived areas, as summarised in Figure 6.3.

It is important to be aware, however, that even if some types of explanation are more common for some types of informal employment than others, there remains tremendous diversity in the rationales for participating in each type of informal employment among different population groups. In other words, there is a rich tapestry of both types of informal employment and reasons for engaging in them in these post-Soviet/socialist societies that cannot be neatly captured by promulgating universal hues. Just as one would not draw universal generalisations about formal waged employment and formal self-employment when evaluating its nature or the reasons for engaging in such work, it is similarly erroneous to do so when considering the informal labour market in post-Soviet/socialist societies.

7 One-to-one unpaid labour, reimbursed family work and paid favours

Introduction

This chapter examines three further forms of work that have in common the fact that they are conducted on a one-to-one basis, namely one-to-one unpaid labour, reimbursed family work and paid favours. The intention is to display the prevalence of these forms of labour in everyday livelihood practices in post-Soviet societies in order to show on the one hand, how the transition to a hegemonic formal market economy is far from achieved and that post-Soviet societies remain characterised by diverse economies, and on the other hand, the role of these informal economies in everyday livelihood practices in the post-Soviet world.

To evaluate, first, one-to-one unpaid labour, second, reimbursed family work and, third, paid favours in post-Soviet spaces, and in order to delve deeper into the role and meaning of such work practices, in each case the Ukrainian and Moscow surveys will be analysed to explore, on the one hand, the extent of each form of work and, on the other hand, the character of such exchanges. The outcome will be an overview of the use of each of these forms of work in post-Soviet societies. This will reveal that contrary to the neo-liberal assumptions that post-Soviet societies are in transition to a fully fledged formal market economy, such informal economic activities continue to play an important role in the livelihood practices of a large segment of the population in the post-Soviet world.

One-to-one unpaid labour

Recent studies in North America reveal that the average American between the ages of 17 and 34 receives the equivalent of two years of unpaid labour from their relatives (Settersten *et al.* 2008). The tasks received include unpaid baby-sitting, household maintenance and repair, driving and care-giving. Indeed, it has been estimated that if one-to-one caregivers in England were paid a minimum wage for their labour, the annual bill would be approximately £87 billion, considerably more than the country's formal healthcare budget of £81 billion (Buckner and Yeandle 2007). A similar finding about the volume and value of one-to-one unpaid labour in the caring sphere has been identified in Canada

(Hollander *et al.* 2009). This, therefore, is not some minor labour practice. One-to-one unpaid labour refers to unpaid labour provided on an individualised level to members of households other than one's own, such as kin living outside one's household, friends, neighbours and acquaintances. Akin to other work practices considered in this book, such one-to-one unpaid labour is of different varieties, ranging from individualised one-way giving (often termed 'informal volunteering') to two-way reciprocity. When reciprocity is involved, such unpaid endeavour often blurs into reimbursed favours since the reciprocity may take the form of either in-kind labour or gifts in lieu of payment. One-to-one unpaid labour also merges at its borders with self-provisioning, given how what constitutes the household and family is becoming blurred in contemporary post-Soviet societies due to the increase in marital separation and divorce. To evaluate the extent and nature of one-to-one unpaid labour in the post-Soviet world, therefore, first, we report the findings from Ukraine and second, from Moscow.

Participation in one-to-one unpaid exchanges in Ukraine

In Ukraine, participation in the provision of unpaid exchanges on a one-to-one basis is widespread. As Table 7.1 displays, some 62 per cent of the participants surveyed had engaged in such one-to-one exchanges in the 12 months prior to interview. However, it is more common among deprived populations. Some 70 per cent of the surveyed population in the deprived neighbourhood of Kyiv had participated in this practice, and 73 per cent in the deprived rural areas, but just 54 per cent in the border town and 52 per cent in the affluent Kyiv neighbourhood

Table 7.1 Participation rates in one-to-one unpaid community exchange in Ukraine: by locality and gross household income

	Percentage of surveyed population participating in one-to-one unpaid community exchanges	*Percentage of 44 tasks last conducted using one-to-one unpaid community exchange*
All areas	62	4
By locality type:		
Affluent Kyiv	52	2
Deprived Kyiv	70	6
Deprived rural	73	5
Border town	54	3
By household income:		
<600	77	5
600–1,399	70	4
1,400–2,199	58	4
2,200–2,999	61	3
3,000–3,799	54	1
>3,800	52	4

Source: Ukraine survey.

studied. This reinforces studies in western countries which display how engaging in one-to-one community exchange is more common in deprived populations (Williams 2005a).

Turning to whether households use one-to-one unpaid community exchanges to get everyday domestic services undertaken, this Ukrainian survey reveals that this is not a widely used practice for getting domestic tasks completed. Just 4 per cent of all the domestic tasks surveyed were last undertaken using one-to-one unpaid community exchanges. However, some populations are more likely to use this mode of exchange than others. One-to-one unpaid community exchanges were last used in 5 per cent of cases in the deprived rural area, 6 per cent of cases in the deprived Kyiv neighbourhood, but just 3 per cent of cases in the border town and 2 per cent of cases in the affluent Kyiv suburb. The tentative conclusion, therefore, is that this is more commonly used among deprived populations to get everyday domestic service tasks completed. This is reinforced when the commonality of the usage of paid favours is compared across households with different levels of income. Lower-income households are more likely to use paid favours to get tasks completed than higher-income households. Some 5 per cent of tasks were last conducted using paid favours in the lowest-income group of households compared with just 1 per cent among some higher-income groups. Moreover, the finding is that lower-income households give and receive some 35 per cent more unpaid community exchanges on a one-to-one basis than the average household, while the higher-income households receive and provide one-third less unpaid exchanges on a one-to-one basis as the average household.

Nature of one-to-one unpaid exchanges in Ukraine

Previous studies highlight the importance and complexities of this labour practice in post-Soviet societies (Ledeneva 1998, 2006; Smith *et al.* 2006; Stenning *et al.* 2006). This study similarly reveals the existence of different types of unpaid community exchange on a one-to-one basis, ranging from kinship exchange (53 per cent of all unpaid one-to-one community exchange), neighbourly exchange (18 per cent) and exchanges with acquaintances (29 per cent). When one unravels unpaid community exchange into its different varieties and explores its configuration in various populations, some marked contrasts in its character can be identified. Comparing relatively affluent and deprived populations, in deprived districts some two-thirds of one-to-one non-monetised labour was for kin, while in the more affluent districts, one-third was for kin and two-thirds for more distant relations and closer to the monetised/non-monetised boundary. Affluent populations therefore use one-to-one monetised exchange more to expand their social networks and consolidate relationships, while such labour in deprived populations revolves more around narrower social networks of kin who are used to deliver material aid. In affluent populations, therefore, it is more about 'getting ahead' while in deprived populations it is more about 'getting by'. Non-monetised labour is therefore perhaps greater among lower-income populations simply because they rely more heavily on kin, lack the financial purchasing power to use money or gifts, and/or physical wellbeing to reciprocate with in-kind labour, so engage by default and out of necessity in non-monetised labour.

These kinship exchanges ranged from baby-sitting and cooking, through repairing appliances, to kitchen and bathroom refurbishment. Examples below demonstrate this taken from both affluent and deprived areas of Kyiv. In the first case here, an interviewee, a high-earning white-collar professional living in an affluent area of Kyiv, describes how she organises child-care:

> I have an eight-year-old son. Normally when I'm at work and in the school holidays, one of his grandmothers will come to our flat and look after him. However, this is sometimes not possible. In such situations, I ask someone who lives in our block of flats to help out. My husband and I have known her for a number of years and we trust her. She loves to spend time with our son and so it works like that.

In another case, Vanya lives in a deprived semi-rural location outside of the city boundaries of Kyiv. He describes how from time to time he does some unpaid labour for neighbours:

> We live in a small private house in the 'dacha zone' of our little town. Most of the dachas are not lived in permanently. However, a few houses down an elderly couple live. They've been friends with my mother for years. When they need something doing, I'll always go round and help. It can sometimes be mending a fence or plastering up a bit of an internal wall.

In these examples the interviewees made it clear that no specific forms of reciprocity occurred. Such forms of labour were more voluntary in their nature. In contrast, an interviewee from a deprived part of Kyiv described how she undertook baby-sitting for a friend who lives in the same apartment block:

> I've known Sveta for over twenty years. We grew up together on this estate, playing and going to the same school. She had a baby two years ago and has now gone back to work. I'm a housewife and so I help out baby-sitting regularly for Sveta. I like to do it, helping out a friend of mine. Also, Sveta always helps me also. Her relatives have a farm out in the countryside. When they receive meat, she always brings me some for my family, which is nice.

Here, therefore, the interviewee makes it clear that 'reciprocity' forms a key role in the nature of the unpaid labour. In the following example, reciprocal relations were also highlighted. Yevgeny lives in an affluent part of central Kyiv and works for a local plumbing firm:

> From time to time, things go wrong with the plumbing in my neighbours' apartments. They get in touch with me and I always endeavour to do what I

> can. I do a few repairs, which normally aren't difficult. In return, I don't receive any payments. Instead, sometimes a neighbour will aid my family. One of the families has a large van and if I ever need to go and collect anything large, like a new piece of furniture or something, the neighbour will go for me for no charge. It works like that and we stay on good terms.

Although deprived populations are more reliant on this labour practice and it is provided for and by closer social relations, they are nevertheless more likely to use this labour out of necessity (65 per cent of instances) while affluent populations do so out of choice (70 per cent of instances). Comparing people living in the affluent and deprived districts of Kyiv, the former were two times more likely to assert that receiving work on this basis was a choice compared with those living in the deprived district. Deprived populations therefore use this when no other options are open to them, whereas for affluent populations such a practice is more a matter of choice rather than due to a lack of choice. This finding is not in antagonistic contradiction to the finding of Brown and Kulcsar (2001) in rural Bulgaria and Clarke (2002) in Russia, that inter-household exchange is more likely among better-off households with greater economic and social resources. One-to-one unpaid exchanges are but one kind of inter-household exchange and one that is used more by deprived households, while affluent populations engage more in other kinds of inter-household exchange, as will be revealed when other forms of exchange are considered.

In sum, unpaid community exchange is more prevalent among lower-income populations in Ukraine, where it is more likely to be conducted for and by kin, not least because they lack the financial purchasing power to use money or gifts, and/or physical wellbeing to reciprocate with in-kind labour, so engage in such exchange in 65 per cent of instances out of necessity. Higher-income populations, in contrast, use one-to-one monetised exchange more to expand their social networks and consolidate relationships and in 70 per cent of instances do so out of choice. Deprived populations therefore use this when no other options are open to them, whereas for affluent populations it is conducted more as a matter of choice.

Prevalence of one-to-one unpaid exchanges in Moscow

In Moscow, 63 per cent of the surveyed population had engaged in unpaid community exchanges on a one-to-one basis in the 12 months prior to the survey. This, therefore, is a common form of labour practice among Muscovite households. However, and akin to Ukraine, Table 7.2 reveals that it is more common among households in deprived populations. Some 72 per cent of the surveyed population in the deprived neighbourhood had participated in this practice, 70 per cent in the mixed neighbourhood and 52 per cent in the affluent neighbourhood surveyed. It is similarly the case when examining participation according to household income. Some 55 per cent of households in the highest-income quartile had conducted paid favours for others, compared with 60 per cent in the

Table 7.2 Participation in and use of unpaid community exchanges in Moscow: by locality and gross household income

	Percentage participating in one-to-one unpaid community exchanges	*Percentage of 44 tasks last conducted using one-to-one unpaid community exchange*
All areas	63	7
By locality type:		
Deprived	72	7
Mixed	70	9
Affluent	52	6
By household income:		
Lowest quartile	72	11
Lower quartile	65	7
Upper quartile	60	6
Highest quartile	55	4

Source: Moscow survey.

upper-middle income quartile, 65 per cent in the lower-middle income quartile and 72 per cent in the lowest-income quartile of households. This clearly intimates that unpaid community exchanges on a one-to-one basis are more common in lower-income populations. In major part, however, this is because higher-income populations have monetised one-to-one reciprocity to a greater extent than deprived populations, as will be discussed below. Although across all populations, roughly equal proportions of the population engage in paid favours and one-to-one unpaid community exchanges, affluent populations are more likely to participate in paid favours and less likely to participate in unpaid community exchanges. Meanwhile, it is the opposite for lower-income populations, who are more likely to participate in unpaid community exchanges and are less likely to participate in paid favours.

Turning to whether households use unpaid community exchange on a one-to-one basis to undertake everyday domestic services, this survey of Muscovite households reveals that this is a fairly common practice. Some 7 per cent of all tasks were last undertaken using unpaid one-to-one exchanges, which is the same proportion as were undertaken using paid favours (see below). The interesting finding here, therefore, is that the sphere of paid favours is about the same size as the realm of unpaid one-to-one community exchanges in the localities studied. However, this is not the case across all populations. Of the everyday domestic services surveyed, the finding is that unpaid one-to-one exchanges were last used in 7 per cent of cases in the deprived district, 9 per cent of cases in the mixed area and 6 per cent in the affluent area. The tentative conclusion, therefore, is that this is more commonly used among deprived and mixed populations to get everyday domestic service tasks completed. This is reinforced when examining its commonality across households with different levels of income. Households in the lowest income quartile use it to undertake 11 per cent of the 44 tasks, 7 per cent among the lower-income quartile, 6 per cent among the upper quartile and 4 per cent among the highest-income quartile.

Comparing the usage of unpaid one-to-one labour across these different populations to get everyday domestic services undertaken, the finding is again that affluent populations rely more on monetised exchanges and lower-income populations more on unpaid community exchanges to get tasks undertaken. Over one-third of one-to-one favours involve monetary payment in the deprived district surveyed, one-half in the mixed district and one-quarter in the affluent district. When kinship exchanges are excluded, where there is a greater willingness to provide and receive unpaid help, in deprived areas over three-quarters of one-to-one material support provided to friends, neighbours and acquaintances involved payment, and even in affluent urban areas payment prevailed in around half of all such instances. This intimates, therefore, that affluent populations are more monetised in terms of their community exchange cultures than lower-income populations.

Nature of one-to-one unpaid exchanges in Moscow

Analysing unpaid help provided either on a one-way or reciprocal basis by or for kin living outside the household, friends, neighbours or acquaintances, just under half of participants in the affluent district and nearly three-quarters in the deprived district engaged in such labour over the previous year, ranging from kinship exchange (45 per cent of all unpaid community exchange), neighbourly exchange (30 per cent) and unpaid exchanges with acquaintances (25 per cent). When non-kin are involved (e.g. neighbours and friends), token payments, gifts or in-kind labour are usually preferred and used whenever feasible. The use of non-monetised labour is greater in deprived populations, therefore, only because they more heavily rely on kin, lack the purchasing power to use money or gifts, and/or the physical wellbeing to reciprocate with in-kind labour, so engage by default in unpaid one-to-one exchange. Indeed, while affluent populations use this one-to-one exchange practice more to expand their social networks and consolidate relationships, deprived populations rely more on narrower social networks of kin as a coping tactic to meet material needs.

Sergey lives in a large deprived housing complex on the edge of Moscow. While his formal employment was working as an engineer in a state-owned enterprise, he would occasionally undertake one-to-one unpaid labour, fixing televisions and other appliances for neighbours:

> As an engineer, I've always enjoyed working with machines. From time to time, a neighbour will knock on our door and ask if I can try and repair a radio or TV. I normally can fix the problem quickly and it doesn't cost me anything. Sometimes, a neighbour might help my family in return but not always. One neighbour works at the cinema and gave my wife some free tickets a year or two ago. Another one kept an eye on our flat whilst we were on holiday.

While this example seems to demonstrate some sort of voluntary but not mandatory reciprocity, the following example highlights the more embedded nature of forms of reciprocal relations based around one-to-one unpaid labour. Natalya lives in an affluent district of Moscow. She works as a lawyer and her husband works for a large construction company:

> We've known our neighbours for over ten years. They are both intelligent people. The husband of my neighbour is the school director where our daughter studies. When they have anything which needs repairing around their apartment, I always ask my husband to do the job. In this fashion, we stay in good relations with our neighbours.

Here, it is clear that Natalya feels it is important to consolidate and nurture her family's relations with their neighbours for the sake of their child by way of her husband undertaking DIY jobs for the neighbours when and where necessary. Comparing people living in the affluent and deprived districts of Moscow, the former were nearly twice as likely to assert that receiving work on this basis was a choice compared with those living in the deprived district. Higher-income populations, in consequence, use one-to-one unpaid labour more to expand their social networks and consolidate relationships, and in two-thirds of instances do so out of choice. Deprived populations, in contrast, use this when no other options are open to them. Interestingly, these findings from Moscow corroborate the findings from Ukraine in general and Kyiv more particularly, and allow the cautious conclusion to be made that while people in deprived districts use forms of one-to-one unpaid labour to 'get by', in more affluent districts individuals use such labour to 'get on'. The chapter now continues with an examination of the prevalence of reimbursed family labour.

Reimbursed family labour

There is often an assumption that paid exchanges exist 'out there' beyond the household and that the household/family unit itself is a realm of unpaid non-exchanged labour. This section seeks to explore whether this is indeed the case in post-Soviet societies. Indeed, it might be assumed that as post-Soviet societies move towards more market-oriented societies, work that previously existed outside of the market realm will be incorporated into the realm of market exchanges. Work within the household is one such instance. It might be argued that as economies become market-oriented, work that was previously conducted on an unpaid non-exchanged basis by a household member for other members of the household might start to become market-oriented, in that monetary exchange may well start to occur. Examining whether work within the household by one household member for other members of the household (what we here term 'family work') is starting to be performed for reimbursement, could therefore be taken as a sign of the marketisation of post-Soviet societies.

Until now, this issue of the monetisation of family work has been seldom, if ever, explicitly considered. Here, therefore, it is put under the spotlight. Of course, and as highlighted in Chapter 3, it is not sufficient to examine solely whether family labour is paid or unpaid, because in lived practice there is more a continuum of practices ranging from paid exchanges at one end and unpaid exchanges at the other end, and in the middle a whole range of other forms of exchange, ranging from one-way giving through in-kind reciprocal exchanges of labour to gifts in the forms of goods.

Seen in this light, reimbursed family work overlaps significantly with other forms of labour. Take, for example, so-called unpaid domestic work or what is sometimes called self-provisioning or even housework. It might well be argued that although unpaid household work, which is where a household member conducts a task on an unpaid basis for other members of the household, is unpaid, there is in lived practice a process of in-kind reciprocity taking place. For example, in the traditional 'male breadwinner' model, where the man is in paid formal employment and the woman conducts the majority of the unpaid housework and caring duties, it might well be considered that there is a very explicit in-kind reciprocal exchange of labour. The man and woman have an explicit understanding between them that one of them earns the money through paid employment and that in exchange the other fulfils the necessary unpaid domestic work and caring functions within the household. This, therefore, is not so much an unpaid exchange of labour as in-kind reciprocity, and consequently, such supposedly 'unpaid' domestic work sits at the boundary between 'unpaid' and 'paid' family work. Usually, however, monetary payments occur only in inter- rather than intra-generational transactions (e.g. from a parent to a child, not between parents, although this blurs in the case of marital breakdown).

There is perhaps also an overlap between 'paid family labour' and 'paid community exchanges'. With the rise in divorce and family breakdown, it is in many cases no longer clear where the 'family' or even 'household' begins and ends. For instance, when a mother is given recompense for caring for a child by the father who no longer lives with them, is this paid family work? And when a woman helps out financially with the support of an ex-partner, such as by helping pay for an occasional cleaner, or by doing some cleaning in exchange for a gift, is this 'paid family labour', paid community exchange, unpaid community exchange or does it sit on the edges of all three forms of labour? The dissolution of families and households, therefore, significantly blurs the divide between what is 'paid family labour' and other forms of labour such as unpaid household work and paid community exchanges. To start to unravel whether such reimbursed family work exists in post-Soviet societies, we here begin to unravel the extent of such labour and the different forms it takes in contemporary post-Soviet societies by examining, first, the study of livelihood practices in Ukraine and, second, the livelihood practices of Muscovite households. This will reveal that despite receiving little, if any, discussion in the literature on livelihood practices and coping tactics, this labour practice is a small but significant practice pursued in post-Soviet societies, albeit more so in affluent populations where inter-generational monetary transfers occur from parents to children for tasks conducted, such as housework. Monetary payments are less common in lower-income populations, where gifts rather than money are more commonplace.

Reimbursed family labour in Ukraine

To evaluate the existence of reimbursed family labour in Ukraine, first, whether such a labour practice exists and the extent to which such a practice occurs is analysed and, second, the different forms this labour practice takes in contemporary Ukrainian society. Examining the extent of participation in paid family labour in Ukraine, the finding is that some 4 per cent of households had used this labour practice in the 12 months prior to the survey. This type of labour practice, however, was more common in the affluent Kyiv locality (where 6 per cent of households had participated in such a labour practice) than in the deprived Kyiv neighbourhood (where the participation rate was just 3 per cent), the border town (4 per cent) or the deprived rural area (2 per cent). The intimation, therefore, is that such a labour practice is more common among affluent populations. This is further reinforced when the use of such a labour practice is analysed across households according to the gross household income. While 8 per cent of the highest income quartile of households had used paid family labour during the past 12 months, this was the case among just 6 per cent of the upper-middle quartile of households, 2 per cent among the lower-middle quartile of households and none of the lowest income quartile of households had used such a labour practice.

Turning to the sources of labour used to conduct everyday domestic services, meanwhile, the finding is that less than 1 per cent of all the tasks conducted had been conducted by household members on a paid basis. The use of family members on a paid basis to conduct these tasks, however, was more common in the affluent Kyiv locality (where 1 per cent of the tasks surveyed had been conducted using this form of labour) and in the deprived Kyiv neighbourhood (where again 1 per cent of tasks were conducted on such a basis), than in the border town and the deprived rural area where well under 1 per cent of tasks were conducted using paid family labour. The intimation, therefore, is that such a labour practice is more common in larger urban areas. It also appears to be more commonly used as a labour practice among more affluent households. While 1 per cent of the domestic service tasks conducted in the past 12 months had been last undertaken using paid family labour in the highest income quartile of households, in lower-income households well under 1 per cent of the tasks had been last conducted using this form of labour. Who, therefore, is conducting this household work for other household members on a paid basis? And what types of endeavour are they engaged in? Starting with who conducts such paid labour for other household members, such labour tends to be exclusively conducted on an inter-generational basis. In other words, the provision of monetary payments between members of a household for tasks conducted is near enough entirely confined to inter-generational exchanges, such as from a parent to a child. No instances were identified where monetary payments occurred between parents or two adults (who were not parent and son/daughter) in the household.

Monetised family labour is slightly more prevalent in affluent populations, where it takes the form almost exclusively of inter-generational monetary transfers from parents to children for tasks conducted. The most common task for which payment is made is either doing various household chores, such as washing up or cleaning, and gardening. For this, the children are recompensed. This, therefore, might be read as a means of teaching children the value of money. Rather than give them 'pocket money' on a weekly or monthly basis to spend, this paid family labour occurs because the intention is to give them this money and to tie it to accomplishing particular tasks. As Sasha commented in relation to giving her teenage son money:

> I give him spending money but he has to earn it. It is not good just giving him it. He would just think that money was easy to come by. By asking him to do some of the household chores, it helps him learn that you need to work to get money. It also gets him used to helping out round the house and learning that the housework doesn't just get done. Otherwise he'll grow up learning nothing about money.

Monetary payments are less common in lower-income populations. Instead, it tends to be small token gifts, rather than money, that are more commonplace in these populations. Here, such gifts often include things such as toys for smaller children, and for older children things such as music CDs or DVDs. Importantly, the value of such gifts rarely equate in monetary value to the work undertaken. Instead, such gifts are very much symbolic and token in their nature. While smaller gifts are seemingly common, there were occurrences of parents buying a larger gift for a child, such as a mobile phone under the condition that the child would do some work around the house for the following calendar year. As Zhennya, a mother of two in the border town, stated:

> My oldest son is in his teens and constantly wants the latest things. He pleaded and pleaded with his father and I for us to buy him a new mobile phone. Eventually, we gave in and bought him the phone on the proviso that he does the vacuuming around our apartment and cleans his father's car. He accepted with a big grin and we're all happy. We feel in this way that he can learn the value of working.

It is not wholly inter-generational however, between parent and child, that such reimbursed family labour occurs. Indeed, when gifts or in-kind reciprocity is involved, the divide between non-exchanged work (i.e. what is often termed self-provisioning) and paid family labour becomes very blurred. Women and men often explicitly state that reciprocity in the form of in-kind labour is expected from their partner, thus calling into question the very depiction of self-provisioning as non-exchanged work. This is displayed in statements like 'I do the cooking and cleaning because he goes out to the workplace and earns money' and 'I do the daily housework and in return, he does the washing up.' Members of couple households therefore often explicitly state that reciprocity in the form of in-kind labour is expected from their partner. For example, a husband in the rural town stated: 'I go out and work hard in my job and in return, my wife is expected to keep a clean and tidy home, and to ensure that I get my meals. This is just the way it works.'

Much so-called non-exchanged work, in consequence, appears to lie at the border with reimbursed family work and to involve in-kind reciprocity, calling into question the very depiction of self-provisioning as not involving exchange. Indeed, the lack of perceived equality in the balance of reciprocity between household members was a major issue frequently voiced by respondents. As one wife in the border town put it:

> We both have jobs and work long hours but he still expects me to do the housework. How is that fair? It's the same for lots of women, lots I work with. We all complain but nothing ever seems to happen. I tried to start saying how much would it cost if you had to pay someone to cook your meals and clean your house. I even threatened to find someone to do the cleaning. He still doesn't change though. He says he will but never does anything about it.

Such responses show a keen sense that although it is often thought that such domestic work is non-exchanged or unpaid, many engaged in such work do in fact have an acute sense of the in-kind reciprocity involved in doing this work and an even acuter sense of this when inequalities arise in the exchanges of in-kind reciprocity. As one woman expressed it:

> He does the finance, sees to the car and household repairs when things go wrong. I have to do all the day-to-day stuff everyday of the week all the time. It never ends. How's that fair? But that's Ukrainian men. They never lift a finger to help out.

Family labour, therefore, is often reimbursed in Ukraine, especially on an inter-generational level, and even when money is not involved there is often a keen sense of whether the in-kind reciprocity is equal or not. Here, we have only considered situations where some form of labour is involved in exchanges. It is also commonplace across all societies to find money being given to different generations without expectation of reciprocity. Unfortunately, this Ukrainian research did not consider such cash transfers between kin. Nevertheless, it is an important aspect of overall livelihood practices and one that should be considered in future research.

Reimbursed family labour in Moscow

Turning to reimbursed family labour in Moscow, we again analyse, first, whether such a labour practice exists and the extent to which it occurs, and second, the different forms this labour practice takes in contemporary Moscow society. Analysing the level of participation in paid family labour in Moscow, the finding is that some 5 per cent of households had used this labour practice in the 12 months prior to the survey, which is higher than Ukraine. This type of labour practice, however, is unevenly spatially distributed. Akin to the finding in Ukraine, the finding is that participation in such a labour practice is more common in affluent than deprived populations. In the affluent district studied, 7 per cent of households had used this labour practice in the past year compared with just 4 per cent in the mixed neighbourhood and 1 per cent in the deprived neighbourhood. This finding that such a labour practice is more common among affluent populations is further reinforced when the use of such a labour practice is analysed according to gross household income. While 11 per cent of households in the highest income quartile had used paid family labour during the past year, this was the case among just 5 per cent of households in the upper-middle quartile, 3 per cent in the lower-middle quartile and 1 per cent of households in the lowest income quartile.

Turning to the sources of labour used to conduct a diverse array of everyday domestic services, meanwhile, the finding is that less than 1 per cent of all the tasks conducted had been conducted by household members on a paid basis. The use of family members on a paid basis to conduct these tasks, however, was more common in the affluent neighbourhood (where 1 per cent of the tasks had been last conducted using this form of labour) than in the mixed and deprived neighbourhoods, where well under 1 per cent had been last conducted using paid family labour. This intimation that such a labour practice is more common in affluent populations is further reinforced when examining the type of households who make use of this labour practice. While 2 per cent of the domestic service tasks conducted in the past year had been last undertaken using paid family labour in the highest income quartile of households, in all other households well under 1 per cent of the tasks had been last conducted using this form of labour. Examining who undertakes this household work for other household members on a paid basis, akin to Ukraine, this labour tends to be exclusively conducted on an inter-generational basis when monetary payment is involved, and this labour practice is concentrated in affluent populations between parents and children. Payments are made for doing various household chores, washing the car, gardening, passing examinations and so forth. The primary rationale of the parents is to teach the children the value of money by only giving them spending money for completing particular tasks. As one father commented: 'I only say that he can have his weekly spending money if he tidies his bedroom and cleans his bathroom. It does them no good just giving them money.'

Few instances of monetary payments were identified in lower-income populations. Instead, they tend to have things bought for them, such as a pair of jeans or shirt, if they do the household chores allocated to them. Similar to the situation in Ukraine, typical gifts to children involved CDs, DVDs and some items of clothing. As one mother states:

> My daughter is a teenager now and has become very fashion-conscious. She wants all the latest clothes, shoes and make-up. Whilst my husband and I try and give her presents of course for her birthday and at the New Year, she often wants new things throughout the year. We've come to an agreement with her. We'll consider buying her new make-up, some new clothes or shoes, in return for her helping around the home. Often I work long hours and so now, my daughter does a lot of the cooking at home. It works like that.

Akin to Ukraine, it was again the case that the boundary between paid family labour and unpaid domestic work was often blurred. Many men and women in couple households often raised the notion that reciprocity in the form of in-kind labour is expected from their partner. As participants stated: 'I earn the money and she looks after the home', 'She cooks so I wash up' and 'I am responsible for the gardening and she is responsible for the housework', thus raising the notion that reciprocity in the form of in-kind labour is expected from their partner. Much of what is supposedly non-exchanged work, in consequence, lies at the border of paid family labour and unpaid domestic work, and to involve in-kind reciprocity, calling into question the very depiction of self-provisioning as non-exchanged work. Indeed, this in-kind reciprocity tends to be voiced most when there is a perceived disparity in what one partner does compared with the other. As a woman asserted:

> I now work mornings and some afternoons. I never used to. But he still doesn't help out around the house. I know it is difficult for him because he doesn't earn a lot and can hardly afford to put food on the table, so I don't want to hurt his feelings, but it sometimes seems totally unfair, especially when I'm tired, that he does so little around the house. But then again, I perhaps expect too much. He is a Muscovite man isn't he? It would hurt his pride.

This response displays a keen awareness of the in-kind reciprocity involved in what is often read as non-exchanged work and the blurring of the edges between unpaid self-provisioning and paid family labour.

Here, therefore, a form of labour has been focused upon that has been seldom discussed either in post-Soviet societies or beyond, namely paid family labour whereby a household member reimburses another household member for work conducted. This reimbursement can be in the form of money, but also in the form of gifts or the in-kind reciprocal exchange of labour. When the latter is involved, it is arguably the case that much of what is normally considered to be unpaid household work, where one member of a household does unpaid work for other members of the household, might well be re-allocated to inhabiting the edges between the realm of unpaid and paid family labour. The overarching finding is that reimbursed family labour constitutes a small but significant livelihood practice in post-Soviet spaces. Mostly involving inter-generational exchanges between a parent and child, such a labour practice is most common in more affluent populations. In lower-income populations where such a labour practice is less frequent, when it does occur, it more commonly involves gifts and/or in-kind reciprocity, rather than monetary exchange.

Paid favours

Paid favours involve one-to-one help provided to kin living outside the household, friends, neighbours or acquaintances, and either a monetary payment and/or a gift is exchanged. As Zelizer (2005) reveals, introducing money does not de-personalise social interactions and turn them into market transactions. People are capable of negotiating their relationship, of creating distinctions between different types of money and the social relations to which they give rise. Until now, nevertheless, few studies have investigated the degree to which money changes hands during one-to-one community exchanges and the nature of the social relations involved. This section aims to fill that gap so far as post-Soviet societies are concerned, thus contributing to the small but important literature emerging regarding the prevalence of the 'moral' or 'social' economy of paid favours in western societies (Cornuel and Duriez 1985; White and Williams 2010; Williams 2005a).

Paid favours in Ukraine

Participating in the provision of paid favours in Ukraine is a widespread practice. As Table 7.3 displays, some 65 per cent of the participants surveyed had engaged in paid favours in the past year prior to interview. This, therefore, is a common form of labour practice among Ukrainian households. However, it is more common among deprived populations. Some 60 per cent of the surveyed population in the deprived neighbourhood of Kyiv had participated in this practice and 63 per cent in the deprived rural areas, but just 30 per cent in the border town and 21 per cent in the affluent Kyiv neighbourhood studied. This reinforces studies in western countries which display how engaging in paid favours is more common in deprived areas (Williams 2005a).

Turning to whether households use paid favours to get everyday domestic services undertaken, this Ukrainian survey reveals that in the realm of domestic services provision, this is not a widely used practice for getting such tasks completed. Just 4 per cent of all tasks were last undertaken using paid favours, which is the same proportion as were undertaken using one-to-one unpaid community exchanges. The interesting finding here, therefore, is that the sphere of paid services is about the same size as the realm of unpaid one-to-one community exchanges in the localities studied. Does this mean, therefore, that one is

Table 7.3 Participation rates in paid and unpaid community exchanges in Ukraine: by locality and gross household income

	Percentage participating in paid favours	*Percentage participating in one-to-one unpaid community exchanges*
All areas	65	63
By locality type:		
Deprived	48	72
Mixed	68	70
Affluent	75	52
By household income:		
Lowest quartile	41	72
Lower quartile	63	65
Upper quartile	74	60
Highest quartile	82	55

Source: Moscow survey.

witnessing a gradual shift of community exchanges from the unpaid to the paid realm? After all, as Ukraine pursues marketisation, it might be expected that there will be a gradual monetisation of such exchanges as marketism takes hold. The first important point to make here is that this is not longitudinal data so no trends can be inferred about the direction of change. The second important point to make, and this will be returned to below, is that just because money changes hands does not mean that one is witnessing the shift of one-to-one community exchange into the realm of profit-motivated market-oriented activity.

Before addressing this issue, however, it is necessary to briefly discuss whether all households are equally likely to use paid favours to undertake domestic service tasks. The finding is that, of the everyday domestic services surveyed, paid favours were last used in 6 per cent of cases in the deprived rural area, 5 per cent of cases in the deprived Kyiv neighbourhood, but just 4 per cent of cases in the border town and 2 per cent of cases in the affluent Kyiv suburb. The tentative conclusion, therefore, is that this is more commonly used among deprived populations to get everyday domestic service tasks completed. This is reinforced when the commonality of the usage of paid favours is compared across households with different levels of income. Lower-income households are more likely to use paid favours to get tasks completed than higher-income households. Some 6 per cent of tasks were last conducted using paid favours in the lowest-income group of households and just 2 per cent in the highest-income group of households. Indeed, examining who provides and receives such paid favours, the finding is that higher-income households give and receive some 41 per cent more paid favours than the average household, while the lowest-income households receive and provide just one-half of the paid favours as the average household. The realm of paid favours, therefore, reinforces rather than reduces the disparities produced by the formal market economy. As a recently retired man explained, 'I can no longer afford to get things done from old friends because I cannot give them a little something. The result is that they no longer get in contact with me to ask for favours.' His ability to receive paid favours is therefore severely curtailed by the inability to offer paid favours in return. The outcome is that although half of one-to-one community exchanges provided outside the household involve monetary payment across all localities surveyed, a greater proportion in affluent than deprived households is in the form of paid favours (three-quarters compared with under one-half), doubtless because of the ability to pay in such populations.

Paid favours are conducted for and by kin, friends, neighbours and acquaintances, often for rationales other than making or saving money. The common finding in studies of western societies has been that the closer the social relations, the more likely are paid favours to be conducted for reasons other than profit, while the more distant the social relations involved, the more likely it is that profit rationales are likely to dominate (Williams 2005a). Similarly, the price charged is more likely to converge towards market prices the more distant the social relations involved, while the closer the social relations, the greater is the divergence from market norms (Cornuel and Duriez 1985; Williams 2004a, 2005a; Williams and Windebank 2001b). Examining all instances where people provide favours to kin, friends and neighbours, this survey finds that some 41 per cent involved payment. Such paid favours, therefore, constitute nearly half of all acts of one-to-one reciprocity in Ukraine. Indeed, some 36 per cent of exchanges with kin who live outside the household are monetised, 56 per cent of exchanges between neighbours and 46 per cent of exchanges between friends.

Nature of paid favours in Ukraine

Examining the character of paid favours when given and received by kin, friends, neighbours and acquaintances, the finding, akin to western societies, is that the closer the social relations involved, the less likely it is that making or saving money is likely to be a dominant motive. However, as the social relations involved between the purchaser and supplier become more distant, the greater is the likelihood that making and saving money becomes dominant. The general rule is that the closer the social relations involved, the more the rationales are social and redistributive, while the more distant the social relations, the greater is the dominance of economic rationales. This monetisation of social relations and reciprocity in contemporary Ukraine, therefore, should not be confused with the penetration of the profit-motive into realms previously occupied by mutual aid. Monetisation of exchange, as shown above, does not always march hand-in-hand with profit-oriented motivations, as is often assumed when these economies are depicted as in transition to marketisation (Williams 2005a). To explain, if one employs kin such as an unemployed cousin living outside the household to undertake a task, such as decorating, the finding is that the principal reason for doing so is often so that one can give them money in a way that does not involve 'charity' (i.e. one is paying them for doing the task of decorating). The motive, therefore, is to help them out by giving them some much needed money. To avoid one's offer of money being rejected, which is highly likely if it is seen as 'charity', one instead asks them to do a task in order that they will accept the offer of money to help them out. Indeed, the prevalence of such motives is displayed in the finding that if the household had not paid the close social relation to undertake the task, some 80 per cent of these tasks either would not have been conducted or the household members would have done the task themselves on a self-provisioning basis.

Closer social relations, therefore, are paid for tasks to redistribute money to them in a benevolent way that avoids any connotation of 'charity' (e.g. when an employed woman paid her adult brother a considerable sum of money for decorating the living room in order to give money to him), or to avoid the favours owed accumulating in situations where it might not be feasible or possible to return them. Paying for favours thus oils the wheels for reciprocity in situations where it might not otherwise feasibly occur, such as when one is physically unable to return favours, or too time-pressured to offer in-kind labour in return. Consequently, money does not de-personalise social interactions and automatically convert them into market transactions (Zelizer 2005). People distinguish between different types of reimbursement and the social relations to which they give rise.

For suppliers, meanwhile, paid favours are conducted to make a little money 'on the side', but at the same time to provide some service to people they know who would otherwise be unable to get the job undertaken, with the balance given to these reasons shifting as one moves along the above spectrum from distant to closer social relations. Moreover, the rationales markedly vary across social groups. In higher-income populations, monetised favours are more commonly towards the profit-motivated end of the spectrum (e.g. doing a kitchen refurbishment for a neighbour for a price a little below the normal market value), while in lower-income populations such favours are usually closer to the redistributive end of the continuum and one-to-one non-monetised exchange. Such scenarios are illustrated in the following examples. Nikolai is a successful businessman who has opened up a small business doing refurbishments for domestic and commercial property. Nikolai explains how in some instances jobs can be taken on which are not solely motivated by economic reasons:

> Last year a neighbour contacted me regarding doing a bathroom refurbishment for his daughter who had recently acquired a new apartment. I agreed that my firm would take on this job. My firm still made a small profit on the job but the neighbour got a really good deal. I've known him for a number of years and I wanted to stay in good relations with him. Maybe one day, I'll ask for a favour back from him and I know he will help.

Grigory, meanwhile, is based in the deprived rural town in Kyiv's hinterland. He works formally in Kyiv in one of the city's large state-owned enterprises, where he has access to the necessary tools to undertake refurbishments in apartments, often at the weekends.

> A couple of years ago my wife asked me to do some work for her sister who lives nearby. She is struggling a little financially after her husband left her and needed some leaks in her apartment sorting out. I went and did the work and just took a small amount of money for the work that I did. She tried to offer to pay me back more money at a later date but I declined this offer. She is family I suppose and my wife wanted to try and help her a little. It worked like that.

As demonstrated in Grigory's example, at the lower end of the socio-economic spectrum, the paid work is undertaken more for social and redistributive reasons than solely for profit. There thus exists a continuum of forms of paid favours from those closer to informal self-employment conducted for profit-motivated rationales through to those more akin to mutual aid in terms of the social relations and motives involved. Those closer to profit-motivated informal self-employment are conducted mostly for more distant acquaintances, and are also more prevalent among higher-income populations, while those where the profit motive is largely absent are redistributive and social rationales prevail, are undertaken largely for closer social relations and are more prevalent in lower-income populations.

Paid favours particularly prevail in the realm of domestic services such as home maintenance and improvement work (e.g. plumbing, installing bathrooms and kitchens, glazing), routine domestic tasks (e.g. cleaning, cooking, gardening) and the provision of caring services (e.g. childcare). In terms of the customers, the following examples again demonstrate the prevalence of paid favours. Irina is a middle-aged businesswoman living in an affluent area in central Kyiv. As she explained, she has little time to do some of the household chores in her apartment and so outsources them to a neighbour:

> I've got a really busy job. I bought a hair salon on the other side of town and have been working hard building up my little business over the past three years. I soon realised that I didn't have time to run my business, spend time with my children and do all the household chores. I contacted one of the older ladies who lives on our floor in the apartment building and we agreed that she would do some cooking, household chores and watch the kids. It has worked well. I pay her a decent amount but below the market rate. It's cash-in-hand. She's happy as she earns some money and doesn't need to leave the apartment building.

While in this case a reasonable amount of money was paid for the labour, in the following example the amount of money was more symbolic and redistributive in its nature. Artem lives in a small private house next to a large housing complex on the edge of Kyiv.

> We've got an old house, which needs constant repairs. I mean that walls sometimes need re-plastering and the fences painted etc. I don't really have

> the time as I'm busy at work. Thus, over the past few years, when a little job needs doing, we've always turned to my wife's cousin. He is out-of-work and so needs some money to keep going himself. He tries to be proud and not accept the money, but we know he needs some money and we want to help him a little without embarrassing him.

In sum, multifarious motives prevail when conducting paid favours which range from more profit-motivated rationales when work is conducted for distant social relations to social and redistributive rationales when conducted for closer social relations.

Paid favours in Moscow

Participating in the provision of paid favours in Moscow is widespread. Some 65 per cent of the participants surveyed had engaged in paid favours in the past 12 months prior to interview. This, therefore, is a common form of labour practice among Muscovite households. However, and contrary to Ukraine, it appears to be more common among households in affluent populations. Some 48 per cent of the surveyed population in the deprived neighbourhood had participated in this practice, 68 per cent in the mixed neighbourhood and 75 per cent in the affluent neighbourhood surveyed. It is similarly the case when examining participation in paid favours according to household income. Some 82 per cent of households in the highest income quartile had conducted paid favours for others, compared with 74 per cent in the upper-middle income quartile, 63 per cent in the lower-middle income quartile and just 41 per cent in the lowest-income quartile of households. This clearly intimates that the sphere of paid favours reinforces, rather than reduces, the disparities produced by the formal market economy. It complements, rather than acts as a substitute for, the formal market economy.

In major part, however, this is because higher-income populations have monetised one-to-one reciprocity to a greater extent than deprived populations, as Table 7.4 reveals. Although across all populations, roughly equal proportions of the population engage in paid favours and one-to-one unpaid community exchanges, affluent populations are more likely to participate in paid favours and less likely to participate in unpaid community exchanges. Meanwhile, it is the opposite for lower-income populations, who are more likely to participate in unpaid community exchanges and are less likely to participate in paid favours. The strong intimation, therefore, is that higher-income populations in Moscow have monetised their community exchange relationships to a greater extent than lower-income populations. Does this mean, therefore, that there has been a marketisation of the work relations involved in community exchange among these higher-income populations? This is by no means certain, as will be returned to below.

Turning to whether households use paid favours to get everyday domestic services undertaken, this survey of Muscovite households reveals that in the realm of domestic services provision, this is fairly common practice for getting such tasks completed. Some 7 per cent of all tasks were last undertaken using

Table 7.4 Use of paid and unpaid community exchange by households to conduct everyday domestic services in Moscow: by locality and gross household income

	Paid favours	*One-to-one unpaid labour*
All areas	7	7
By locality type:		
Deprived	4	7
Mixed	8	9
Affluent	9	6
By household income:		
Lowest quartile	4	11
Lower quartile	6	7
Upper quartile	8	6
Highest quartile	10	4

Source: Moscow survey.

paid favours, which is the same proportion as were undertaken using one-to-one unpaid community exchanges. The interesting finding here, therefore, is that the sphere of paid services is about the same size as the realm of unpaid one-to-one community exchanges in the localities studied (see Table 7.4). Again, this does not mean that one is witnessing a gradual shift of community exchanges from the unpaid to the paid realm. Just because money changes hands does not mean that one is witnessing the shift of one-to-one community exchange into the realm of profit-motivated market-oriented activity.

Before examining this, it is important to highlight the differences between higher- and lower-income populations in their engagement in community exchange. Of the everyday domestic services surveyed in terms of the form of work used the last time they were undertaken, the finding is that paid favours were last used in 4 per cent of cases in the deprived rural area, 8 per cent of cases in the mixed area and 9 per cent in the affluent area. The tentative conclusion, therefore, is that this is more commonly used among affluent populations to get everyday domestic service tasks completed. This is reinforced when the commonality of the usage of paid favours is compared across households with different levels of income. Lower-income households are less likely to use paid favours to get tasks completed than higher-income households. Some 4 per cent of tasks were last conducted using paid favours in the lowest-income group of households, 6 per cent in the lower quartile, 8 per cent in the upper quartile and 10 per cent in the highest-income quartile.

When one compares these different populations in terms of their usage of paid and unpaid community exchanges to get everyday domestic services undertaken, however, the finding is again that affluent populations rely more on monetised exchanges and lower-income populations more on unpaid community exchanges to get tasks undertaken. Paid favours involve the provision of one-to-one help to either kin living outside the household, friends, neighbours or acquaintances where monetary payment is exchanged. When gifts and/or in-kind labour are exchanged, it lies at the border with unpaid favours. Until now, this economic practice has been seldom investigated. However, over one-third of one-to-one favours involve monetary payment in the deprived district surveyed, one-half in the mixed district and one-quarter in the affluent district. When kinship exchanges are excluded, where there is a greater willingness to provide and receive unpaid help, in deprived areas over three-quarters of material support provided to friends, neighbours and acquaintances involved payment, and even in affluent urban areas payment prevailed in around half of all such instances. In consequence, payment appears to be common whenever favours are exchanged. The suggestion again, therefore, is that affluent populations are more monetised in terms of their community exchange cultures than lower-income populations. Does this mean that they are also more profit-motivated when giving and receiving such one-to-one exchanges?

Nature of paid favours in Moscow

Examining all instances where people provide favours to kin, friends and neighbours, this survey first finds that some 51 per cent involved payment. Such paid favours, therefore, constitute over half of all acts of one-to-one reciprocity in the Moscow districts surveyed. Indeed, some 30 per cent of exchanges with kin who live outside the household are monetised, 65 per cent of exchanges between neighbours and 62 per cent of exchanges between friends. This realm therefore provides some support for the complementary perspective towards the informal economy. This is because higher-income households give and receive some five times more paid favours than the average household, while the lowest-income households receive and provide just one-fifth of the paid favours as the average household, displaying how this informal work reinforces the socio-spatial disparities of the formal economy.

It should be noted, however, that kinship exchange has largely not been monetised. Instead, kinship exchange is mostly either unpaid or gifts (but not money) are given and accepted, as Ledeneva (1998) has shown in her in-depth discussions of *blat*, networking and informal exchange. This socially embedded own account work, therefore, only applies to non-kinship exchange such as friends and neighbours. Indeed, some two-thirds of favours for friends and neighbours involve monetary payments, displaying that such paid favours are a key mechanism for the delivery of community self-help. Analysing the character of paid favours when given and received by kin, friends, neighbours and acquaintances, the finding, akin to Ukraine, is that the closer the social relations involved, the more the rationales are social and redistributive, while the more distant the social relations, the greater is the dominance of making and saving money. This monetisation of social relations and reciprocity in contemporary Moscow, therefore, should not be confused with the penetration of the profit-motive into realms previously occupied by mutual aid.

Take, for example, a young female student who looked after the preschool child of her neighbour each afternoon. For this student, this task was conducted to make a little 'extra money' to fund her studies, but just as importantly, also to help out the woman who would otherwise be unable to work and make ends meet. For the mother of the child, meanwhile, this was not only 'saving money' compared with formal childcare but, importantly, she saw it as a way of helping the student to finance her studies. Another instance of the existence of paid favours is a self-employed plumber who had a sliding scale of rates for different groups ranging from what he called 'massive' rates well above market prices for affluent foreigners to the 'token payments' he asked from neighbours and friends so they would not think he was offering them 'charity'. For him, however, these were seen as charitable acts since, as he put it, 'they wouldn't be able to afford to get the boiler repaired or heating fixed otherwise'. Similar to this, Vladimir explains how this works in his home removal business:

> Essentially, we have two price lists in our business. One is the official price, quoted on the Internet and over the phone. There are lots of rich people now who when they need something done quickly, will pay for these services. At the same time, we have prices for acquaintances and for our friends and extended families. These prices are much lower, but we still make a small profit from them. It keeps the business moving forwards and works like that.

An example of the more symbolic nature of paid labour is provided by Natalya, a young nail manicurist, who lives on the edge of Moscow:

> I work as a nail manicurist in a salon in the centre of Moscow. At the salon, people come and pay large prices. It's often part of 'showing-off' that you have the means to pay such prices. However, back here I do a little extra work for my friends who live on this estate. They come to my apartment and we have a good chat, catch up and I charge them a really small amount for their nails! It's a way for me to stay close to my friends here. If in the future, I might need something, I'll be able to turn to them for help.

For suppliers, in consequence, paid favours are conducted to make a little money 'on the side' but at the same time to provide some service to people they know who would otherwise be unable to get the job undertaken, with the balance given to these reasons shifting as one moves along the above spectrum from distant to closer social relations. Moreover, the rationales markedly vary across social groups. In higher-income populations, monetised favours are more commonly towards the profit-motivated end of the spectrum (e.g. doing a kitchen refurbishment for a neighbour for a price a little below the normal market value), while in lower-income populations such favours are usually closer to the redistributive end of the continuum and one-to-one non-monetised exchange.

For customers, meanwhile, closer social relations are paid for tasks to redistribute money to them in a benevolent way that avoids any connotation of 'charity', or to avoid the favours owed accumulating in situations where it might not be feasible or possible to return them. Sveta, a housewife in an affluent part of Moscow, demonstrates such a scenario:

> My husband has a brother who has only just arrived in Moscow. He is from a village in the region and came to Moscow to try and earn some money for his family back in the countryside. Whenever we need some things doing, like washing the family car or repairs at our dacha in the countryside, we ask him to do it. We give him a decent amount of money. It is well below the market rate for these services but it works well I think. We get these things done for us by a guaranteed person and he gets to earn some extra roubles to send back to his family.

While in Sveta's example the monetary transaction was important for both parties, in Alena's example below, the transfer of monies was much more symbolic in nature. Alena was a married mother of two living in a deprived housing complex on the edge of Moscow:

> Both my husband and I work long hours, both travelling into central Moscow every day. Last year, I decided to speak to my mother-in-law who lives close by. She is on her own and receives a miserly state pension. After some discussion, she finally agreed that we give her a small amount of money for looking after our children sometimes when we're at work and also doing some chores around our apartment.

Paid favours particularly prevail in the realm of domestic services such as home maintenance and improvement work (e.g. plumbing, installing bathrooms and kitchens, glazing), routine domestic tasks (e.g. cleaning, cooking, gardening) and the provision of caring services (e.g. childcare). This survey uncovers that 57 per cent of all off-the-books work is conducted for closer social relations and for rationales other than making or saving money. Women in more than two-thirds (64 per cent) of cases conduct such activities.

Conclusions

This chapter has examined the prevalence and nature of three forms of one-to-one exchange in post-Soviet societies, namely one-to-one unpaid labour, reimbursed family work and paid favours. To evaluate the extent and nature of such activities in post-Soviet spaces, and in order to delve deeper into the role and meaning of such exchanges, the surveys conducted in Ukraine and Moscow have been analysed. This has revealed that in both Ukraine and Moscow, unpaid one-to-one labour is more prevalent among lower-income populations, where it is more likely to be conducted for and by kin, not least because they lack the financial purchasing power to use money or gifts, and/or physical wellbeing to reciprocate with in-kind labour, so engage in such exchange out of necessity. Higher-income populations, in contrast, use one-to-one monetised exchange more to expand their social networks and consolidate relationships, and do so more out of choice. Deprived populations therefore use this when no other options are open to them in order to 'get by', whereas for affluent populations it is conducted more as a matter of choice, in order to 'get on'.

The chapter then examined the nature of a form of labour that has been seldom discussed either in post-Soviet societies or beyond, namely paid family labour whereby a household member reimburses another household member for work conducted. This reimbursement can be in the form of money but also in the form of gifts or the in-kind reciprocal exchange of labour. The overarching finding is that reimbursed family labour constitutes a small but significant livelihood practice in post-Soviet spaces. Mostly involving inter-generational exchanges between a parent and child, such a labour practice is most common in more affluent populations. In lower-income populations where such a labour practice is less frequent, when it does occur, it more commonly involves gifts and/or in-kind reciprocity, rather than monetary exchange. The notion that the existence of such a labour practice marks the advent of a marketisation of the domestic realm, however, does not appear to be valid. When one examines the rationales underpinning such exchanges, there is little notion that the participants in such practices view themselves as engaged in market-like profit-motivated exchanges. Broader social and redistributive rationales, such as the desire to impart an understanding of the meaning of money, seem to be more to the fore in terms of the participants' motives than profit-motivated rationales, and neither do they perceive these exchanges as akin to market-oriented exchanges conducted for the purpose of profit.

Finally, concerning the nature of paid favours, the chapter reveals in both Ukraine and Moscow the existence of a continuum of forms of paid favours from those closer to informal self-employment conducted for profit-motivated rationales through to those more akin to mutual aid in terms of the social relations and motives involved. Those closer to profit-motivated informal self-employment are conducted mostly for more distant acquaintances, and are also more prevalent among higher-income populations, while those where the profit motive is largely absent are redistributive and social rationales prevail, are undertaken largely for closer social relations and are more prevalent in lower-income populations.

8 Formal and informal unpaid employment

Introduction

A widespread assumption has been that when one engages in formal labour, it is paid. However, it takes but a moment's reflection to realise that some formal employment is not paid. To see this, one has only to think about unpaid internships in the private, public and third sectors of the economy, which many people now undertake in order to gain work experience and improve their employability. It is also the case that potential employees of an organisation sometimes undertake one-week or one-month trials on an unpaid basis so that employers can judge their suitability for the post. In these instances, the unpaid worker usually expects an offer of paid formal employment at the end of the unpaid trial period. There is often an overlap, therefore, between paid formal employment and this so far little discussed realm of unpaid formal employment.

Although such unpaid formal employment occurs in the private and public sectors and appears to be a burgeoning realm, it is not perhaps the most significant segment of unpaid formal employment in post-Soviet societies. It is in third sector organisations (TSOs) that this practice is perhaps most prevalent, where it is more commonly termed 'formal volunteering', which refers to 'giving help through groups, clubs or organisations to benefit other people or the environment' (Low *et al.* 2008: 11). Volunteering is composed of two major types of engagement: formal volunteering, which is a form of unpaid formal labour; and informal volunteering, which involves the provision of one-to-one help on an unpaid basis to others who do not live in one's household but in the wider community. This latter type of work practice was considered in Chapter 7. Here, we focus upon formal volunteering as a form of unpaid formal employment that sits further along the formal/informal continuum towards informality than unpaid formal employment in private and public sector organisations, but nevertheless sits firmly in this category of unpaid formal employment.

Second, this chapter addresses a work practice that has seldom been analysed in post-Soviet societies, namely informal unpaid employment. This is where somebody is employed by an organisation on an unpaid basis, as above, but the employer or employee does not adhere to all the rules and regulations required. This applies to those working on an unpaid basis in private, public and TSOs. To understand what is covered by this work practice, let us take the example of somebody engaged in unpaid volunteering by giving help through groups, clubs or organisations to benefit other people or the environment. Unlike formal volunteering, where the person adheres to all the regulations attached to such an endeavour, such as having the licences to do so, 'informal' unpaid employment/volunteering does not. Sometimes, for example, those engaged in unpaid volunteering in community-based groups might do so illegitimately or informally. This is what we here mean by unpaid informal employment. For example, it might occur when a community-based group is set up to care for children, but without the required licences to act as child carer. Alternatively, it might take place when operating a sporting group, community fund-raising or music event without the necessary licences. Until now, this labour practice has been little discussed in any literature.

To evaluate the extent and nature of unpaid formal labour in post-Soviet societies, we will first review previous research on both unpaid formal employment in the private and public sectors and formal volunteering in post-Soviet societies. Second, we will turn our attentions to unravelling the extent and character of this labour practice in Ukraine, along with a slightly richer and more textured understanding of its role and meanings, followed in the third section by a similar review of its magnitude and character in Moscow. Following this, and to assess the extent and nature of the more 'informal' forms of unpaid employment in the private and public sectors and how formal volunteering can sometimes be conducted informally, we will first interrogate the interviews conducted in Ukraine to evaluate the extent to which this is a livelihood practice and its nature, and following this, we will evaluate the Moscow interviews to again evaluate its extent and character in this post-Soviet context. The outcome will be a review of some economic practices that have so far received little attention in the literature on post-Soviet societies.

Formal unpaid employment

Formal unpaid employment, to repeat, can take the form of either unpaid internships or trial periods in the private and public sectors, or it can occur in TSOs where it is more commonly referred to as 'formal volunteering'. In this section, we first review what is known about the extent of such a labour practice in post-Soviet societies and then, having shown the limited empirical evidence so far available, provide an analysis of the extent and nature of this labour practice from our fieldwork in both Ukraine and the Russian city of Moscow. This will provide not only an assessment of the magnitude of such a practice in post-Soviet societies, but also a richer and more textured evaluation of its character and the attitudes of people towards this form of work than has perhaps so far been the case.

Formal unpaid employment in the private and public sector

In the private and public sectors, as stated, formal unpaid labour can take the form of unpaid internships or one-week or more trials, and people often do this expecting paid employment at the end. Although this is an increasingly widely used practice in post-Soviet societies and beyond, little if any empirical evidence is available so far on either the extent to which this labour practice is being employed in post-Soviet societies or the characteristics of such endeavours. Neither, so far as is known, are there any studies on the ways in which employers use this form of labour in their overall recruitment strategies or the attitudes of potential employees to engaging in such unpaid internships and trial periods. Indeed, the only related research so far available in post-Soviet societies is on how businesses sometimes fail to pay their formal employees for protracted periods (Shevchenko 2009), which in itself is a form of unpaid formal employment. As discussed in Chapter 5, many formal businesses often do not pay their formal employees either their formal wage or the additional undeclared 'envelope' wage that is so prevalent in the post-Soviet labour market, meaning that formal employees often end up working on an unpaid basis for their formal employees. Below, therefore, we will report some of the first evidence available on the extent to which formal unpaid employment is used in the private and public sectors in post-Soviet societies, as well as the character of this labour practice in such societies by reporting evidence from both Ukraine and the Russian city of Moscow. Unlike formal unpaid employment in the private and public sectors, however, much greater evidence exists on the extent and character of such a labour practice in the third sector in post-Soviet societies.

Formal volunteering in post-Soviet societies

To understand the contemporary use of formal volunteering in post-Soviet societies, it is important to understand how its current configuration has been influenced by the Soviet legacy. During the Soviet period, social, economic and political activity was closely controlled by the state (Howard 2002). This allowed the Communist regime to suppress formal autonomous organisations and the development of mass-movements other than the Communist Party (Evans 2006). Close control of all social organisations provided an effective way of creating 'good Communist citizens' outside the official political party framework (Evans 2006). This is not to say that informal associations did not exist, but unlike western civil society arrangements, the realm of 'voluntary' associations representing civil society was not separate from the state. Such arrangements left a legacy of paternalistic state–society relations. Effectively, this meant that Soviet civil society was institutionalised within the state (Rose 1995). Participation was a patriotic duty for Soviet citizens (Evans 2006), not a voluntary and freely chosen activity. This hindered the development of a culture of voluntary participation (Smolar 1996). Consequently, as a space for action, civil society was not perceived as an arena which would aggregate, represent, and articulate interest and facilitate collective action between the individual and the state, but was instead seen as organised and an aspect of social control.

Despite the controlled and institutionalised nature of civil society arrangements, small and 'illegal' grass-roots networks did exist (Fish 1991). These independent grass-roots movements and organisations formed around intelligentsia groups, which consisted of 'opposition-minded intellectuals [in] tight-knit, highly insular, and mutually suspicious circles' (Mendelson and Gerber 2007: 57). Furthermore, most ordinary Soviet citizens relied on personal networks and close 'contact groups' (Kharkhodin 1998: 958) in order to offset any arising shortage and uncertainty present throughout the Communist regime (Rose 1995). These networks helped Soviets to mitigate the effect of the continuous scarcity of basic consumer goods, and facilitated access to other necessary resources (Ledeneva 1998). This culture favoured 'circles of intimacy and trust among family members and close friends' (Evans 2006: 47) and helped Russians to become proficient at circumventing the authorities and the state. Along with the institutionalised and forced nature of official civil society, it also resulted in the constriction of the space available to civil society (Crotty 2006). For Rose (1995) and Mishler and Rose (1997), these arrangements represent an hourglass society, which by definition consisted of two halves. The top-half was characterised by a rich political and social life among ruling elites (Rose 1995). Networks of cooperation existed in an informal manner, allowing individuals to secure their own (mainly political) goals. The bottom-half was also characterised by a rich social life (Rose 1995). These networks were based around the nuclear family and friends. Rose (1995) observed that this specific network organisation and hourglass nature of society led to the 'insulation' of the top from the bottom. As a result, there was limited interaction between the elites and ordinary citizens during the Soviet period (Rose 1995). Official civil society was managed and controlled by the state; other civic activity was informal and focused on economic rather than political objectives.

In the 1990s, continuing the process of liberalisation and faced with economic and fiscal hardship, the state apparatus withdrew from various activities and social responsibilities. This process has been labelled 'over-withdrawal' (Sil and Chen 2004: 363) and had a detrimental impact on ordinary citizens. As a result of this 'over-withdrawal', citizens had to continue to rely on their personalised informal networks because the withdrawal took place without the emergence of institutions or organisations able to take on these roles and responsibilities (Poznanski 2001). Consequently, large parts of the population in countries such as Russia, including the disabled, veterans and politically repressed, were effectively 'forgotten' by the state (Henderson 2008). Despite this, many still expected the state to provide for many of these abandoned basic services (Crotty 2003). However, as a result of the economic difficulties (Hanson 2003; Lavgine 2000), the state all but ceased its support for former Soviet-era TSOs. TSOs, which enjoyed virtual monopolies in providing care and services, were now unable to do so (Sundstrom and Henry 2006). A gap for independent TSOs to take on these tasks had therefore opened up.

In an environment of over-withdrawal and democratisation, civil society had the opportunity to expand its constricted space by taking on and replacing activities formerly undertaken by the state. However, many of Kharkhordin's (1998) collectives or other informal networks exploited the subsequent political weakness of the state. With the desire to survive as forms of association, such networks engaged in activities that led to criminal extortion or self-enrichment rather than engaging in activities conducive to the building of an autonomous civil society sphere (Yurchak 2002; Volkov 2002). TSOs which did not engage in such anti-modern behaviour (Rose 1996) formed around networks outside political elites and they attempted to engage in civil activities, but faced a number of problems due to cultural and social legacies inherited from the Soviet past. Another aspect which constrained TSOs in engaging the public was the fact that the majority of post-Soviet TSOs typically sprung out of tight-knit pre-existing family and friendship networks (Cook and Vinogradova 2006), which were hostile towards outsiders. Human rights organisations predominantly reflect this development trajectory of TSOs (Mendelson and Gerber 2007). These networks did not actively pursue activities and strategies to engage the public as they were originally conceived to protect the members from the state. However, the inability and/or unwillingness to connect and engage the public aggravated the societal detachment of TSOs. This hindered TSOs in pluralising the democratic arena and impeded the institutionalisation of civil society as a space between the individual and the state. As a result, civil society remained a constricted space and further accentuated the hourglass society (Crotty 2006).

Post-Soviet civil society has not inhabited the middle ground between the state and society and is still dominated by 'informal' networks existing at either end of the hourglass rather than an autonomous middle ground. In addition to these inherent developmental difficulties for the third sector, the state has not shown any interest in facilitating a civil society based on collective action, interest aggregation and promoting democratisation. Hence, structures and institutions which enable such civil society arrangements to develop and operate; for example a functioning and independent judiciary, a system of social contracting or formalised vehicles for state–civil society interaction (Henderson 2008), have been notable by their absence. In combination with the above-mentioned persistent lack of generalisable trust, this constrained civil society development as a space in which autonomous intermediary agents were able to act. The lack of trust in institutions and the legacy of the specifics of Soviet forms of civil society have meant that levels of formal volunteering in post-Soviet Russia and Ukraine remain low. According to the Charities Aid Foundation's World Giving Index 2011, both Russia (130th) and Ukraine (105th) maintain low positions in comparison with other countries (World Giving Survey 2011). Similar figures are confirmed by the European Values Survey of 1999, with Ukraine and Russia holding the third and second lowest levels of formal volunteering among European countries. These results are confirmed again by the results of the European Values Survey in 2008, in which Ukraine and Russia are positioned second bottom and bottom according to participation rates in formal volunteering. The results indicate lower levels in general for post-socialist societies compared with western European societies.

Why, therefore, do people engage in unpaid formal volunteering in post-Soviet societies? An analysis of Table 8.1 reveals that in the Russian Federation, the reasons people participate in unpaid formal volunteering is more to do with meeting their own social, emotional and personal development needs rather than the material needs of others. They engage in such endeavours for personal reasons, such as a sense of moral obligation, social reasons, bringing about the social changes they want and personal development reasons such as gaining new skills and experiences. The needs of those they are serving tend to be lower down the list of reasons given, such as helping disadvantaged people, solidarity with the poor and disadvantaged and compassion with those in need. Given this, the strong intimation is that relying on formal volunteering as a means of meeting the material needs of others is unlikely to be effective in such post-Soviet societies, since this is not the reason that most people become involved in such endeavours. It is more about meeting their own social, emotional and personal development needs, not the material needs of those they are helping.

In some instances, however, and as will be revealed later in this chapter, such formal volunteering can become 'off-the-radar' unpaid labour, where help is provided through groups to benefit other people or the environment but the required formalities required by law are not all fulfilled. For the moment, nevertheless, this is left aside. Instead, attention here turns to a more qualitative analysis of the role and meaning of such unpaid formal labour in people's livelihood practices. To do this, we first report evidence from the 600 face-to-face interviews conducted in Ukraine, and following this, the 313 interviews conducted in Moscow.

Table 8.1 Reasons for engaging in voluntary work in the Russian Federation

	Percentage stating:				
	Unimportant	*2*	*3*	*4*	*Very important*
Sense of duty, moral obligation	7.0	5.8	14.2	25.6	47.3
For social reasons	9.8	6.1	16.9	23.3	43.8
Bring about social or political change	14.2	7.3	16.0	23.7	38.9
Gain new skills and useful experience	12.9	9.0	14.6	27.3	36.1
Make a contribution to my local community	13.2	6.9	18.5	27.7	33.6
Opportunity to repay something	18.0	10.8	20.2	17.8	33.2
Compassion for those in need	8.2	10.6	23.1	25.7	32.4
Time on my hands	20.7	11.6	15.9	25.0	26.9
Solidarity with the poor and disadvantaged	14.6	10.8	27.1	20.8	26.5
Help disadvantaged people	20.0	12.1	26.3	21.1	20.3
Identifying with people who suffer	13.9	13.9	26.3	25.9	19.9
Personal satisfaction	42.5	13.0	17.2	14.9	12.6
Did not want to but could not refuse	44.5	13.2	19.7	12.5	10.1
Religious belief	66.2	13.0	7.6	6.1	7.1

Source: World Values Survey (2008).

Formal unpaid labour in Ukraine

Participating in unpaid formal labour in Ukraine is not a minority practice. As Table 8.2 displays, some 4 per cent of participants had engaged in formal unpaid labour in the private or public sector in the 12 months prior to interview and a further 25 per cent had engaged in formal unpaid labour in the third sector in the last 12 months, or what is termed formal volunteering. This, therefore, is a common form of labour practice among Ukrainian households. However, it is more common as a labour practice among some population groups than others. Although formal unpaid labour in the private and public sector is fairly evenly distributed among all locality types, formal unpaid labour in the third sector (henceforth referred to as 'formal volunteering') is unevenly distributed spatially, with those living in the affluent locality surveyed in Kyiv being more likely to engage in such endeavours than those living in the deprived locality types studied. This reinforces previous studies in other countries, which display a statistically significant relationship between formal volunteering and the level of affluence of an area (Williams 2005a).

This is further reinforced when the relationship between participation in formal unpaid labour and household income is analysed. Not only is there a strong relationship between participation in unpaid formal labour in the private and public sectors and household income, with more affluent households engaging in higher levels of such endeavours, but so too is a similar pattern identified between participation in formal volunteering and household income. This is not perhaps surprising. Not only are more affluent households likely to be more able to invest time

Table 8.2 Participation rates in formal unpaid labour in Ukraine: by locality and gross household income

	Percentage participating in:	
	Formal unpaid labour in public and private sector	*Formal unpaid labour in third sector*
All areas	4	25
By locality type:		
Affluent Kyiv	4	31
Deprived Kyiv	5	15
Deprived rural	3	19
Border town	4	33
By household income:		
<600	1	10
600–1,399	2	21
1,400–2,199	3	25
2,200–2,999	5	21
3,000–3,799	8	30
>3,800	4	40

Source: Ukraine survey.

and resources in engaging in unpaid internships, for example, so as to increase their employability, but so too are they more likely to participate in formal volunteering in order to build their social capital and provide help to others.

Turning to whether households use unpaid formal labour to get everyday domestic services undertaken, this Ukrainian survey reveals that in the realm of domestic services provision, this is not a widely used practice for getting such tasks completed. As Table 8.3 reveals, no households used formal unpaid labour to get these everyday domestic tasks completed, and less than 1 per cent used formal volunteering to undertake these tasks. Indeed, where formal volunteering was used, it was mostly confined to fulfilling caring functions such as for children, elderly kin and pets.

This, therefore, provides evidence to support the hypothesis discussed above that in post-Soviet states, and reflecting the Soviet legacy, most people become involved in such endeavours to meet their own social, emotional and personal development needs. Very little formal volunteering is about meeting the material needs of some client group that they are helping. This provides a clear signal that in Ukraine civil society does not represent a resource that might be drawn upon to meet the needs of marginalised groups. Is this also the case, therefore, in the Russian city of Moscow?

Formal unpaid labour in Moscow

As Table 8.4 reveals, participating in unpaid formal labour in Moscow is not a minority practice. Some 3 per cent of participants had engaged in formal unpaid

Table 8.3 Use of formal unpaid labour by Ukrainian households to conduct 44 everyday domestic services: by locality and gross household income

	Percentage participating in:	
	Formal unpaid labour in private and public sector	*Formal unpaid labour in third sector*
All areas	0	<1
By locality type:		
Affluent Kyiv	0	<1
Deprived Kyiv	0	<1
Deprived rural	0	<1
Border town	0	<1
By household income:		
<600	0	1
600–1,399	0	<1
1,400–2,199	0	<1
2,200–2,999	0	<1
3,000–3,799	0	0
>3,800	0	0

Source: Ukraine survey.

Table 8.4 Participation rates in formal unpaid labour in Moscow: by locality and gross household income

	Percentage participating in:	
	Formal unpaid labour in the private and public sectors	*Formal unpaid labour in the third sector*
All areas	3	28
By locality type:		
Deprived	2	18
Mixed	3	24
Affluent	3	37
By household income:		
Lowest quartile	1	17
Lower quartile	2	31
Upper quartile	2	33
Highest quartile	4	34

Source: Moscow survey.

labour in the private or public sector in the 12 months prior to interview, and a further 28 per cent in formal volunteering. However, participation is again unevenly distributed across the Muscovite population. Although formal unpaid labour in the private and public sector is fairly evenly distributed among all locality types, formal volunteering is again not. Those living in the affluent locality are more likely to engage in formal volunteering than those living in the deprived or mixed area, similar to Ukraine.

This is further reinforced when the relationship between participation in formal unpaid labour and household income is analysed. Not only are higher-income households more likely to participate in unpaid formal labour in the private and public sectors, but so too are they more likely to participate in formal volunteering. Akin to Ukraine, therefore, such households are more likely to be able to invest time and resources in engaging in unpaid internships, for example, so as to increase their employability, but so too are they more likely to participate in formal volunteering in order to build their social capital, seek emotional and social support themselves and provide help to others. Turning to whether households use unpaid formal labour to get everyday domestic services undertaken, meanwhile, this Moscow survey reveals that it is not widely used. As Table 8.5 displays, no households used formal unpaid labour in the private and public sectors to get these everyday domestic tasks completed, and less than 1 per cent used formal volunteering to do so. Indeed, where formal volunteering was used, and akin to Ukraine, it was mostly confined to fulfilling caring functions such as for children, elderly kin and pets.

Given this review of the extent to which these two forms of unpaid formal labour are used in Ukraine and Moscow, attention now turns to unravelling the role and meaning of such work to those engaged in it.

Table 8.5 Use of formal unpaid labour by Muscovite households to conduct everyday domestic services: by locality and gross household income

	Percentage participating in:	
	Formal unpaid labour in the private and public sectors	*Formal unpaid labour in the third sector*
All areas	0	<1
By locality type:		
Deprived	0	1
Mixed	0	<1
Affluent	0	<1
By household income		
Lowest quartile	0	<1
Lower quartile	0	<1
Upper quartile	0	<1
Highest quartile	0	<1

Source: Moscow survey.

Lived experiences of formal unpaid employment in the private and public sectors in Ukraine and Moscow

In Ukraine, often people work unpaid for a trial period when offered a formal job in the private or public sectors. Indeed, 30 per cent of respondents starting a new formal job in the private sector over the year prior to interview had been asked to do so, especially younger people. In Moscow, the figure was 15 per cent of respondents. A significant minority had not been offered employment at the end of their trial period. The respondents often asserted this to be a deliberate employer strategy to get 'free labour'. For example, a person working as a courier had been told after a two-week trial that the business did not after all have any positions available and that he was not wanted, yet job advertisements for the same job appeared in the newspaper the next day. Similar stories were recounted with regard to retail stores and kiosks continuously employing people on an unpaid trial basis and saying that they were not wanted at the end of their free trial. Another example came from the financial sector, where Lesya, a graduate in finance, had been given a trial period working at one of the leading banks in Kyiv:

> I was offered the job and told that there was a compulsory one-month trial period and after that, the wages being offered looked good. I worked hard and did well throughout the month but at the end of it, I was told that things had changed and there were now no vacancies. I felt disappointed obviously. Several of my friends have also had this experience.

In Moscow, Artem recounts a similar experience:

> I graduated from a good Moscow university with a degree in economics. I searched hard for a good job but it was difficult. Eventually, I found a

> position at an insurance firm. I applied and was offered a job on condition of undertaking a six-week unpaid trial period. I was assured that this was simply company policy and that all would be OK. Anyway, at the end of this trial period, I was released from the firm, with the manager telling me that the firm had some financial difficulties etc. I understood what had happened straightaway.

Whether this is a valid depiction of an employer practice or simply a result of potential employees being inappropriate for the job is a question that needs to be asked. Although in some cases this is of course due to the individual being inappropriate for the role, meaning they are asked to leave and not taken on to a paid formal job after the trial period, this is not always the case. The evidence suggests that, given the widespread nature of this employment practice, it is in large part a tactic pursued by employers to access unpaid labour and is often an ongoing practice employed by them. As a graduate from a good university in Ukraine explains:

> I left university with a degree in accounting and economics. I found a job in a bank.... I had to work for three months on a trial basis, without pay, and then my wage would start at quite a good level. I decided to give it a go and was 'lucky' enough to get the job. However, almost at the end of the three month trial period, my boss one day simply told me that I was not good enough at my job and there was no future at the bank for me.... At no time before was my performance discussed. I thought about complaining to someone, but to whom and what would be the point? It's always the same in our country, the rich and powerful act as they please, enrich themselves and don't care about normal people.

In the public sector, meanwhile, this practice of unpaid trial periods was less commonly used. Although there were instances identified of individuals undertaking unpaid internships, such as over the summer months when they are students in order to gain work experience and develop their employability skills, there were few instances identified among the respondents of any tactic among public sector employers of deliberately releasing them. Instead, this practice of using unpaid internships appeared to be much more in the unpaid employee's interest than that of the employer when undertaken in the public sector. Indeed, gaining access to such unpaid internships was highly competitive and those who gained access to them often had to engage in '*blat*' in order to gain access to such internships, or else pay straight 'bribes' to the government officials involved in order to get such a placement. In Ukraine, two examples, one from Kyiv and one from the border town, confirm such practices:

> Before you graduate from university, you need to gain some practical experience. Jobs now are very competitive and thus you need some experience before applying. It is even difficult to get an unpaid internship. For me,

> I used a friend of my father's to get me an internship in a state ministry. I worked hard for two months.
>
> After finishing my studies, I wanted to work in local administration in my home city. The jobs are difficult to come by and you need some help from a contact to get 'through the door'. I worked for three months on a summer internship unpaid after my father used a contact to get me the place. At the end of the internship, I was taken on for a probationary one-year period.

In Moscow, Larisa, a medical graduate, explained a similar situation:

> Before completing my studies at the medical university, I searched for some work experience at some of Moscow's hospitals. I soon found out that in order to get a placement, money needed to be given to the right person at the hospital. It was crazy; I ended up paying for the privilege of working for three months unpaid! I got my work experience though and have now begun my final year of studies.

Indeed, these are not the only examples of unpaid formal labour in post-Soviet states. Some 20 per cent of the private sector employees surveyed asserted that their weekly or monthly wage had not been paid to them over the past year. On the whole, this was the undeclared (envelope) wage component that had not been paid. Many Ukrainian respondents stated how, since the onset of the global financial crisis which hit Ukraine's economy harder than most, such a situation has become more common and thus, the receipt of declared and undeclared (envelope) wages very unpredictable. An interviewee who holds a white-collar office job in Kyiv outlines such a situation below:

> Our wages are very unstable now. Previously, we received an official wage and then a 'top-up' wage in an envelope every month. Over the previous two years, we don't really know what we will receive each month. Sometimes, we receive our full wages, as agreed with the boss including the envelope wage. Sometimes though this isn't the case.

Moreover, 8 per cent asserted that even the declared wage had not been paid in full. This, therefore, is a significant minority of all formal employees who were in effect working not as paid formal employees for their employer, but were also engaging in unpaid formal labour since a portion of their salary owed to them was not being paid. Such a situation is confirmed by an International Labour Office report on the effect of the financial crisis in Ukraine after 2008. The report notes how after significant decreases in wage arrears in Ukraine from 2000–2007, the arrears grew by 2.5 times during 2008–2009, being particularly problematic in the public administration, construction and healthcare segments of the economy (Kulikov and Blyzniuk 2010). Irina, a healthcare worker in the rural town outside of Kyiv, illustrates the prevalence of declared wages not fully paid:

> We receive a miserly wage from the state and even that often is not paid in full. It's been particularly bad over the past year or so, with sometimes 20 per cent of our wage unpaid. What can you do though? We continue to go to work and hope that in time, we'll receive our wage arrears.

In Moscow, the figures in comparison with Ukraine were lower. Fifteen per cent of the private sector employees surveyed asserted that their weekly or monthly wage had not been paid to them at some point in the past year prior to the survey. On the whole, this was the undeclared (envelope) wage component that had not been paid, although 4 per cent asserted that the official declared wage had not.

Lived experiences of formal unpaid labour in the third sector

In Ukraine, one-fifth of all respondents had engaged in formal volunteering in the 12 months prior to the survey, with participation rates greater among affluent populations, as displayed in Table 8.2. In Moscow, some 28 per cent of all respondents had engaged in formal volunteering in the 12 months prior to the survey, with participation rates greater among affluent populations, as displayed in Table 8.3. Such formal volunteering, however, does not on the whole deliver material support to others. As Table 8.3 displays, less than 1 per cent of the common domestic services surveyed were provided in this way in Ukraine, and as Table 8.5 displays, less than 1 per cent of the common domestic services surveyed were provided in this way in Moscow. Instead, in Ukraine 90 per cent of cases and in Moscow 85 per cent of cases when people engaged in formal volunteering, the primary reason respondents engaged was to seek social or emotional support for themselves rather than to help others. Common responses were 'it is a good opportunity to mix' and 'it provides a way of discussing things with others who are sympathetic'. This suggests that developing participation in community-based groups in Ukraine and Moscow will not meet material needs unmet by the formal market economy. It is a way of meeting the social and emotional needs of those who engage in such formal volunteering, rather than a vehicle for delivering help to others. In Ukraine, just 10 per cent (15 per cent in Moscow) participated for the primary purpose of providing material aid to others.

Informal unpaid employment

Unpaid employment is not always conducted on a wholly formal basis. Often, people are employed by a private, public or third sector organisation on an unpaid basis, but the employer or employee does not adhere to all of the rules and regulations required for this to be legitimate activity, such as the necessary licences. To start to unpack this form of work which, so far as is known, has been seldom, if ever, discussed in a post-Soviet context, we first outline the extent of this practice in Ukraine and Moscow, and following this, begin to unpack its character from the interviews conducted. This will reveal that despite receiving little, if any, discussion in the literature on coping tactics, such a practice is a small but nevertheless regular practice pursued in post-Soviet societies.

Extent of informal unpaid employment in Ukraine and Moscow

On analysing the level of participation in informal unpaid employment in Ukraine, the finding is that 1 per cent of households had participated in this labour practice in the 12 months prior to the survey. This type of labour practice, however, is unevenly spatially distributed. Participation in such a labour practice is more common in the deprived rural population (where 2 per cent had engaged in such an endeavour) compared with the deprived urban locality of Kyiv and border town (where 1 per cent had done so) or the affluent Kyiv suburb where nobody had done so. This finding that such a labour practice is more common among relatively deprived populations is further reinforced when the use of such a labour practice is analysed according to gross household income. Although none of the poorest households had engaged in such a practice, and neither had any of the most affluent households, this endeavour was very much clustered among the middle-income households. This labour practice, however, was little used to undertake everyday domestic services. Well under 1 per cent of the 44 household services were conducted by people working on an unpaid informal basis. Indeed, the only instance where it was used was associated with home repair and maintenance services where some of the labour provided by businesses in the home repair and improvement sector was provided on an unpaid informal basis.

Examining the level of participation in unpaid informal employment in Moscow, and akin to Ukraine, just 1 per cent of households participated in this labour practice in the 12 months prior to the survey. This type of labour practice, nevertheless, is unevenly distributed and, akin to Ukraine, is again concentrated in deprived populations where 2 per cent had participated in this form of work, compared with 1 per cent in the mixed area and nobody in the affluent area. This concentration of such work in lower-income populations is further reinforced when analysing the distribution of such work according to household income. In Moscow, and similar to Ukraine, it is the lower-to-middle income households that have the highest participation rates. In the lowest income quartile, 2 per cent of households participate, compared with 3 per cent in the lower-middle income quartile of households, 1 per cent in the upper-middle income quartile of households and nobody in the highest income quartile of households.

Character of informal unpaid employment in Ukraine and Moscow

Informal unpaid employment in post-Soviet societies such as Ukraine and Russia takes three forms, depending on the sector in which it takes place. First, there is informal unpaid employment in the third sector. This is where somebody engages in unpaid voluntary and/or community activity either in community-based groups or unpaid voluntary and/or community activity on a one-to-one basis, but does not adhere to all of the legal responsibilities attached to this activity such as the labour laws. As will be shown, it tends to arise because many people consider that current statutory and legal responsibilities and regulations only apply, such as when caring for others' children, if the activity is paid. If the activity is unpaid, there is a widespread perception that regulations and legal responsibilities are somehow not applicable. The outcome is that many engaged in unpaid voluntary and/or community activity, either in community-based groups or a one-to-one basis, in effect operate on an informal basis because they are not aware of their statutory and legal responsibilities to which they need to adhere, such as when caring for children. An example of this was the unpaid voluntary work undertaken by an interviewee, Svetlana in Kyiv:

> I've worked in the local dance centre for a few years now. It was set up to encourage local children to do some Ukrainian traditional dancing after school. I've always enjoyed dancing and enjoy working with children too. I don't get paid and we don't register anything really. There are a few of us and we simply help out in the centre when we can, in terms of organising the classes, keeping in contact with parents.

Similarly, in the rural town Volodymyr outlined his role in a local sports club for teenage boys:

> I've worked at the local sports club for a couple of years. My son goes there and enjoys it so I decided to help out when and where I could. I don't do much, just normally driving the boys in my van to different places if they have a match. I'm not registered at the club; it's just a group of people who are interested in helping the club develop.

Turning to Moscow, Yuliya, a mother of two and housewife, lives in a large housing complex on the edge of Moscow. As well as looking after her two young children, she often undertakes unpaid voluntary work on the estate in a small community club:

> The club was set up a while ago now and offers a place for children to go to and be supervised, often after nursery clubs finish. More and more parents now are working longer hours and struggle to pick up their children from the nursery on time. I try and help out there a couple of times a month with a friend of mine who works there also. I don't get paid but it's nice to help out and I stay in contact with lots of other parents in our area.

Second, informal unpaid employment occurs in the private sector. For example, in many family businesses, individual family members may help out on an unpaid basis from time-to-time, such as when there are peaks in demand. It is often the case in Ukraine that such workers are not registered, have not undertaken any necessary health and safety training and do not adhere to a multiplicity of other regulatory requirements when working in the business. Such informal unpaid employment also occurs when people are employed on unpaid internships, for example, as discussed above, but do not adhere to all the regulatory requirements regarding their employment. Again, this is often because employers are sometimes not aware that the same regulatory conditions apply to those who work in their business on an unpaid basis as to those who are employed on a paid basis. Just because somebody is not paid when dealing with a customer, for example, does not mean that the organisation is not subject to the same legal liabilities regarding customer safety.

For example, a builder operating on a self-employed basis in the border town used their teenage child as an unpaid labourer on jobs, with the child helping by things such as carrying the tools and equipment, building materials and sweeping up and tidying afterwards. Similarly, in Kyiv a small business owner, Natalya, uses her son to undertake deliveries in her flower business:

> I set up the business three years ago and it is going steadily. The business involves ordering flowers over the Internet. When we have deliveries, often I ask one of my sons to help out. He is a taxi-driver and thus has the means to do this. He takes the flowers and drives to our clients all over Kyiv. He isn't registered in our business as he is registered as a taxi driver.

In Moscow, Gennady explained how he also used his vehicle as a means to help out a friend who owns a small café:

> I have a large jeep and about once a month I go to a depot and pick up a lot of goods for a friend who owns a small café in our neighbourhood. I don't get paid for this and I don't even ask for the petrol money. I just offered to help a while ago and the situation hasn't changed. I'm not registered as working for the café or anything like that; it's just the way we do things.

Similarly, Pavel explains how his friend also often helps him out in his small business:

> I own a small printing firm. As we all know, the Internet has become more and more important in business. When I have some difficulties with the Internet and the firm's website, my friend comes and tries to sort the problem out. We've known each other for years since we were at university together. There is no payment involved.

Third, there is informal unpaid employment in the public sector. As discussed above, it is often the case that people engage in unpaid internships in order to gain work experience and improve their employability. However, it is similarly the case that the regulatory conditions attached to their employment are similar to the regulatory conditions attached to the employment of those who receive a salary. Leonid, an engineer at a large public sector organisation in Kyiv, explains how such a form of labour manifests itself:

> My son is studying at university at present, like me to become an engineer. On several occasions, he's come and worked with my team and I on a project. This is unpaid work but it gives him experience of the real world. It's not enough now to simply have a degree, you need a degree and experience in order to gain a good job.

In a different setting in the public sector, Irina, a schoolteacher in the rural town outside of Kyiv, explains how such informal unpaid employment works:

> We are a very small school and we get little money from the education authority. Sometimes, if we have a small problem, we ask friends or acquaintances to come into the school and help. The two most common situations are problems with the lighting and with the computers. We have a couple of guys who come to the school and sort these issues out. One of them has a son at the school and is an electrician and another is a husband of one of the teachers. It works like that; we try and get by as well as we can.

In Moscow, Ludmilla, again a schoolteacher, outlines the character of such informal unpaid employment:

> Regularly we have school trips for our children. We take them often into Moscow and go to the theatre or something like that. We often need volunteers to help us organise the visit. We have three or four local people who often come and help. We've known them for a long time and their children used to study at our school. They often come and help supervise the children when we travel into Moscow on the bus and then on the metro system.

Furthermore, in both countries parents talked about how they were obliged to provide unpaid informal labour to their children's schools. This might be the clearing of snow, undertaking a 'deep clean' of classrooms before the school year starts and decorating. While this is an accepted practice, which was widely used in the Soviet period, there is a feeling that some schools receive funding for such activities and free labour is used instead and the money diverted elsewhere.

Conclusions

This chapter has reviewed the extent and nature of formal and informal unpaid labour in post-Soviet societies. Concerning formal unpaid labour, we have examined its existence and character in, first, the private and public sectors, and second, the third sector where it is often referred to as 'formal volunteering'. The finding is that formal unpaid labour certainly exists in the private and public sectors. In these sectors, young people, in order to gain much needed work experience and often to get a 'foot in the door', often undertake it. In the private sector, though, there is evidence that employers potentially use this method as a deliberate way to employ 'free' labour so as to reduce labour costs and hence increase a firm's profitability. Moreover, there is also evidence of formal unpaid labour occurring when employers (in both the private and public sectors) fail to pay employees' full wages. While this problem has considerably improved since the chaotic days of the 1990s, when wage arrears were a major problem, the problem still exists and is one which has seemingly been exacerbated in the aftermath of the global financial crisis and its effect on Russia and Ukraine's economies. Regarding unpaid labour in the third sector, this certainly exists, but importantly is rarely used to meet the material needs not met by other fields of provision, such as the formal market economy. Individuals engage in community-based associations to fulfil their own needs rather than to deliver material support to others. As such, if the intention in Ukraine and Russia is to encourage the development of civil society in order to meet material needs not met by the formal private and public sectors, or even other forms of informal delivery, then developing participation in community-based groups is inappropriate.

Second, this chapter has begun to unravel a form of work that has so far been seldom discussed in post-Soviet spaces or beyond, namely unpaid informal employment. This takes many forms depending on the sector in which it occurs. What distinguishes it from paid informal employment is that although it is unregistered and unregulated by the state, it is not paid but unpaid endeavour, and what distinguishes it from unpaid formal employment is that while unpaid formal employment adheres to workplace regulations and other statutory responsibilities, unpaid informal employment does not, in whole or in part, do so. This is often because employers do not realise that the legal responsibilities that apply to paid employment are also applicable to unpaid employment, such as indemnity insurance or health and safety legislation. In sum, this chapter has revealed the diverse array of forms of paid and unpaid informal employment and how these vary according to whether such activity is conducted in the private, public or third sectors of post-Soviet society. Hopefully, therefore, this chapter will start to encourage others to begin to further unravel the different manifestations of this work practice in post-Soviet societies. If it does so, then this chapter will have achieved its objective.

9 The internal economies of the household

Introduction

It has been often assumed that self-provisioning is a leftover from a previous mode of accumulation and that the small vestiges that remain will eventually disappear as the formal market economy becomes ever more dominant (e.g. Smuts 1971). Over the last decade or so, however, there has been an emergent recognition that self-provisioning is not some minor practice in post-Soviet societies and beyond, but is extensively used by the vast majority of households in their everyday livelihood practices (Bennholdt-Thomson 2001; Bittmann *et al.* 1999; Gershuny 2000; Marcelli *et al.* 2010; Williams 2003, 2005b, 2007, 2008; Williams and Nadin 2010; Williams and Round 2008, 2010). To explain this, a range of competing explanations have emerged which variously depict those engaged in self-provisioning either as rational economic actors, dupes, seekers of self-identity or simply as doing so out of necessity or choice. Despite this, few have evaluated either the importance and prevalence of, or rationale for, participation in self-provisioning. This chapter bridges that gap.

To commence, therefore, the first section will briefly review the various perspectives towards self-provisioning in relation to both its prevalence and the reasons for engaging in such work. To evaluate critically these contrasting perspectives, the second section will then evaluate the extent of, and reasons for, self-provisioning in Ukraine, while the third section covers Moscow. This will reveal not only how self-provisioning is extensively used in the post-Soviet world, but also through a process of induction, how one can differentiate between 'willing' (rational economic actors, choice, identity seeking) and 'reluctant' (economic and market necessity, dupes) participants in self-provisioning. Having then reviewed in the fourth section the particular role of the dacha in post-Soviet societies, the concluding section will call for wider recognition of the persistence of self-provisioning in the contemporary post-socialist world and its centrality in livelihood practices. At the outset, however, self-provisioning must be defined, or what is variously referred to as 'subsistence production', 'housework', 'domestic work' or 'do-it-yourself activity'. Self-provisioning here refers to work undertaken on an unpaid basis by household members for themselves or for some other member of their household that might otherwise be undertaken in the formal economy (Reid 1934; Williams 2005a). To distinguish between self-provisioning and leisure, this definition thus uses a 'third person' approach. That is, if the activity could be undertaken by somebody in formal employment, then it is self-provisioning rather than leisure. As will become apparent later, this issue of whether it 'could' be undertaken by somebody in formal employment and why it is currently not is very important in understanding the persistence of self-provisioning.

Perspectives towards self-provisioning

To review the competing perspectives towards subsistence work, first, the contrasting views on the magnitude of such production in the contemporary economic landscape will be reviewed, followed by the competing views on the reasons for engagement in such self-provisioning.

Views on the prevalence of self-provisioning

During much of the previous century, self-provisioning was perceived as a residue or leftover from some previous era that the formal market economy was steadily replacing (Braverman 1971; Smuts 1971). It was thus caricatured as a 'peasant' or 'backward' form of production (Watts 1999). This '*modernisation*' perspective assumed that over the long run of history there had been a shift from household production for domestic consumption to a situation in which household members work for employers in exchange for wages. Individuals were viewed as increasingly selling their labour as a commodity within the labour market rather than producing goods that satisfy their own immediate needs. This was seen to have resulted in a separation or dispossession of people from the means of production, as well as a separation of the home from production. Those who previously had made goods for their own use began 'for the first time, to use their new factory wages to purchase factory-made items in the marketplace' (Rifkin 2001: 81). The result in this view has been the disappearance of self-provisioning as the tentacles of the formal market economy stretch out to envelope every nook and cranny of the modern world. However, this 'modernisation' perspective, representing self-provisioning as disappearing in the modern world and persisting only in a few minor enclaves, is highly contestable. It depicts the economy as increasingly composed of a single mode of production (i.e. the formal market economy) and people as reliant on only one form of work (i.e. formal employment) for their livelihood.

By reconceptualising self-provisioning as one of a plurality of labour practices used by households to secure a livelihood, then a very different perspective towards such work emerges. Adopting a 'diverse economies' or 'whole economy' perspective towards self-provisioning, the argument is that the subsistence 'economy' (i.e. people and households relying on this as their principal mode of production) hardly exists today. Indeed, Williams (2010b) identifies that just 6 per cent of all households in Central and Eastern Europe rely primarily on self-provisioning for their livelihood. However, self-provisioning has not disappeared. Even if goods production has moved out of the household, households still engage in an extensive range of self-servicing, ranging from routine housework, cleaning windows, cooking, gardening, child- and elder-care through to car maintenance, as well as home maintenance and improvement activity. The movement of goods production into the marketplace, therefore, seems to have been only partially followed by a shift of service provision (Williams and Nadin 2010; Williams and Round 2008, 2010; Williams and Windebank 2001a). As Bennholdt-Thomsen (2001: 224) puts it:

> Anyone who thinks a subsistence orientation should be banished 'to the stone age' or 'to the Middle Ages' or to the Third World, because in our developed society we have allegedly outgrown both self-provision and worries about subsistence, has failed to recognize that subsistence does not disappear, but rather changes through history and takes different forms in different contexts.

Seen through this 'diverse economies' lens, self-provisioning is ubiquitous. Every day, members of households cook meals, clean, tidy, mow, iron, repair and maintain goods. The interesting question, of course, is whether the extent of such work is relatively minor compared with the formal economy. Until now, there have been few evaluations of the extensiveness of self-provisioning relative to other labour practices. The only exception is time-budget studies which reveal that in many developed economies, over half of working time is spent engaged in unpaid work (Gershuny 2000; Williams 2005a). These time-budget studies, however, do not signify the importance of self-provisioning in overall livelihood practices, or explain why people use self-provisioning to undertake tasks.

Explaining self-provisioning

Two broad approaches have been adopted when explaining self-provisioning. On the one hand, wider theorisations of consumption and the consumer have been applied. On the other hand, a structure/agency debate has been played out, viewing it as conducted out of economic necessity and/or as a matter of choice. As will now be shown, both approaches suffer from intractable problems. Those applying broader theorisations of consumption and the consumer have explained self-provisioning in three contrasting ways. First, a rational utility maximisation model of consumption and the consumer has been employed, which derives from neo-classical economic thought. Here, participants in self-provisioning are believed to view their home as a business investment and to wish to maximise the market value of their property. As such, they weigh up the costs of their subsistence work against their investment return and the opportunity costs of doing this rather than spending their time on other activities (Brodersen 2003).

A second theorisation of consumption and the consumer adopted to explain self-provisioning portrays the consumer as a dupe or passive subject whose aspirations are formed and manipulated by the mass media, served and fuelled by retail businesses (Slater 1997). Here, self-provisioning is seen to have been co-opted by the market economy, such as DIY retailers, and those participating in self-provisioning are portrayed as passive subjects and dupes fooled by the latest marketing-inspired fads (Mintel 2002, 2005, 2006). A third and final theorisation of consumption and the consumer used to explain self-provisioning represents consumers as manipulating commodities to produce symbolic meanings and constitute identities (e.g. Buck-Morss 1989; Campbell 2005; Crewe 2000; McCracken 1988; Willis 1991; Wolff 1985). Seen through this lens, self-provisioning is conducted to realise effects which convey individuality and self-identity. The problem with all these theories, however, is that they focus upon why households decide to undertake particular tasks (e.g. building a summer house). They do not consider why one labour practice (e.g. self-provisioning) is used rather than another (e.g. formal employment). Building a summer house, for example, may of course be a product of: a rational economic person seeking to improve the market value of their property; a consumer responding to media-inspired aspirations, and an attempt to express individuality by acting as a manipulator of symbols. However, one does not need to use self-provisioning to build the summer house to achieve these ends. These ends could just as easily be achieved by employing a tradesperson. Such theories therefore tell us little in practice about the rationales for self-provisioning.

A second approach towards explaining self-provisioning adopts a structure/agency analytical lens, considering whether such endeavour is conducted out of economic necessity and/or as a matter of choice (Williams 2004a, 2004b, 2008). Earlier studies of various forms of self-provisioning, such as DIY, assumed it was conducted out of economic necessity because households could not afford to outsource the task to a tradesperson. However, there has been a growing recognition that some do so out of choice (Davidson and Leather 2000; Mintel 2002; Munro and Leather 2000; Williams 2004b). The intractable problem, however, is that this structure/agency dualism often does not exist in practice. As Williams (2004a) identifies in urban England, in over 80 per cent of instances where DIY was used, both economic necessity and choice were co-present in participants' motives. At present, in sum, competing perspectives exist regarding the importance and prevalence of self-provisioning, as well as the rationales for participation in such endeavour. Few studies, however, have evaluated critically these competing perspectives. Here, therefore, we start to bridge this gap.

Evaluating self-provisioning in Ukraine

As Krantz-Kent (2009: 48) remarks, self-provisioning occurs when people 'perform services for themselves or their households rather than purchasing those services', and as Budlender (2010) demonstrates, such self-provisioning is prevalent in economies across the globe. Ukraine is no exception. As noted in Chapter 4, although less than 1 per cent of surveyed households relied solely on self-provisioning to ensure their livelihoods, almost 8 per cent relied on this as their main source of livelihood, with a secondary livelihood practice to support them, and 17 per cent said it was their second most importance practice. Therefore, self-provisioning, in all its forms, including, for example, the self-growing of food, plays a significant role in Ukrainian households, as over 25 per cent state it plays an important role in their lives. Its importance is demonstrated further when households were asked the form of labour that was used to last complete a range of everyday tasks ranging from household chores such as cleaning to significant repairs. As Table 9.1 shows, 71 per cent were last undertaken on a self-provisioning basis.

Clearly, not all tasks are equally likely to be conducted using self-provisioning, with the least likely being installing double-glazing (15 per cent), hairdressing (29 per cent), improving the bathroom (32 per cent), improving the kitchen (33 per cent), plumbing (37 per cent) and flooring (39 per cent). Given that the tasks more likely to be completed using self-provisioning are small

Table 9.1 Percentage of everyday tasks undertaken using self-provisioning in Ukraine, by task

Task	*Percentage of all tasks last conducted using self-provisioning*
Wash dishes	93.7
Wash/iron clothes	93.4
Cooking	93.4
Shopping	93.3
Book-keeping	92.9
Routine housework	92.8
Clean inside windows	89.5
Evening childcare	84.5
Daytime childcare	79.1
Tutoring	77.1
Wallpapering	71.6
Tend sick	71.6
Make/repair tools	65.0
Replace broken window	64.0
Indoor painting	57.7
Make/repair furniture	51.6
Make/repair clothes	51.1
Make/repair curtains	54.1
Maintain appliances	46.4
Improve flooring	39.5
Plumbing	37.0
Improve kitchen	33.5
Improve bathroom	32.3
Hairdressing	29.3
Double glazing	15.4
ALL	70.7

Source: Ukraine survey.

tasks, it obviously seems that it is more common for larger, more complex projects to be outsourced. However, this does not mean that they necessarily then fall into the formal sphere, as only 48 per cent said that they paid someone formally. The remainder either used friends or family who have the skills and tools to complete such work, or they paid an 'outsider' cash in hand to undertake it. Such findings directly support the arguments in Chapter 3 that the modernisation thesis must be challenged as it assumes that self provisioning is no longer an important practice in modern societies. There is some variation, however, in the prevalence of such practices across income groups. As Table 9.2 highlights, lower income households are more likely to use self-provisioning, with the lowest income groups doing so in 76 per cent of instances compared with 38 per cent in the highest income households.

While this might suggest that lower-income households undertake such tasks out of necessity, this is not always the case, as will now be shown.

Motives for self-provisioning in Ukraine

Why, therefore, is self-provisioning used by households? Rather than design the survey using closed-ended questions so that responses had to fit into pre-defined categories (e.g. cost, choice), the decision was taken at the survey design stage to generate more grounded theory using an open-ended question and a follow-up probe, namely 'what was your primary reason for doing the task in this way?' and 'is that the only reason?'. Having generated these qualitative responses, the next task was to group them together according to the common phrases and terms used to explain the reasons for participation in self-provisioning. Table 9.3 displays examples of the responses given, along with how they have been clustered into groups of explanations.

The outcome of this inductive approach is a more grounded typology of the reasons for self-provisioning that reflects how participants represent themselves as either 'reluctant' or 'willing'. Those viewing themselves as 'reluctant' engage in such endeavours either because they cannot afford to outsource the task or due to problems with regard to finding and using tradespeople, such as getting a

Table 9.2 Percentage of everyday tasks undertaken as self-provisioning in Ukraine, by income category

	Percentage of tasks last conducted using self-provisioning
All	70.7
<600	75.8
600–1,399	79.2
1,400–2,199	72.9
2,200–2,999	59.3
3,000–3,799	62.8
>3,800	38.3

Source: Ukraine survey.

Table 9.3 Typology of motives for self-provisioning

Examples of rationales	*Reason for self-provisioning*	*Type of self-provisioning*
'I did it to save money' 'I didn't have the money'	Economic necessity	
'You cannot find reliable tradespeople' 'Tradesman are not available to do this job'	Reliability of tradesperson to turn up	Reluctant self-provisioning
'Tradesman do bad workmanship' 'I am wary of tradesmen' 'Tradesmen do bad jobs'	Reliability of tradesperson with regard to quality and trust	
'I increased the value of my home' 'It was an investment in my house'	Rational economic calculation	
'I enjoy doing creative things' 'I got satisfaction doing it' 'Because it was pleasurable to do'	Pleasure gained from self-provisioning	Willing self-provisioning
'To create something unique' 'To personalise my home' 'To show who we are' 'So our home displays our identity'	Individualising end-product/self-identity	

tradesperson to turn up, the perceived inferior quality of the end-product and trust issues related to leaving them alone in the home. For these participants, self-provisioning was often not their first choice but their chosen option. For 'willing' self-providers, meanwhile, self-provisioning was more often their first choice and undertaken for reasons ranging from an economic desire to maximise the value of their home (akin to the neo-classical model of the consumer), the pleasure they get from self-service activity (akin to the choice model) or the satisfaction received from creating an individualised end-product, completing a job, mastering a skill or simply doing something for oneself (supporting post-modern theories of the consumer). Table 9.4 reports the results. This reveals that people are more likely to cite 'willing' rather than 'reluctant' reasons with two-thirds of tasks conducted on a self-provisioning basis being conducted by willing participants and one-third by reluctant participants. However, this varies according to household income, with high-income households more likely to be willing while lower-income households are more likely to use self-provisioning reluctantly.

Thus, it can be seen that only about 20 per cent of tasks within the household are undertaken out of economic necessity, although this rises to 38 per cent in lower-income households. Therefore, it cannot be stated that this is the dominant reason. However, no other competing theory as to the rationale behind such practice offers a fuller explanation. For those who argue, from a neo-classical viewpoint, that every task is undertaken as an economically rational calculation aimed at getting the best return on inputs, the above shows that only around

Table 9.4 Primary reason for conducting self-provisioning in Ukraine: by household income

	Reason for engaging in self-provisioning (%)			
	All households	*Lowest income third*	*Middle income third*	*Upper income third*
Reluctant self-provisioning	34	48	30	25
Economic necessity	20	38	18	10
Tradesperson access problems	10	5	9	11
Tradesperson quality, trust, etc.	4	5	3	4
Willing self-provisioning	66	52	70	75
Rational calculation	26	18	26	29
Pleasure from process	20	17	21	22
Individualisation of end-product/self-identity	20	17	23	24
Total	100	100	100	100

Source: Ukraine survey.

one-quarter of tasks were completed through this prism. The 'cultural turn' approach, which would suggest that people would make such decisions out of a wish to enjoy the practices, can be observed in around 20 per cent of the undertakings. A similar percentage could be ascribed to a post-modernist argument whereby people want individualised outcomes. This, however, is more common in higher-income households, so care must be taken not to ascribe this more widely. The remaining 14 per cent can be seen to be around issues of trust and the inability to find someone suitable to undertake it. Thus, it is clear that there is not a dominant rationale across households for self-provisioning, but all rationales can be observed to a significant degree.

Evaluating self-provisioning in Moscow

To analyse the prevalence and importance of self-provisioning, the Muscovites surveyed were again asked for the work practice the household primarily and secondarily relied on to secure a livelihood. The finding is that one in 17 households (6 per cent) relied chiefly on self-provisioning to secure their livelihood. Moreover, when those relying on self-provisioning as their second most important livelihood practice are included, 10 per cent of households rely chiefly or secondarily on self-provisioning to secure their livelihood. The strong intimation, therefore, is that self-provisioning is not some minor residue existing in a few peripheral enclaves of the Muscovite economic landscape. One in ten households relies primarily or secondarily on such a practice to secure their livelihood in this post-socialist global city.

This perceived importance of self-provisioning is further reinforced when participation rates in different labour practices are analysed. Participation in self-provisioning is ubiquitous; all households engaged in this form of labour. This is not the same with other labour practices. Only just over one-third (37 per cent) had engaged in formal employment over the past year and 22 per cent in employment in the private sector. Compared with self-provisioning, therefore, participation in the formal labour market is confined to small pockets of the Muscovite population and is highly variable, ranging from 25 per cent in the deprived district through 40 per cent in the mixed district to 54 per cent in the affluent district. Examining participation rates, therefore, it is not self-provisioning which is a minor practice, existing in a few peripheral enclaves of the Muscovite population. It is participation in formal employment. This re-reading of the prevalence and importance of self-provisioning is further reinforced when examining the labour practices used by households to complete everyday tasks. As Table 9.5 reveals, the last time households undertook these tasks ranging from everyday household chores to home improvement work, over two-thirds (67 per cent) were undertaken on a self-provisioning basis. Formal labour, meanwhile, was last used in just 7 per cent of instances and only 26 per cent even involved monetary exchange. The implication is that self-provisioning is the major labour practice used to complete these everyday tasks. This is an important finding. The modernisation perspective assumes that self-provisioning is some minority practice. However, this survey reveals that self-provisioning remains the dominant labour practice used.

Nevertheless, there are variations in the tendency to use self-provisioning both spatially and according to household income. Self-provisioning is more heavily relied on by those living in deprived districts, as do households in the lowest and lower income quartile compared with more affluent households.

Socio-spatial variations prevail not just in the degree to which self-provisioning is used, but also in the nature of the self-provisioning undertaken. Lower-income households undertake a wider range of tasks on a self-provisioning basis and a greater proportion of all tasks, but these tend to be

Table 9.5 Percentage of everyday tasks last conducted using self-provisioning in Moscow: by locality and gross household income

	Percentage last completed using self-provisioning
All areas	67
By district:	
Deprived	78
Mixed	67
Affluent	62
By household income:	
Lowest quartile	79
Lower quartile	74
Upper quartile	64
Highest quartile	51

Source: Moscow survey.

smaller, mundane tasks. Outsourcing, meanwhile, is primarily used to conduct urgent maintenance and repair jobs, such as mending a broken window, which often needs to be outsourced in order to be completed. Relatively affluent households, in contrast, conduct a narrower range of tasks on a self-provisioning basis, but these tend to be larger home improvement projects, such as building an extension. Indeed, higher-income households seem to externalise many of the mundane routine domestic tasks to external service providers in order to create free time to engage in more rewarding home improvement projects on a self-provisioning basis. Hence, there is a qualitative difference in not only the prevalence and importance of self-provisioning across populations, but also the nature of the self-provisioning conducted.

Rationales for self-provisioning in Moscow

To explore why households made the choices they did, and akin to Ukraine, the survey asked, in an open-ended manner, 'what was your primary reason for doing it in this way?' and 'is that the only reason?'. The responses were then classified into two broad categories, 'reluctant' or 'willing'. Table 9.6 investigates the results. This reveals that the ratio of reluctant-to-willing self-provisioning across the surveyed population is 2:1; for every self-provisioning activity conducted on a willing basis, two are conducted on a reluctant basis. There are, however, statistically significant variations in the reasons for undertaking subsistence work across different household income levels. Among

Table 9.6 Reasons for conducting subsistence work in Moscow: by household income

	Reason for engaging in subsistence work (%):				
	All households	*Lowest income quartile*	*Lower income quartile*	*Higher income quartile*	*Highest income quartile*
Reluctant subsistence worker	64	90	81	60	25
Economic necessity	40	60	54	35	10
Tradesperson access problems	14	17	15	18	8
Tradesperson quality, trust, etc.	10	13	12	7	6
Willing subsistence worker	36	10	19	40	75
Rational calculation	12	4	7	10	25
Pleasure from process	8	3	5	10	15
Individualisation of end-product/self-identity	16	3	7	20	35
Total	100	100	100	100	100
X^2	–	129.74	73.24	29.92	163.86

Source: Moscow survey.

Note

$X^2 > 16.750$ in all cases, leading us to reject H_0, within a 99.5 per cent confidence interval, that there are no household income variations in the reasons for engaging in subsistence work.

higher-income populations, people are statistically significantly more likely to be willing participants in self-provisioning, while lower-income populations are significantly more likely to reluctantly engage in self-provisioning.

Unravelling the more detailed reasons for participating in self-provisioning, 40 per cent of such activity was conducted for reasons associated with economic necessity, although this rose to 60 per cent in the lowest-income households studied. Although this explanation, as might be expected, is significantly more relevant in lower-income populations, it does not explain all self-provisioning. Another reason is what can be termed 'market failure', namely the shortage of tradespeople, including plumbers, plasterers and so forth. Although the problem of trust has been raised when examining outsourcing (de Ruijter and Weesie 2007), the shortage of reliable tradespeople has not been before raised as an additional barrier and explanation for self-provisioning. In this survey, however, 14 per cent of self-provisioning was primarily undertaken because of the problems associated with finding a tradesperson and getting them to turn up, and a further 10 per cent due to problems with the quality of tradespersons and associated issues related to trust. Hence, one-quarter (24 per cent) of self-provisioning is a direct product of market failure.

For those portraying every aspect of personal and domestic life as operating according to market rationality, participation in self-provisioning is similarly a rational economic calculation pursued to maximise profits or save money (Brodersen 2003). However, only 12 per cent of self-provisioning was conducted for this reason. This displays that self-provisioning is not always embedded in market-like, profit-motivated, rational economic calculations. Muscovites do not view their home and labour purely as a commodity (cf. Hochschild 2003). In recent years, previous economic theorisations of consumption have been increasingly replaced by a 'cultural turn' that puts greater emphasis on agency. The notion that self-provisioning is conducted primarily out of choice, such as due to the pleasure gained from the process, however, is found to apply to around 8 per cent of self-provisioning, and such an explanation is more prevalent among higher income quartiles. Similarly, when evaluating the post-modern argument that self-provisioning is conducted by willing participants seeking to individualise the end-product for reasons associated with their self-identity, the finding is that one in six instances of self-provisioning (16 per cent) are motivated by such an objective, and this is especially the case among higher-income households where over one-third is conducted for this rationale. However, to assert that such a rationale is more widely applicable would be to impute a rationale popular among higher-income groups onto the wider population.

The role of the dacha in household economies

Having examined the self-provisioning that takes place within Russian and Ukrainian households, we here turn our attention to look at the role of the dacha, a plot of land outside of the urban area, in the household economy. The dacha is a plot of rural land that normally has some form of accommodation on it, ranging from the most basic 'hut' to the multi-million dollar homes of the newly rich. Typically, time is spent on the dacha during weekends during the spring and then for an extended period over the summer, although there is a growing tendency for richer families to build properties that can be lived in all year round. During the Soviet period, land was given to households by the state, usually via their employer. Thus, there are regions of land where mainly military personnel or workers from a certain ministry, for example, have their dachas (see Lovell 2003, for an excellent historical overview). In the Soviet period, when overseas travel was not available, for the majority the dacha was a holiday from the city and a place where food was grown to bypass shortages.

The role of the dacha during the post-Soviet period has gained much academic attention. The majority of these studies have explored the economic reasoning behind the domestic production of food and which income groups were undertaking this self-provisioning practice (see, for example, Clarke 2002; Southworth 2006; Wegren 2004). Seeth *et al.* (1998) and Clarke (2002) were dismissive of the importance of domestically grown food to the incomes of poorer households, while Southworth (2006) argued that as production had increased during times of economic crisis, it must have some importance. However, as Round (2006), Pallot and Moran (2000) and Pickup and White (2003) argue, reducing domestic food production to economic rationality overlooks the multitude of ways in which the outputs are utilised in everyday life.

Across the household surveys conducted in Ukraine and Moscow, 26 per cent of respondents stated that they have access to land where food is grown for their consumption and 24 per cent have land where no food is grown, where the dacha is used mainly as a site of relaxation, an 'escape from the city'. However, the relationships of this latter group to food grown in the region reveal much about post-Soviet informal practices. When interviewing households who have land but do not grow food, many discussed how they obtain food from the surrounding area. This could be bought from street markets, exchanged with neighbours, given freely from family and friends who do grow food and/or foraged from common land. As an interviewee in Kyiv recalled:

> We get our meat from the village [where their dacha is located]. Everyone has relatives in the village who can get products. You cannot trust the meat that is sold in shops so we get it from relatives who work on the farms as it is 'home grown' [and] therefore of good quality.

Many interviewees also picked berries from common land, which are often taken back to the city and stored for the winter. For many, though, the dacha is a site of relaxation and recuperation from the city and its stresses:

> I would die without my dacha. I am too old to grow food there as the soil is of a poor quality and requires a lot of work which I now cannot do. So I spend my time just relaxing. Growing flowers and talking to my friends who also spend the summer there is how I spend my days. The air is so good

> here I feel healthier the moment I arrive. It allows me to regain my health and when I leave in September I feel prepared for the coming winter months.

While this is an extreme example, numerous interviewees discussed how they are so exhausted from their multiple informal practices, they do not know how they would cope without the relaxation the dacha provides. Turning to the findings of the survey in relation to the importance of domestically grown food to the household, the results in both Ukraine and Moscow contradict the assertions of those who dismiss its role as a provider of food. Among those with land, 74 per cent stated that the produce was either 'very important' or 'important' to their diet. However, only 20 per cent said that they would be unable to buy the food if they did not grow it. Consequently, the rationales must be analysed further. For the majority, the food they grow has a substitutive role in the household, by which is here meant that they could afford the good they grow but by growing it themselves they can spend the money on other items. As a construction worker says about his growing of food:

> We don't buy fruits and vegetables as we have all this in our vegetable garden. We grow things all year round and in the summer we preserve what we grow to help us through the winter. Our garden is very important in our life and family budget as we have children so there is always something we need to buy for them. If we had to spend all our money on food we would really struggle.

It is common among interviewees to grow food that is expensive to buy but which requires little effort, such as berries. Such products would be unobtainable otherwise for families living on or near the subsistence minimum. As opposed to Clarke (2002), the surveys in both Ukraine and Moscow showed that the importance of domestic production was linked to household income. Using the respondent definition of a realistic subsistence figure, it was found that 82 per cent living below this figure said that their domestic food production was important to the household, compared to 50 per cent with incomes above this level. The food-growing process is also important to them. The outputs are seen as 'organic' and interviewees discussed with great pride the fact that they were able to produce their own food:

> What we are eating here we just picked an hour or so ago. It is fresh and it is healthy as we know there are no chemicals on it. It tastes much better and we know it is the result of our hard work.

With so much uncertainty surrounding one's position in the formal labour market (see Chapter 5), regaining some sense of control over everyday life is of valuable importance to many of those interviewed (see also Caldwell 2011 for further discussion on the importance of the food's organic nature). As the example at the very beginning of this book highlighted, some households sell some of the food they produce. This practice was observed more among senior citizens, having few other economic opportunities open to them. For some households, this practice is of great importance, as the following woman in Kyiv discussed:

> My husband is disabled and I cannot work as I need to look after him. Our only formal income is his benefit payment, therefore the income we can get from selling what we grow on our land is of vital importance to our lives. We try and save as much as we can over the summer as it is impossible to stand on the streets to sell things when it reaches minus thirty in the winter!

Although the daily income from selling such produce is often relatively low, given that pensions are so small, it still makes an important contribution to the household budget. As an interviewee from Uzhgorod states:

> I work twelve hours per day from late April to late September to earn enough to survive the winter. I start working on my land before the snow melts; something like in April. Then I dig and plant radish, dill, and onion. Usually they are the first things I sell on the market. In a good month I can earn more than my pension. I have no idea how I will live when I am not able to dig or to carry my goods to the market.

As such quotes display, the domestic growing of food by this group for sale is not an alternative economic practice, a resistance to capitalism or a return to a pre-modern era of self-provisioning, but one borne out of marginalisation and in many cases out of desperation. The process is labour intensive and although they gain pride in their ability to survive, it often comes at a cost to their health. As discussed in Chapter 6, such practices are seen by the state as an attempt to cheat it out of tax revenues. This group would argue that it is the actions of the state (i.e. low pensions, poor healthcare services and the need to pay bribes) that forces them into such endeavours. For the elderly the food grown by relatives is also of great importance. The vast majority of interviewees discussed how they received a considerable amount of their fresh food from relatives with dachas. This enables them to spend their meagre pensions on other essential products. The dacha, therefore, despite some who have espoused the contrary, reflecting the lives of rich Russians and Ukrainians, remains for many an important resource in their livelihood practices without which they would be suffering far more than is currently the case.

Conclusions

Until now, few studies have evaluated either the contrasting views on the prevalence of self-provisioning or the rival explanations for participation in such endeavours in post-Soviet societies. Analysing the pervasiveness and importance of self-provisioning, this chapter has found little support for the 'modernisation' perspective which portrays this endeavour as a residue or leftover from a previous era persisting in just a few minor enclaves of the modern economy. Not only is self-provisioning a ubiquitous practice which a significant minority of households in both Ukraine and Moscow rely heavily on to secure their livelihood, but the vast majority of everyday tasks in households are conducted on a self-servicing basis. The clear implication is that everyday life in Ukraine and Moscow is more a 'do-it-yourself' rather than a 'do it for me' culture. Some households, moreover, do more on a self-provisioning basis than others. Indeed, the lowest-income households conduct more on a self-provisioning basis than the highest-income households. This, however, is not because self-provisioning is purely a product of economic necessity.

Economic necessity is more common as an explanation in lower-income households, but cannot be relied on exclusively to explain all self-provisioning. A fuller and more comprehensive explanation for self-provisioning requires a move beyond this simplistic explanation. As has been here revealed, some self-provisioning is conducted on a 'willing' basis by those who engage in such endeavours either as a rational economic calculation, for pleasure or to seek self-identity from the end-product, while other self-provisioning is conducted on a 'reluctant' basis by those forced into such endeavour either for economic reasons or due to problems with finding and using tradespeople. The finding is that although reluctant self-provisioning is more likely among lower-income populations, in higher-income populations people are markedly more likely to be willing participants.

In sum, this chapter has revealed that self-provisioning in these post-Soviet economies is not some minor residue left over from a previous era as the modernisation perspective asserts. Instead, it is a persistent, important and pervasive feature of the economic landscape in the post-Soviet world. With this in mind, we now turn our attention to drawing some conclusions about the role of informal economies in the post-Soviet world.

10 Conclusions

Introduction

The aim of this book has been to contest the belief that there is an inevitable, inescapable and irreversible shift towards a formal market economy in post-Soviet societies by re-evaluating the role of informal economies in this region of the world. In this chapter we synthesise the findings from the previous chapters to reach some conclusions on the role of informal economies in post-Soviet societies. To do this, and following the structure of the book, first, we review the theoretical and conceptual framework we have advocated for rethinking the role of informal economies in the post-Soviet world and, second, display how using this as a lens enables one to more fully understand not only that households draw upon a plurality of economic practices to secure their livelihood in post-Soviet spaces, but also how the nature, role and meaning of these diverse work practices vary across different population groups.

(Re)theorising transition economies

In order to understand the role that informal economic practices play in securing a livelihood and getting by in post-Soviet spaces, Part I of this book outlined a theoretical and conceptual framework for rethinking this issue. In Chapter 2 we revisited the recurring question of transition in order to dispute not only the past hegemony of the command economy system, but also the notion that there is a universal linear trajectory of development in post-Soviet spaces towards a hegemonic ideal-type formal market economy system as some end-point. Instead, we called for a more nuanced argument to be adopted that allows it to be recognised how there has been a transformation of post-Soviet economies in varying ways from different starting points and along different economic development trajectories.

Chapter 3 then turned its attention to contesting the myth that the advent of a hegemonic formal market economy is an inevitable and natural process and that no other options exist regarding the trajectory of economic development. On the issue of the inevitability of a formal market economy, this chapter made it very clear that a future where the formal market economy becomes hegemonic is not cast in stone. Indeed, to assert that the formal market economy is unavoidable is to fly in the face of the empirical evidence on the trajectories of post-Soviet economies. On the issue of whether the advent of a formal market economy is a natural process, meanwhile, this chapter revealed that the formal market economy is not an autonomous sector that grows with little or no help. Rather, it is argued to have been energetically facilitated and sustained by a barrage of intervention. Taking this into account, it has been asserted that one has to consider quite how widely and deeply the formal market economy would have permeated the post-Soviet world without such massive intervention and encouragement. If the formal market economy has only captured such a minor share of all economic activity even when governments have so actively intervened to encourage its growth, then one does wonder quite how expansive the formal market realm would have been if left to its own devices. Given this continuous and ongoing nurturing and support by government, it is thus obvious that the formal market economy is not an organic process. Once recognised, then the future trajectory of economic development becomes more open. Seeking to develop the formal market economy through controlled interventionism and paying little heed to the development of work beyond the formal market economy becomes clearly recognised as but one option available regarding the trajectory of economic development.

The outcome has been a rethinking of the 'economic' and an opening up of economic development as an 'undefined, open-ended, heterogeneous transformative process' (Chowdhury 2007: 10). Rather than view post-Soviet spaces as lagging behind the west by reducing difference to backwardness, this chapter opened up the future to other possibilities beyond a totalising formal market economy. Our project, therefore, has been to deconstruct the familiar notion of economic development as a transition to a formal market economy by revealing that formal market economic practices are just one of a plurality of economic practices in post-Soviet spaces, thereby decentring the formal market economy and recovering alternative futures for economic development so as to disrupt dominant economic discourses about the future of post-Soviet economies as being towards a totalising formal market economy. However, our intention has not been to replace one universal conceptualisation of the trajectory of economic development with another alternative universal.

Instead, we have argued that not only is the informal and non-market economy persistent and even growing in many post-Soviet spaces (negating the formalisation and marketisation theses), but also that the role they play in contemporary post-Soviet spaces is not always the same and that it varies according to both the type of informal work being considered and the population groups and places being evaluated. Reviewing the competing theoretical perspectives on the role of informal economies in contemporary economies, Chapter 3 concluded by raising the possibility that some forms of informal work might be a by-product of the changes in the formal market economy in some places and among some populations groups, while other forms of informal work will act as complements and yet others as alternatives to the formal market economy.

To move beyond an understanding of the economic and economy which is centred on the impending hegemony of a formal market economy and to gain greater understanding of the role that informal economies continue to play in people's livelihood practices, chapter 4 adopted a 'whole economy' perspective and constructed an analytical lens for understanding the multiple labour practices which exist in contemporary economies. Transcending the simplistic formal/informal economy dichotomy, and developing the 'total social organisation of labour' conceptual framework proposed by Glucksmann (2005), this conceptualised a spectrum from formal-oriented to informal-oriented labour practices, which is cross-cut by another spectrum ranging from wholly monetised to wholly non-monetised labour practices.

The resultant outcome is to capture the plurality of labour practices that exist in post-Soviet societies in a manner which shows how they all seamlessly merge into each other.

Having developed this analytical lens for understanding the 'diverse economies' of the post-Soviet world, Chapter 4 then used this to provide an overarching understanding of the multifarious labour practices used in Ukraine and Russia. Analysing the results of 600 interviews conducted across various populations in Ukraine and 313 interviews conducted in Moscow, this revealed the shallow permeation of the formal market economies in Ukraine and Russia that have been supposedly undergoing a 'transition' to formal market economies. It also revealed the existence of diverse work cultures across different populations, along with marked socio-spatial variations in the nature of individual labour practices. To begin to develop a deeper understanding of these socio-spatial variations in individual labour practices, Part II then evaluated the various labour practices that are used to secure a livelihood in post-Soviet societies.

The lived experiences of transition

To begin to develop a deeper understanding of the role that informal economic activities play in securing a livelihood in post-Soviet societies, as well as the socio-spatial variations, each form of informal economic activity has been evaluated in turn. Displaying the need to transcend the formal/informal economy dichotomy, Chapter 5 examined the role played by formal employment in securing a livelihood, and more precisely how in post-Soviet societies the formal economy is so infused with informality that it is difficult, if not impossible, to differentiate formal and informal labour practices. Chapter 6 then evaluated the role played by informal employment, Chapter 7 the roles played by paid favours, reimbursed family work and one-to-one unpaid labour, Chapter 8 formal unpaid employment and informal unpaid employment and Chapter 9 self-provisioning. The intention in doing so has been to display the prevalence of these forms of labour in everyday livelihood practices in post-Soviet societies in order to show, on the one hand, how the transition to a hegemonic formal market economy is far from achieved, and on the other hand, the prominent role of informal economic activities in everyday livelihood practices in the post-Soviet world.

In Chapter 5 it was revealed that despite all of the hyperbole about the hegemony of the formal market economy, just 59.2 per cent of the working-age population is employed in the formal economy. This means that four in every ten people of working age in the post-Soviet world do not participate in the formal economy. Even this, however, is an exaggeration of the reach of formalisation in post-Soviet societies. Many of those who are in formal employment are in jobs infused with informality. Some one in eight formal employees receive an envelope wage and this on average amounts to 38 per cent of their wage packet. The result is that even if 59 per cent of the working-age population is engaged in formal employment, one in eight of these occupy quasi-formal jobs. This not only blurs the divide between formal and informal jobs, but also means that the proportion in purely formal employment is even lower than previously assumed. This, however is not the only way in which the formal economy is infused with informality. As the case studies of kindergartens, schools, the university system, entry into the graduate labour market and healthcare provision revealed, the formal economy in post-Soviet societies remains riddled with crime, informality and corruption. In doing so, this chapter revealed that it is impossible to view the formal and informal economies as separate and discrete spheres. Informality is an inherent feature of the formal economy in post-Soviet societies.

Chapter 6 then turned its attention to the role played by informal employment and showed that it is not some small residue that is steadily disappearing from view in post-Soviet economies. As Schneider (2012) reveals, its magnitude is equivalent to 32.6 per cent of GDP across post-Soviet economies, and although it has declined slightly over the last few years relative to the formal economy, it remains a sizeable feature across all post-Soviet societies. Indeed, examining the results of the surveys conducted in Ukraine and Moscow, informal employment was found to play a central role in the livelihood practices of a large proportion of households. Indeed, some 40 per cent of Ukrainian households cite informal employment as either the principal or secondary contributor to their living standard and 43 per cent in Moscow. Examining their reasons for engaging in informal employment, moreover, in Ukraine 30 per cent of informal employment is explained purely in terms of exclusion from the formal economy, 35 per cent purely to avoid the costs, time and effort of formal registration and in preference to formal employment, and 13 per cent purely for social and/or redistributive reasons, with the remaining 22 per cent a mix of these rationales. Similar levels of reliance on informal employment and diversity in the rationales among those engaged in informal employment was identified in Moscow.

Despite this heavy reliance on informal employment in both countries and similar rationales being expressed for engaging in this work, the configuration of informal employment differs markedly across the two countries. The finding is that in Moscow 78 per cent is informal self-employment and 22 per cent is waged informal employment. In Ukraine, in contrast, 38 per cent is informal self-employment and 62 per cent waged informal employment. Yet despite this, the rationales for engagement in each type of informal employment and by each population group are markedly similar in both countries. Voluntarism, and therefore the neo-liberal and post-structuralist theorisations, is more commonly cited by those engaged in informal self-employment and those living in higher-income households, rural and affluent localities. Exclusion from the formal economy, meanwhile, is more commonly cited among those engaged in waged informal employment and among low-income households, and those living in urban and deprived areas.

It is important to be aware, however, that even if some types of explanation are more common for some types of informal employment than others, there remains tremendous diversity in the rationales for participating in each type of informal employment among different population groups. In other words, there is a rich tapestry of both types of informal employment and reasons for engaging in them in these post-Soviet societies that cannot be neatly captured by promulgating universal hues. Just as one would not draw universal generalisations about formal waged employment and formal self-employment when evaluating its nature or the reasons for engaging in such work, it is similarly erroneous to do so when considering the informal labour market in post-Soviet societies.

Chapter 7 then turned its attention to the prevalence and nature of three forms of one-to-one exchange in post-Soviet societies, namely one-to-one unpaid labour, reimbursed family work and paid favours. This revealed that in both Ukraine and Moscow unpaid one-to-one labour is more prevalent among lower-income populations, where it is more likely to be conducted for and by kin, not least because they lack the financial purchasing power to use money or gifts, and/or physical wellbeing to reciprocate with in-kind labour, so engage in such exchange out of necessity. Higher-income populations, in contrast, use one-to-one monetised exchange more to expand their social networks and consolidate relationships and do so more out of choice. Deprived populations therefore use this when no other options are open to them, in order to 'get by', whereas for affluent populations it is conducted more as a matter of choice, in order to 'get on'.

The chapter then examined the nature of a form of labour that has been seldom discussed in post-Soviet societies or beyond, namely paid family labour whereby a household member reimburses another household member for work conducted. This reimbursement can be in the form of money, but also in the form of gifts or the in-kind reciprocal exchange of labour. The overarching finding was that reimbursed family labour constitutes a small but significant livelihood practice in post-Soviet spaces. Mostly involving inter-generational exchanges between a parent and child, such a labour practice is most common in more affluent populations. In lower-income populations where such a labour practice is less frequent, when it does occur, it more commonly involves gifts and/or in-kind reciprocity rather than monetary exchange. The notion that the existence of such a labour practice marks the advent of a marketisation of the domestic realm, however, does not appear to be valid. Examining the rationales underpinning such exchanges, there is little notion that the participants in such practices view themselves as engaged in market-like profit-motivated exchanges. Broader social and redistributive rationales, such as the desire to impart an understanding of the meaning of money, were found to be more to the fore in terms of the participants' motives than profit-motivated rationales, and nor did they perceive these exchanges as akin to market-oriented exchanges conducted for the purpose of profit.

Turning to paid favours, Chapter 7 then revealed in both Ukraine and Moscow the existence of a continuum of forms of paid favours from those closer to informal self-employment conducted for profit-motivated rationales through to those more akin to mutual aid in terms of the social relations and motives involved. Those closer to profit-motivated informal self-employment are conducted mostly for more distant acquaintances, and are also more prevalent among higher-income populations, while those where the profit motive is largely absent, are redistributive and social rationales prevail are undertaken largely for closer social relations and are more prevalent in lower-income populations.

Chapter 8 then transcended the widespread assumption that when one engages in formal employment, it is always paid labour. Reviewing the persistence and even growth of unpaid internships in the private, public and third sectors of the economy, which many people now undertake in order to gain work experience and improve their employability, as well as the existence of trials on an unpaid basis so that employers can judge the suitability of an applicant for a post, as well as the growth of formal volunteering in the third sector, this revealed that formal unpaid labour certainly exists in the private and public sectors. In these sectors, young people, in order to gain much needed work experience and often to get a 'foot in the door', often undertake it. In the private sector, though, there is evidence that employers potentially use this method as a means of employing 'free' labour so as to reduce labour costs and hence increase a firm's profitability. Moreover, there is also evidence of formal unpaid labour occurring when employers (in both the private and public sectors) fail to pay employees' full wages. While this problem has considerably improved since the chaotic days of the 1990s, where wage arrears were a major problem, the problem still exists and one which has seemingly been exacerbated in the aftermath of the global financial crisis. Regarding unpaid labour in the third sector, this certainly exists but importantly is rarely used to meet the material needs not met by other fields of provision, such as the formal market economy. Individuals engage in community-based associations to fulfil their own needs rather than to deliver material support to others. As such, if the intention in Ukraine and Russia is to encourage the development of civil society in order to meet material needs not met by the formal private and public sectors, or even other forms of informal delivery, then developing participation in community-based groups is inappropriate. This chapter then addressed a labour practice that has seldom been analysed in post-Soviet societies, namely informal unpaid employment, which is where somebody is employed by an organisation on an unpaid basis, but the employer or employee does not adhere to all the rules and regulations required. This revealed that such work often prevails because employers and workers engaged in unpaid employment do not realise that the legal responsibilities that apply to paid employment are also applicable to unpaid employment, such as indemnity insurance, or health and safety legislation.

Chapter 9 then addressed the practice of self-provisioning, often assumed to be a leftover from a previous mode of accumulation, and that the small vestiges that remain will eventually disappear as the formal market economy became ever more dominant (e.g. Smuts 1971; Watts 2001). This reveals the extensiveness of self-provisioning in post-Soviet societies and how it is possible to differentiate between 'willing' (rational economic actors, choice, identity seeking) and 'reluctant' (economic and market necessity, dupes) participants in self-provisioning. Not only is self-provisioning a ubiquitous practice which a significant minority of households in both Ukraine and Moscow rely heavily on to secure their livelihood, but the vast majority of everyday tasks in households are conducted on a self-servicing basis. The clear implication is that everyday life in Ukraine and Moscow is more a 'do-it-yourself' rather than a 'do it for me' culture. Some households, moreover, do more on a self-provisioning basis than others. Indeed, the lowest-income households conduct more on a self-provisioning basis than the highest-income households. This, however, is not because it is purely a product of economic necessity.

Economic necessity is more common as an explanation in lower-income households, but cannot be relied on exclusively to explain all self-provisioning. A fuller and more comprehensive explanation for self-provisioning requires a move beyond this simplistic explanation. As has been here revealed, some self-provisioning is conducted on a 'willing' basis by those who engage in such endeavour either as a rational economic calculation, for pleasure, or to seek self-identity from the end-product, while other self-provisioning is conducted on a 'reluctant' basis by those forced into such endeavour either for economic reasons or due to problems with finding and using tradespeople. The finding is that although reluctant self-provisioning is more likely among lower-income populations, in higher-income populations people are markedly more likely to be willing participants. Overall, however, self-provisioning in these post-Soviet economies is a persistent, important and pervasive feature of the economic landscape in the post-Soviet world. With this in mind, we now turn our attention to drawing some conclusions about the role of informal economies in the post-Soviet world.

The role of informal economies in the post-Soviet world

Since the demise of the socialist bloc, the recurring belief has been that post-Soviet societies are in transition to capitalism. Indeed, Kostera (1995) has likened the intervention and investment to facilitate this advent of capitalism to a religious crusade, with management educators and consultants acting like missionaries spreading the cult of what Parker (2002) calls 'market managerialism'. However, this book has revealed that in post-Soviet societies a plurality of labour practices are pursued. One important finding is the relatively shallow penetration of the formal market economy although the depth to which it has permeated everyday life varies socio-spatially. Another finding is that work cultures also vary. Those living in affluent populations adopt more formal and monetised work cultures, while those in lower-income populations are more reliant on community exchanges between closer social relations, both of the monetised and non-monetised variety, as well as self-provisioning (see Figure 10.1).

The character of each labour practice also varies socio-spatially. On the whole, affluent populations engage in a greater range of labour practices, and do so out of choice, while deprived populations employ a narrower range of practices which they engage in more out of necessity in the absence of alternatives. The outcome is that uneven development in Moscow and Ukraine is not characterised by affluent populations being more formalised and monetised. Rather, uneven development is characterised by a polarisation between 'work busy' populations engaging in a wide array of labour practices and doing so more commonly out of choice, and 'work deprived' populations engaging in a narrower range of labour practices which they do more commonly out of necessity. Depending on the types of informal work and populations studied, different representations of the informal economy are appropriate. When considering the limited number of households pursuing subsistence modes of production, for example, and how very few households remain untouched by the formal economy, the residue perspective appears valid. Indeed, this is further reinforced by subsistence households, especially in the deprived rural area of Ukraine, who assert that their numbers are dwindling as the young leave the countryside and move to the towns in search of formal employment.

When considering other types of informal work, however, it is the representation of the informal economy as a by-product of a new emergent form of capitalism that is using informal working arrangements to compete and off-loading onto the informal sector those no longer of use to it which is valid. Support for this comes not only when examining forms of informal waged employment such as 'envelope wages' and sweatshop-like work, as well as routine self-provisioning, but also when wider trends are recognised such as that participation in the informal economy is much greater among lower-income populations. Yet to depict all of the informal economy in this manner is a misnomer.

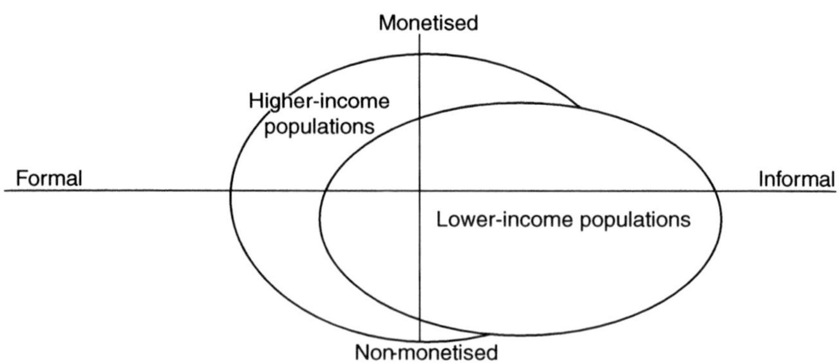

Figure 10.1 Configuration of labour practices in post-Soviet spaces: by gross formal income of household.

As the evidence in support of the representation of the informal economy as a complement to the formal economy clearly displays, informal work, at least in some of its varieties, is often not a sphere inhabited purely by the marginalised, but rather, is a realm which reinforces, rather than reduces, the socio-spatial disparities in the formal economy. This is exemplified in the realm of do-it-yourself activity, for example, as well as the sphere of paid favours. There are also types of informal work that are a chosen alternative to the formal economy. Not only is there a culture of resistance to immersion in the formal economy, at least among some engaged in subsistence production as their primary work strategy, but the extensive 'hidden enterprise culture' of off-the-books enterprise and entrepreneurship being pursued as a widespread resistance practice to the (in their eyes) over-excessive regulation and state corruption, provides solid support for the depiction of informal work as a chosen alternative.

The result is that although varying discourses are appropriate as representations of different types of informal work, no one articulation fully captures the diverse nature and multiple meanings of the informal economy in Ukraine and Moscow. However, if we transcend the view that these are competing discourses and recognise that each is a depiction of particular types of informal work, as Chen (2006) most prominently has suggested, then it becomes quickly obvious that by incorporating all of them a finer-grained and more comprehensive understanding of the complex and diverse meanings of the informal economy can be achieved.

How, therefore, might these articulations be coupled together to reach this more holistic understanding? At first glance, this appears unachievable. On the one hand, in the representations of the informal economy as a residue and an alternative, the formal and informal economies are viewed as discrete and separate, while in the discourses of the informal economy as a complement to, and by-product of, the formal economy, they are viewed as inextricably inter-related. Indeed, much of the contemporary literature that views formal and informal work as entangled vehemently opposes any notion of separateness (e.g. Smith 2004; Smith and Stenning 2006).

In lived practice, however, some forms of informal work are relatively entangled in the formal economy and others relatively separate. 'Envelope wages', where formal employees are paid a portion of their wages on a cash-in-hand basis, for example, provide solid support for the depiction of formal and informal work as inextricably inter-related. Yet this intimate entanglement of formal and informal work is not apparent when examining most forms of self-provisioning. There is a case to be made, therefore, for recognising a spectrum of informal work ranging from varieties that are relatively separate from the formal sphere to those that are relatively intertwined with the formal economy (e.g. 'envelope wages'). On the other hand, while the residue and by-product perspectives universally attribute the informal economy with exclusion or necessity, the complementary and alternative approaches do the inverse and view such practices to result from a desire to exit the formal realm or choice. However, it is again wholly feasible to conceptualise a continuum of types of informal work ranging from those where choice is more likely to prevail (e.g. paid favours, unpaid community exchange, informal entrepreneurship) to those where exclusion is more prevalent (e.g. exploitative 'sweatshop'-like informal waged employment).

These discourses, therefore, do not need to be seen as rival and contradictory representations of the informal economy. Instead, they can each be read as valid depictions of particular types of informal work which need to be integrated together to achieve a finer-grained and fuller understanding of the diverse nature of the informal economy. Indeed, this is now starting to be recognised (e.g. Chen 2006). How they can be joined together to provide a more holistic understanding, nevertheless, has not been so far discussed. Here, a first attempt is made to do so. Figure 10.2 provides a graphic representation of how this might be accomplished. The four contrasting discourses are here used to depict particular types of informal work that exist on, first, a spectrum that ranges from forms of informal work that are relatively separate from the formal economy to types that are heavily embedded in the formal economy, and second, a spectrum

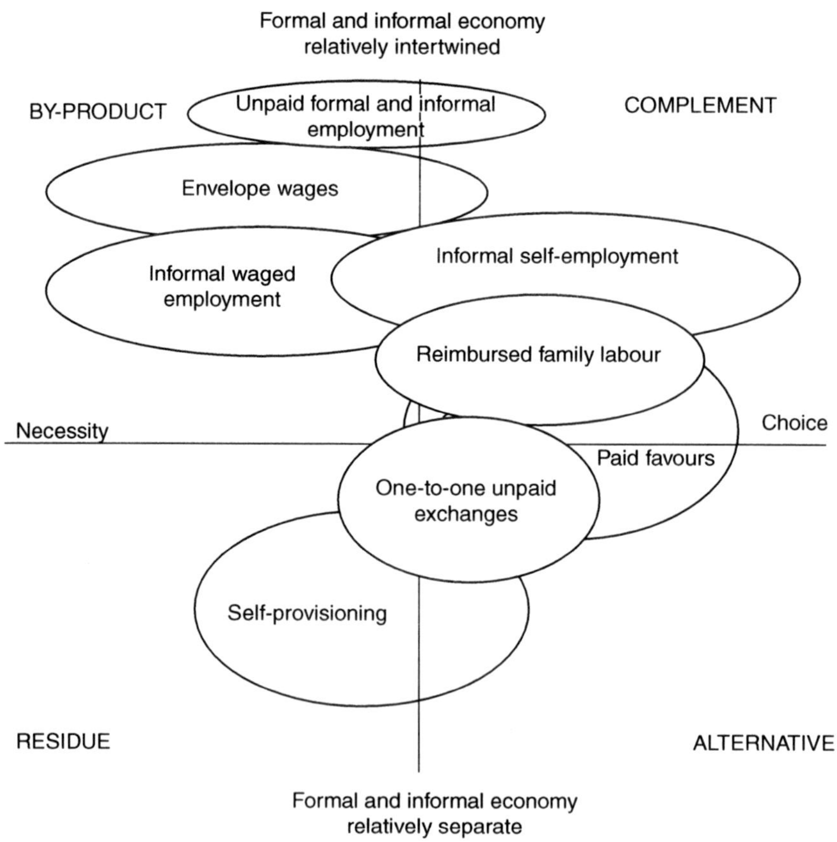

Figure 10.2 Representations of informal economic activities in post-Soviet societies.

of the reasons for engagement from pure exclusion at one end to pure exit at the other.

If adopted when analysing the informal economy, this integrative conceptual framework that facilitates an understanding of the multifarious nature of labour practices would have important impacts on how we think about informal work. First, adopting such a conceptual framework would enable the persistent debates between rival discourses that contest each others' viewpoint despite them talking about different forms of informal work (e.g. neo-liberals on informal self-employment and post-Fordists on informal waged employment) to be transcended. It might also begin to put a stop to the all-too-common occurrence whereby discourses simply focus upon those forms of informal work conforming to their depiction of informal work while ignoring those that do not. As Samers (2005) has highlighted, for instance, post-development theorists viewing informal work as a chosen alternative seem to display a myopic disregard for forms of informal work that do not conform to their depiction, such as low-waged sweatshop-like informal employment. This, however, is not unique to these commentators. It applies across the spectrum of discourses.

Second, adopting this more integrative conceptual framework might also start to result in more nuanced policy approaches towards informal work. At present, a largely negative approach predominates, reflecting the dominance of the residue and by-product perspectives. This is particularly the case when considering what needs to be done about undeclared work where the dominant approach is to eradicate such work by increasing the probability of detection and the penalties if caught (Williams 2004a, 2006b). It is similarly the case when considering other forms of informal work. Few, if any, governments move beyond an employment-centred discourse when discussing economic development. If the above conceptual framework were adopted, however, then this would help identify those forms of informal work that need to be eradicated and those that need to be either transformed into formal employment or tacitly condoned rather than adopting a 'one size fits all' public policy approach which treats all types the same.

Third, and perhaps most importantly, this more holistic framework might also help the long-standing but simplistic arguments about whether formalisation or informalisation is the path to progress to be finally transcended. Rather than an 'on–off' decision about whether formalisation or informalisation is the way forward for economic development, more nuanced and finer-grained debates about the nature and direction of urban and regional economic development could perhaps start to emerge that pursue a more 'pick and mix' approach so far as various types of informal (and formal) work are concerned.

In sum, this book finds that the representation of market hegemony has prevented the recognition, valuing and even developing of other (and 'othered') labour practices beyond the formal market economy. In this book an alternative theoretical framework and analytical lens for capturing and ordering these multiple labour practices has been developed which portrays labour practices more fluidly, showing how they are not separate discrete practices but are seamlessly entwined and conjoined. This has enabled a rethinking of labour relations and the lived practice of economic transition in post-Soviet societies. If it is now applied more widely to understanding the multiplicity of labour practices in not only the post-socialist world but also so-called advanced western economies and the majority (third world), then this book will have achieved its principal intention. If this then begins to stimulate deliberation of the feasibility of, and possibilities for, alternative futures beyond market hegemony, then it will have achieved all of its objectives.

Bibliography

Aarva, P., Ilchenko, I., Gorobets, P. and Rogacheva, A. (2009) 'Formal and informal payments in health care facilities in two Russian cities, Tyumen and Lipetsk', *Health Policy and Planning*, 24, 5: 395–405.

Abbot, P. and Wallace, C. (2009) 'Patterns of participation in the formal and informal economies in the Commonwealth of Independent States', *International Journal of Sociology*, 39, 2: 12–38.

Acker, J. (2006) *Class Questions: Feminist Answers*, Lanham, MD: Rowman & Littlefield.

Agranovich, M. (2008) Podstava na ekzamene: kazhdyj vtoroj rossiyanin ubezhden, chto postupit' v vuz mozhno tol'ko s pomoshch'yu vzyatki, [Impersonators on the test: every second Russian is certain that the only way to enter a university is through bribes], *Rossiyskaya gazeta*, 4736, (www.rg.ru/2008/08/26/kantorovich.html, accessed 9 June 2010).

Ahmad, A. (2008) 'Dead men working: time and space in London's ("illegal") migrant economy', *Work, Employment and Society*, 22, 2: 301–318.

Ahmed, M. (2012) *Financial Support for Arab Countries in Transition* (http://blog-imfdirect.imf.org/2012/08/07/financial-support-for-arab-countries-in-transition, accessed 20 November 2012).

Albert, M. (1993) *Capitalism Against Capitalism*, London: Whurr.

Alden, J. (1982) 'A comparative analysis of moonlighting in Great Britain and the USA', *Industrial Relations Journal*, 13, 1: 21–31.

Alexeev, Michael. (1986) 'Factors influencing distribution of housing in the USSR', Duke University, Durham NC, Department of Economics.

Alexeev, M. and Pyle, W. (2003) 'A note on measuring the unofficial economy in the former Soviet Republics', *Economics of Transition*, 11, 1: 1–23.

Amin, A., Cameron, A. and Hudson, R. (2002) *Placing the Social Economy*, London: Routledge.

Anderson, B. (2000) *Doing the Dirty Work? The Global Politics of Domestic Labour*, London: Zed Books.

Anderson, G. and Boettke, P. (1997) 'Soviet venality: a rent-seeking model of the communist state', *Public Choice*, 93: 37–53.

Anderson, J. and Gray, C. (2006) *Anticorruption in Transition 3: Who is Succeeding and Why?*, World Bank (http://siteresources.worldbank.org/INTECA/Resources/ACT3.pdf, accessed 9 June 2010).

Apel, M. (1994) *An Expenditure-based Estimate of Tax Evasion in Sweden*, RSV Tax Reform Evaluation Report No. 1.

Aristei, D. and Perugini, C. (2012) 'Inequality and reforms in transition countries', *Economic Systems*, 36: 2–10.

Arnsberg, K.-L. and Borén, T. (eds) (2003) *Everyday Economy in Russia, Poland and Latvia*, Stockholm: Almqvist and Wiksell International.

Ashwin, S. (1998) 'Endless patience: explaining Soviet and post-Soviet social stability', *Communist and Post-Communist Studies*, 31, 2: 187–198.

Ashwin, S. (1999) *Russian Workers: The Anatomy of Patience*, Manchester: Manchester University Press.

Ashwin, Sarah and Clarke, S. (2003) *Russian Trade Unions and Industrial Relations in Transition*, New York: Palgrave Macmillan.

Åslund, A. (1995) *How Russia Became a Market Economy*, Washington, DC: Brookings Institution.

Åslund, A. (2002) *Building Capitalism: The Transformation of the Former Soviet Bloc*, Cambridge: Cambridge University Press.

Åslund, A. (2007) *Russia's Capitalist Revolution: Why Market Reform Succeeded and Democracy Failed*, Washington, DC: Peterson Institute for International Economics.

Åslund, Anders (2011) 'Revisiting the end of the Soviet Union', *Problems of Post-Communism*, 58, 4: 46–55.

Atkins, F.J. (1999) 'Macroeconomic time series and the monetary aggregates approach to estimating the underground economy', *Applied Economics Letters*, 6, 9: 609–611.

Bajada, C. (2002) *Australia's Cash Economy: A Troubling Issue for Policymakers*, Aldershot: Ashgate.

Bajada, C. and Schneider, F. (2003) *The Size and Development of the Shadow Economies in the Asia Pacific*, University of Linz Department of Economics discussion paper.

Bartlett, B. (1998) *The Underground Economy*, National Center for Policy Analysis, (http//:www.ncpa.org/ba/ba273.html, accessed 9 June 2010).

Bartlett, B. (1990) 'The underground economy: Achilles' heel of the state?' *Economic Affairs*, 10, 5: 24–26.

Basharina, E.N. (2008) 'Vliyaniye gosudarstvennovo regulirovaniya na razvitiye instituta korporativnoi sotsialnoi otvestvennosti', Gosudarstvennoye Upravleniye. *Elekronnyii Vestnik, Vipusk*, 14, (http://e-journal.spa.msu.ru/images/File/2008/14/Basharina.pdf, accessed 9 June 2010).

Bayat, A. (2007) 'Radical religion and the habitus of the dispossessed: does Islamic militancy have an urban ecology?' *International Journal of Urban and Regional Research*, 31, 3: 579–590.

Becker, K. (2004) *The Informal Economy*, Stockholm: Swedish International Development Agency.

Beissinger, M. (2002) *Nationalist Mobilization and the Collapse of the Soviet State*, Cambridge: Cambridge University Press.

Bender, D. (2004) *Sweated Work, Weak Bodies: Anti-Sweatshop Campaigns and Languages of Labor*, New Brunswick, NJ: Rutgers University Press.

Bennholdt-Thomsen, V. (2001) 'What really keeps our cities alive, money or subsistence?', in V. Bennholdt-Thomsen., N. Faraclas. and von C. Werlhof (eds), *There is an Alternative: Subsistence and Worldwide Resistance to Corporate Globalization*, London: Zed.

Berardi, L. (2001) 'Globalization and poverty in Chile', *Discourse and Society*, 12, 1: 47–58.

Berger, S. and Dore, R. (eds) (1996) *National Diversity and Global Capitalism*, Ithaca, NY: Cornell University Press.

Berliner, J. (1978) *The Innovation Decision in Soviet Industry*, Cambridge, MA: MIT Press.

Beveridge, W. (1948) *Voluntary Action: A Report on Methods of Social Advance*, London: George, Allen and Unwin.

Bittman, M., Matheson, G. and Meagher, G. (1999) 'The changing boundary between home and market: Australian trends in outsourcing domestic labour', *Work, Employment and Society*, 13, 2: 249–273.

Bloch, J. and Parry, M. (1989) *Money and the Morality of Exchange*, Cambridge: Cambridge University Press.

Block, S. (2002) 'Political business cycles, democratization, and economic reform: the case of Africa', *Journal of Development Economics*, 67: 205–228.

Boeke, J.H. (1942) *Economies and Economic Policy in Dual Societies*, Haarlem: Tjeenk Willnik.

Bogdanov, K. (2012) 'The queue as narrative: a Soviet case study', in A. Baiburin, C. Kelly and N. Vakhtin (eds), *Russian Cultural Anthropology After the Collapse of Communism*, London: Routledge.

Boren, T. (2003) 'What are friends for? Rationales of informal exchange in Russian everyday life', in K. Arnstberg and T. Boren (eds), *Everyday Economy in Russia, Poland and Latvia*, Stockholm: Almqvist and Wiksell International.

Boswell, J. (1990) *Community and the Economy*, London: Routledge.

Bradley, H. (2007) *Gender*, Cambridge: Polity.

Braverman, H. (1971) *Labour and Monopoly Capital*, New York: Monthly Review Press.

Broadman, H. (1998) *Russian Enterprise Reform: Policies to Further the Transition*, Washington, DC: World Bank.

Brodersen, S. (2003) *Do-it-yourself Work in North-Western Europe: Maintenance and Improvement of Homes*, Copenhagen: Rockwool Foundation.

Brooke, C. (2006) *Moscow: A Cultural History*, Oxford: Oxford University Press.

Brown, D. and Kulcsar, L. (2001) 'Household economic behaviour in post-socialist rural Hungary', *Rural Sociology*, 66: 157–180.

Brown, G., Kraftl, P., Pickerill, J. and Upton, C. (2012) 'Holding the future together: towards a theorisation of the spaces and times of transition', *Environment and Planning A*, 44, 7: 1607–1623.

Bruck, T. and Lehmann, H. (2012) 'Economic and social consequences of industrial restructuring in Russia and Ukraine: an introduction', in T. Brück and H. Lehmann (eds), *In the Grip of Transition: Economic and Social Consequences of Restructuring in Russia and Ukraine*, London: Palgrave Macmillan.

Bruff, I. and Horn, L. (2012) 'Varieties of capitalism in crisis?' *Competition and Change*, 16, 3: 161–168.

Buck-Morss, S. (1989) *The Dialectics of Seeing: Walter Benjamin and the Arcades Project*, Cambridge, MA: MIT Press.

Buckner, L. and Yeandle, S. (2007) *Valuing Carers: Calculating the Value of Unpaid Care*, London: Carers UK.

Budlender, D. (ed.) (2010) *Time Use Studies and Unpaid Care Work*, New York and Oxford: Routledge/UNRISD.

Burau, V. (2012) 'Transforming health policy and services: Challenges for comparative research', *Current Sociology*, 60, 4: 569–578.

Burawoy, M. (1996) 'The state and economic involution: Russia through a China lens', *World Development*, 24, 6: 1105–1117.

Burawoy, M. (1998) 'The extended case method', *Sociological Theory*, 16, 1: 4–33.

Burawoy, M. (2001) 'Transition without transformation: Russia's involutionary road to capitalism', *East European Politics and Societies*, 15, 2: 269–290.
Burawoy, Michael (2006) 'A public sociology for human rights', in J. Blau and K. Lyall Smith (eds), Public Sociologies Reader, Lanham, MD: Rowman & Littlefield.
Burawoy, M. and Verdery, K. (1999) *Uncertain Transitions*, Lanham, MD: Rowman and Littlefield Publishers.
Burawoy, M., Krotov, P. and Lykina, T. (2000) 'Involution and destitution in capitalist Russia', *Ethnography*, 1,1: 43–65.
Burki, S. and Perry, G. (1998) *Beyond the Washington Consensus: Institutions Matter*, Washington, DC: World Bank.
Burova, N. and Ozmidova, E. (2012) 'Questions of business ethics in Russian higher education', *Center for Entrepreneurship, E-Bulletin*, 15 (www.cfe.ru/en/resource_center/bulletin/issue1791/1789.htm, accessed 24 October 24 2012).
Burrell, K. (2011) 'Opportunity and uncertainty: young people's narratives of "double transition" in post-socialist Poland', *Area*, 43, 4: 413–419.
Butler, J. (1990) *Gender Trouble: Feminism and the Subversion of Identity*, London: Routledge.
Byrne, K., Forest, R., Gibson-Graham, J.K., Healy, S. and Horvath, G. (2001) *Imagining and Enacting Non-capitalist Futures*, Rethinking Economy Project Working Paper no. 1 (http//:www.arts.monash.edu.au/projects/cep/knowledges/byrne.html, accessed 15 June 2010).
Caldwell, M. (2004) *Not by Bread Alone: Social Support in the New Russia*, Berkeley, CA: University of California Press.
Caldwell, M. (2011) *Dacha Idylls, Living Organically in Russia's Countryside*, Berkeley, CA: University of California Press.
Campbell, C. (2005) 'The craft consumer: culture, craft and consumption in a postmodern society', *Journal of Consumer Culture*, 5, 1: 23–42.
Caridi, P. and Passerini, P. (2001) 'The underground economy, the demand for currency approach and the analysis of discrepancies: some recent European experience', *The Review of Income and Wealth*, 47, 2: 239–250.
Carothers, T. (2002) 'The end of the transition paradigm', *Journal of Democracy*, 13, 1: 5–21.
Carrier, J.G. (1998) 'Introduction', in J.G. Carrier and D. Miller (eds), *Virtualism: A New Political Economy*, Oxford: Berg.
Carrier, J. and Miller, D. (1998) *Virtualism: A New Political Economy*, Oxford: Berg.
Carroll, Toby (2010) *Delusions of Development: The World Bank and the Post-Washington Consensus in Southeast Asia*, New York: Palgrave Macmillan.
Carruthers, B. and Babb, S. (2000) *Economy/Society: Markets, Meanings and Social Structure*, Thousand Oaks, CA: Pine Forge Press.
Carter, M. (1984) 'Issues in the hidden economy: a survey', *Economic Record*, 60, 170: 209–221.
Castells, M. and Portes, A. (1989) 'World underneath: the origins, dynamics and effects of the informal economy', in A. Portes, M. Castells and L.A. Benton (eds), *The Informal Economy: Studies in Advanced and Less Developing Countries*, Baltimore, MD: John Hopkins University Press.
Castree, N., Coe, N., Ware, K. and Samers, M. (2004) *Spaces of Work: Global Capitalism and the Geographies of Labor*, London: Sage.
Chakrabarty, D. (2000) *Provincializing Europe: Postcolonial Thought and Historical Difference*, Princeton, NJ: Princeton University Press.

Charmes, J. (2009) 'Concepts, measurement and trends', in J.P. Jutting and J.R. Laiglesia (eds), *Is Informal Normal? Towards More and Better Jobs in Developing Countries*, Paris: OECD.

Chatterjee, S., Chaudhury, K. and Schneider, F. (2002) *The Size and Development of the Indian Shadow Economy and a Comparison with 18 Asian countries: An Empirical Investigation*, University of Linz Department of Economics Discussion Paper.

Chen, M. (2006) 'Rethinking the informal economy: linkages with the formal economy and the formal regulatory environment', in B. Guha-Khasnobis, R. Kanbur and E. Ostrom (eds), *Linking the Formal and Informal Economy: Concepts and Policies*, Oxford: Oxford University Press.

Cherneyshev, I. (2006) *Socio-economic Activity and Decent Work in Ukraine: A Comparative view and Statistical Findings*, Working Paper no. 76, ILO.

Chernova, Z. (2012) 'New pronatalism? Family policy in post-Soviet Russia', *REGION: Regional Studies of Russia, Eastern Europe, and Central Asia*, 1, 1: 75–92.

Chowdury, S. (2007). *Everyday Economic Practices: The 'Hidden Transcripts' of Egyptian Voices*, London: Routledge.

Christiansen, T., Petito, F. and Tonra, B. (2000) 'Fuzzy politics around fuzzy borders: the European Union's near abroad', *Cooperation and Conflict*, 35, 4: 389–415.

Ciscel, D. and Heath, J. (2001) 'To market, to market: imperial capitalism's destruction of social capital and the family', *Review of Radical Political Economics*, 33: 401–414.

Clarke, S. (2002) *Making Ends Meet in Contemporary Russia: Secondary Employment, Subsidiary Agriculture and Social Networks*, Cheltenham: Edward Elgar.

Coates, D. (2002) *Models of Capitalism: Debating Strengths and Weaknesses*, Cheltenham: Edward Elgar.

Cocco, M.R. and Santos, E. (1984) 'A economia subterranea: contributos para a sua analisee quanticacao no caso Portugues', *Buletin Trimestral do Banco de Portugal*, 6, 1: 5–15.

Colton, T. (1986) *The Dilemma of Reform in the Soviet Union*, Washington, DC: Council on Foreign Relations.

Comelieau, C. (2002) *The Impasse of Modernity*, London: Zed Books.

Community Economies Collective (2001) 'Imagining and enacting noncapitalist futures', *Socialist Review*, 28: 93–135.

Cook, L.J. and Vinogradova, E. (2006) 'NGO's and policy making in Russia's regions', *Problems of Post-Communism*, 53, 28–41.

Cox, R. (2006) *The Servant Problem: Domestic Employment in a Global Economy*, London: I.B. Tauris.

Cooper, N. and May, C. (2012) 'The informal economy and dignified work', in S. Bolton (ed.), *Dimensions of Dignity at Work*, London: Routledge.

Cornuel, D. and Duriez, B. (1985) 'Local exchange and state intervention', in N. Redclift and E. Mingione (eds), *Beyond Employment: Household, Gender and Subsistence*, Oxford: Basil Blackwell.

Cowling, K. and Tomlinson, P. (2011) 'Post the "Washington Consensus": economic governance and industrial strategies for the twenty-first century', *Cambridge Journal of Economics*, 35: 831–852.

Cremin, C. (2012) 'The Social logic of late capitalism: guilt fetishism and the culture of crisis industry', *Cultural Sociology*, 6, 1: 45–60.

Crewe, L. (2000) 'Geographies of retailing and consumption', *Progress in Human Geography*, 24, 2: 275–290.

Crisp, B. and Kelly, M. (1999) 'The socio-economic impacts of structural adjustment', *International Studies Quarterly*, 43, 3: 533–552.

Crnkovic-Pozaic, S. (1999) 'Measuring employment in the unofficial economy by using labor market data', in E.L. Feige and K. Ott (eds), *Underground Economies in Transition: Unrecorded Activity, Tax Evasion, Corruption and Organized Crime*, Aldershot: Ashgate.

Crompton, R. (2006) *Employment and the Family: The Reconfiguration of Work and Family Life in Contemporary Societies*, Cambridge: Cambridge University Press.

Crompton, R. and Lyonette, C. (2006) 'Work–life balance in Europe', *Acta Sociologica*, 49, 4: 379–393.

Cross, J. (2000) 'Street vendors, modernity and postmodernity: conflict and compromise in the global economy', *International Journal of Sociology and Social Policy*, 20, 1: 29–51.

Cross, J. and Morales, A. (2007) 'Introduction: locating street markets in the modern/postmodern world', in J. Cross and A. Morales (eds), *Street Entrepreneurs: People, Place and Politics in Local and Global Perspective*, London: Routledge.

Crotty, J. (2003) 'Managing civil society: democratisation and the environmental movement in a Russian region', *Communist and Post-Communist Studies*, 36, 4: 489–508.

Crotty, J. (2006) 'Reshaping the hourglass? The environmental movement and civil society development in the Russian Federation', *Organization Studies*, 27, 9: 1319–1338.

Crotty, J. and Rodgers, P. (2012) 'Sustainable development in the Russia Federation: the limits of greening within industrial firms', *Corporate Social Responsibility and Environmental Management*, 19, 3: 178–190.

Crouch, C. (2012) 'Sustainability, neoliberalism, and the moral quality of capitalism', *Business and Professional Ethics Journal*, 31, 2: 363–374.

Crouch, C. and Streek. W. (1997) *L'avenir du Capitalisme Diversifié*, Paris: La Découverte.

Dafflon, D. (2009) *Youth in Russia: The Portrait of a Generation in Transition*, Biel: Swiss Academy for Development.

Davidson, M. and Leather, P. (2000) 'Choice or necessity? A review of the role of DIY in tackling housing repair and maintenance', *Construction Management and Economics*, 18, 5: 747–756.

Davies, R.W. (2001) 'Making economic policy' (www.uh.edu/~pgregory/4davies.doc, accessed 4 March 2013).

Davis, C. (2001) 'Country survey XVI: the defence sector in the economy of a declining superpower: Soviet Union and Russia, 1965–2001', *Defense and Peace Economics*, 13, 3: 145–177.

Davis, M. (2006) *Planet of Slums*, London: Verso.

De Certeau, M. (1988) *The Practice of Everyday Life: Living and Cooking Vol. 2*, Minneapolis , MN: University of Minnesota Press.

Del Boca, D. and Forte, F. (1982) 'Recent empirical surveys and theoretical interpretations of the parallel economy', in V. Tanzi (ed.), *The Underground Economy in the United States and Abroad*, Lexington, MA: Lexington Books.

Demidova, O. and Signorelli, M. (2012) 'Determinants of youth unemployment in Russian regions', *Post-Communist Economies*, 24, 2: 191–217.

Derrida, J. (1967) *Of Grammatology*, Baltimore, MD: Johns Hopkins University Press.

De Ruijter, E. and Weesie, J. (2007) 'Working your way in: trust problems and social embeddedness affect the behaviour of home maintenance suppliers', *Rationality and Society*, 19, 1: 35–64.

De Soto, H. (1989) *The Other Path*, London: Harper and Row.

De Soto, H. (2001) *The Mystery of Capital: Why Capitalism Triumphs in the West and Fails Everywhere Else*, London: Black Swan.

Dicken, P. (2003) *Global Shift*, 4th edition, London: Sage.

Dickson-Swift, V., James, E., Kippen, S. and Liamputtong, P. (2007) 'Doing sensitive research: what challenges do qualitative researchers face?' *Qualitative Research*, 2, 7: 327–353.

Dilnot, A. and Morris, C.N. (1981) 'What do we know about the black economy?', *Fiscal Studies*, 2, 1: 58–73.

Dixon, A. (2011) 'Variegated capitalism and the geography of finance: towards a common agenda', *Progress in Human Geography*, 35, 2: 193–210.

Dzvinka, R. (2002) 'How does the unofficial economy interact with the official one?' Economics Education and Research Consortium MA thesis, National University of Kyiv-Mohyla Academy.

EBRD. (2011) *Transition Report 2011: Crisis and Transition – The People's Perspective*, London: European Bank for Reconstruction and Development.

EBRD. (2012) *Transition Report 2012: Integration Across Borders*, London: European Bank for Reconstruction and Development.

Eikenberry, A. (2009) 'Refusing the market a democratic discourse for voluntary and nonprofit organizations', *Nonprofit and Voluntary Sector Quarterly*, 38, 4: 582–596.

Elkin, T. and McLaren, D. (1991) *Reviving the City: Towards Sustainable Urban Development*, London: Friends of the Earth.

Escobar, A. (1995) *Encountering Development: The Making and Unmaking of the Third World*, Princeton, NJ: Princeton University Press.

Escobar, A. (2001) 'Culture sits in places: reflections of globalism and subaltern strategies of localization', *Political Geography*, 20: 139–174.

Espenshade, J. (2004) *Monitoring Sweatshops: Workers, Consumers and the Global Apparel Industry*, Philadelphia, PA: Temple University Press.

Essers, C. (2009) 'Reflections on the narrative approach: dilemmas of power, emotions and social location while constructing life-stories', *Organization*, 16, 2: 163–181.

Esteva, G. (1985) '"Beware of participation" and "Development: metaphor, myth, threat"', *Development: Seeds of Change*, 3: 77–79.

European Commission. (1998) *Communication of the Commission on Undeclared Work* (http://europa.eu.int/comm/employment_social/empl_esf/docs/com98-219_en.pdf, accessed 12 April 2007).

European Commission. (2007) *Stepping up the Fight Against Undeclared Work*, Brussels: European Commission.

European Commission (2011) *Employment and Social Developments in Europe 2011*, Brussels: European Commission.

Eurostat. (2007) *Taxation Trends in the European Union: Data for the EU Member States and Norway*, Brussels: Eurostat.

Eurostat. (2011) *Taxation Trends in the European Union: Main Results*, Brussels: Eurostat.

Evans, A.B. (2006) 'Valdimir Putin's design for civil society', in A.B. Evans, L.A. Henry. and L.M. Sundstrom (eds), *Russian Civil Society: A Critical Assessment*, Armonk, NY: M.E. Sharpe.

Feige, E.L. (1979) 'How big is the irregular economy?', *Challenge*, November/December: 5–13.

Feige, E.L. (1990) 'Defining and estimating underground and informal economies', *World Development*, 18, 7: 989–1002.

Feige, E.L. (1999) 'Underground economies in transition: non-compliance and institutional change', in E.L. Feige and K. Ott (eds), *Underground Economies in Transition: Unrecorded Activity, Tax Evasion, Corruption and Organized Crime*, Aldershot: Ashgate.

Feige, E.L. and Ott, K. (eds) (1999) *Underground Economies in Transition: Unrecorded Activity, Tax Evasion, Corruption and Organized Crime*, Aldershot: Ashgate.

Feige, E.L. and Urban, I. (2008) 'Measuring underground (unobserved, non-observed, unrecorded) economies in transition countries: can we trust GDP?' *Journal of Comparative Economics*, 36: 287–306.

Fernandez-Kelly, P. (2006) 'Introduction', in P. Fernandez-Kelly and J. Shefner (eds), *Out of the Shadows: Political Action and the Informal Economy in Latin America*, University Park, PA: Pennsylvania State University Press.

Field, G. (2012) *Working Hard, Working Poor: A Global Journey*, New York: Oxford University Press.

Fine, B. and Milonakis, D. (2011) '"Useless but true": economic crisis and the peculiarities of economic science', *Historical Materialism*, 19, 2: 3–31.

Fish, S. (1991) 'The emergence of independent associations and the transformation of Russian political society', *Journal of Communist Studies*, 7: 299–334.

Fitoussi, J.-P. and Saraceno, F. (2012) *European Economic Governance: The Berlin–Washington Consensus*, Paris: OFCE working paper.

Flavin, P., Pacek, A.C. and Radcliff, B. (2011) 'State intervention and subjective well-being in advanced industrial democracies', *Politics and Policy*, 39: 251–269.

Fotaki, M. (2009) 'Informal payments: a side effect of transition or a mechanism for sustaining the illusion of "free" health care? The experience of four regions in the Russian Federation', *Journal of Social Policy*, 38, 4: 649–670.

Foucault, M. (1981) 'The order of discourse: inaugural lecture at the College de France, given 2 December 1970', in R. Young (ed.), *Untyping the Text: A Poststructuralist Reader*, London: Routledge and Kegan Paul.

Foucault, M. (1977) *Discipline and Punish: The Birth of the Prison*, London: Penguin.

Freeland, C. (2000) *Sale of the Century: The Inside Story of the Second Russian Revolution*, London: Little, Brown.

Freud, D. (1979) 'A guide to underground economics', *Financial Times*, 9 April, 16.

Friedman, E., Johnson, S., Kaufmann, D. and Zoido-Lobaton, P. (2000) 'Dodging the grabbing hand: the determinants of unofficial activity in 69 countries', *Journal of Public Economics*, 76: 459–493.

Frye, T. (2011) 'Belarus and its implications for the study of transition economies: an introduction', *Eurasian Geography and Economics*, 52, 6: 747–749.

Fukuyama, F. (1992) *The End of History and the Last Man*, New York: Free Press.

Gabrisch, H. and Hölscher, J. (2006) *The Successes and Failures of Economic Transition*, London: Palgrave Macmillan.

Gaddy, C. and Ickes, B. (1998) 'Russia's virtual economy', *Foreign Affairs*, 77, 5: 53–67.

Gaetz, S. and O'Grady, B. (2002) 'Making money: exploring the economy of young homeless workers', *Work, Employment and Society*, 16: 433–456.

Gallin, D. (2001) 'Propositions on trade unions and informal employment in time of globalization', *Antipode*, 19, 4: 531–549.

Geertz, C. (1963) *Old Societies and New States: The Quest for Modernity in Asia and Africa*, Glencoe, IL: Free Press.

Gerber, T. and Mayorova, O. (2010) 'Getting personal: Networks and stratification in the Russian labor market, 1985–2001', *American Journal of Sociology*, 116, 3: 855–908.

Gershuny, J. (2000) *Changing Times: Work and Leisure in Post-industrial Society*, Oxford: Oxford University Press.

Gershuny, J. and Jones, S. (1987) 'The changing work/leisure balance in Britain 1961–84', *Sociological Review*, 33, 1: 9–50.

Gershuny, J., Godwin, M. and Jones, S. (1994) 'The domestic labour revolution: a process of lagged adaptation?', in M. Anderson, F. Bechhofer and J. Gershuny (eds), *The Social and Political Economy of the Household*, Oxford: Oxford University Press.

Gerxhani, K. (2004) 'The informal sector in developed and less developed countries: a literature survey', *Public Choice*, 120, 2: 267–300.

Ghezzi, S. (2010) 'The fallacy of the formal and informal divide: lessons from a post-Fordist regional economy', in E. Marcelli, C.C. Williams and P. Joassart (eds), *Informal Work in Developed Nations*, London: Routledge.

Ghodsee, K. (2011) *Lost in Transition: Ethnographies of Everyday Life After Communism*, Durham, NC: Duke University Press.

Gibson-Graham, J.K. (1996) *The End of Capitalism (as we knew it)? A Feminist Critique of Political Economy*, Oxford: Blackwell.

Gibson-Graham, J.K. (2003) 'Poststructural interventions', in T. Sheppard and A. Barnes (eds), *Companion to Economic Geography*, Oxford: Blackwell.

Gibson-Graham, J.K. (2006) *Post-Capitalist Politics*, Minnesota, MN: University of Minnesota Press.

Giddens, A. (1998) *The Third Way: The Renewal of Social Democracy*, Cambridge: Polity.

Giles, D. (1999a) 'Measuring the hidden economy: implications for econometric modelling', *The Economic Journal*, 109, 456: 370–380.

Giles, D. (1999b) *Modelling the Hidden Economy in the Tax Gap in New Zealand*, Victoria: University of Victoria.

Giles, D. and Tedds, L. (2002) *Taxes and the Canadian Underground Economy*, Canadian Tax Paper No. 106, Canadian Tax Foundation.

Gilman, M. (2010) *No Precedent, No Plan: Inside RUSSIA'S 1998 Default*. Cambridge, MA: MIT Press.

Gimpelson, V. (2009) 'Strasti po bezrabotitsa (Horror of unemployment)', *Vedomost'*, 18 March.

Gimpelson, V., Kapeliushnikov, R. and Lukiyanova, A. (2010) 'Stuck between surplus and shortage: demand for skills in Russian industry', *Labour*, 24, 3: 311–332.

Glucksmann, M. (1995) 'Why work? Gender and the total social organisation of labour', *Gender, Work and Organisation*, 2, 2: 63–75.

Glucksmann, M. (2000) *Cottons and Casuals: The Gendered Organisation of Labour in Time and Space*, Durham: Sociology Press.

Glucksmann, M. (2005) 'Shifting boundaries and interconnections: extending the "total social organisation of labour"', *The Sociological Review*, 53, 2: 19–36.

Glucksmann, M. (2009) 'Formations, connections and divisions of labour', *Sociology*, 43: 878–895.

Godfrey, P. (2011) 'Toward a theory of the informal economy', *The Academy of Management Annals*, 5,1: 231–277.

Goldschmidt-Clermont, L. (1982) *Unpaid Work in the Household: A Review of Economic Evaluation Methods*, Geneva: International Labour Office.

Goldschmidt-Clermont, L. (1998) *Measuring and Valuing non-SNA Activities: Handbook of National Accounting, Household Accounting – Experiences in the Use of Concepts and Their Compilation – Household Satellite Extensions*, New York: United Nations.

Goldschmidt-Clermont, L. (2000) *Household Production and Income: Some Preliminary Issues*, Geneva: International Labour Office.
Golubchikov, O. and Phelps, N. (2011) 'The political economy of place at the post-socialist urban periphery: governing growth on the edge of Moscow', *Transactions of the Institute of British Geographers*, 36, 3: 425–440.
Gough, I. (2000) *Global Capital, Human Needs and Social Policies*, Basingstoke: Palgrave.
Gradskova, Y. (2010) 'Should I send my child to kindergarten, and should i pay the teacher? Parenting, gender, and preschool educational institutions in internet forums', *Laboratorium: Russian Review of Social Research*, 3: 178–183.
Graham, L. (1993) *The Ghost of the Executed Engineer: Technology and the Fall of the Soviet Union*, Cambridge, MA: Harvard University Press.
Granovetter, M. (1973) 'The strength of weak ties', *American Journal of Sociology*, 78, 6: 1360–1380.
Granovetter, M. (1983) 'The strength of weak ties: a network theory revisited', *Sociological Theory*, 1, 1: 201–233.
Gregory, A. and Windebank, J. (2000) *Women and Work in France and Britain: Theory, Practice and Policy*, Basingstoke: Macmillan.
Gregory, C. (1982) *Gifts and Commodities*, London: Academic Press.
Gregory, Paul R. (1987) 'Productivity, slack, and time theft in the Soviet economy', in J.R. Millar, *Politics, Work, and Daily Life in the USSR: A Survey of Former Soviet Citizens*, Cambridge: Cambridge University Press, pp. 241–75.
Gregory, P. and Stuart, R. (1994) *Soviet and Post-Soviet Economic Structure and Performance*, New York: HarperCollins.
Grishina, K. and Korchinsky, V. (2006) 'Kak postupit v VUZ, ne davaya na "lapu"? [How to enter a HEI without paying a bribe]', *Segodnya*, July 17, (www.osvita.org.ua/articles/123.html, accessed 23 May 2009).
Gros, D. and Steinherr, A. (1995) *Winds of Change: Economic Transition in Central and Eastern Europe*, London: Longman.
Grossman, G. (1977) 'The second economy studies in comparative in the USSR', *Problems of Communism*, 16, 5: 25–40.
Guariglia, A. and Kim, B.Y. (2006) 'The dynamics of moonlighting in Russia', *Economics of Transition*, 14, 1: 1–45.
Gudeman, S. (2001) *The Anthropology of Economy*, Oxford: Blackwell.
Günther, I. and Launov, A. (2012) 'Informal employment in developing countries: opportunity or last resort?', *Journal of Development Economics*, 97, 1: 88–98.
Gupta, A. (1998) *Postcolonial Development: Agriculture in the Making of Modern India*, Durham, NC: Duke University Press.
Güven, A. (2012) 'The IMF, the World Bank, and the global economic crisis: exploring paradigm continuity', *Development and Change*, 43, 4: 869–898.
Hann, C. (2006) *Not the Horse We Wanted!: Postsocialism, Neoliberalism and Eurasia*, Munster: Lit Verlag.
Hanson, M. (2006) *Transition in Ukraine*, NATO Parliamentary Assembly, report number 065, Escew 06 E.
Hanson, P. (2003) 'The Russian economic recovery: do four years of growth tell us that the fundamentals have changed?', *Europe-Asia Studies*, 55: 365–382.
Hanson, P. and Teague, E. (2007) 'Russian political capitalism and its environment', in D. Lane (ed.), *Varieties of Capitalism in Post-Communist Countries*, London: Palgrave Macmillan.

Hansson, I. (1982) 'The underground economy in Sweden', in V. Tanzi (ed.), *The Underground Economy in the United States and Abroad*, Lexington, MA: Lexington Books.

Hapke, L. (2004) *Sweatshop: The History of an American Idea*, New Brunswick, NJ: Rutgers University Press.

Harrison, M. (2002) 'Coercion, compliance, and the collapse of the Soviet command economy', *Economic History Review*, 3: 397–433.

Harvey, David (1982) *The Limits to Capitalism*, Oxford: Blackwell.

Harvey, David (1989) *The Conditions of Postmodernity: An Enquiry into the Origins of Cultural Change*, Oxford: Blackwell.

Harvey, D. (2000) *Spaces of Hope*, Edinburgh: Edinburgh University Press.

Harvey, D. (2011). *The Enigma of Capital: and the Crises of Capitalism*, London: Profile Books.

Hazans, M. (2005) 'Latvia: working too hard?', in D. Vaughan-Whitehead (ed.), *Working and Employment Conditions in the new EU Member States: Convergence or Diversity?*, Geneva: ILO-EU.

Hellberger, C. and Schwarze, J. (1986) *Umfang und struktur der nebenerwerbstatigkeit in der Bundesrepublik Deutschland*, Berlin: Mitteilungen aus der Arbeits-market- und Berufsforschung.

Henderson, S.L. (2008) 'Shaping civic advocacy: international and domestic policies towards Russia's NGO sector' (http://evans.washington.edu/files/HendersonAdvocacy-Chapter.pdf, accessed 12 August 2010).

Henry, J. (1976) 'Calling in the big bills', *Washington Monthly*, 5: 6.

Heyneman, S. (2007) 'Three universities in Georgia, Kazakhstan and Kyrgyzstan: the struggle against corruption and for social cohesion', *Prospects: Quarterly Review of Comparative Education*, 37, 3: 305–318.

Heyneman, S. (2010) 'A comment on the changes in higher education in the former Soviet Union', *European Education: Issues and Studies*, 42, 1: 76–87.

Heyneman, S., Anderson, K. and Nuraliyeva, N. (2008) 'The cost of corruption in higher education', *Comparative Education Review*, 52, 1: 1–26.

Howard, M.M. (2002) 'Post-communist civil society in comparative perspective', *Demokratizatsiya*, 10: 285–306.

Hickel, J. and Khan, A. (2012) 'The culture of capitalism and the crisis of critique', *Anthropological Quarterly*, 85, 1: 203–227.

Hochschild, A.R. (2003) *The Commercialization of Intimate Life: Notes from Home and Work*, Berkeley, CA: University of California Press.

Hoffman, D. (2011) *The Oligarchs: Wealth and Power in the New Russia*, New York: Public Affairs.

Hollander, M.J., Liu, G. and Chappell, N.L. (2009) 'Who cares and how much? The imputed economic contribution to the Canadian healthcare system of middle-aged and older unpaid caregivers providing care to the elderly', *Healthcare Quarterly*, 12, 2: 42–49.

Hollingsworth, R. and Boyer, R. (eds) (1997) *Contemporary Capitalism*, Cambridge: Cambridge University Press.

Holmes, L. (2008) 'Corruption and organised crime in Putin's Russia', *Europe–Asia Studies*, 60, 6: 1011–1031.

Howard, M.M. (2002) 'Post-communist civil society in comparative perspective', *Demokratizatsiya*, 10: 285–306.

Hudson, R. (2005) *Economic Geographies: Circuits, Flows and Spaces*, London: Sage.

Humphrey, C. (2002) *The Unmaking of Soviet Life. Everyday Economies After Socialism*, New York: Cornell University Press.

ILO (2002a) *Decent Work and the Informal Economy*, Geneva: International Labor Office.
ILO (2002b) *Women and Men in the Informal Economy: A Statistical Picture*, Geneva: International Labour Office.
ILO (2012) *Global Employment Trends 2012: Preventing a Deeper Jobs Crisis*, Geneva: International Labour Office.
ILO (n.d) *Key Indicators of the Labour Market* (KILM) (http://kilm.ilo.org/kilmnet, accessed 15 August 2010).
Isachsen, A.J., Klovland, J.T. and Strom, S. (1982) 'The hidden economy in Norway', in V. Tanzi (ed.), *The Underground Economy in the United States and Abroad*, Lexington, KY: D.C. Heath.
Jensen, C. (2011) 'Marketization via compensation: health care and the politics of the right in advanced industrialized nations', *British Journal of Political Science*, 41, 4: 907–926.
Jessop, B. (2010) 'From hegemony to crisis? The continuing ecological dominance of neo-liberalism', in K. Birch and V. Mykhnenko (eds), *The Rise and Fall of Neo-liberalism*, London: Zed Books.
Jessop, B. (2011) 'Imagined recoveries, recovered imaginaries: a cultural political economy perspective', *Economy and Society*, forthcoming.
Jessop, B. (2012) 'The world market, variegated capitalism, and the crisis of European integration', in P. Nousios, H. Overbeek and A. Tsolakis (eds), *Globalisation and European Integration: Critical Approaches to Regional Order and International Relations*, London: Routledge.
Juster, F. and Stafford, F. (1991) 'The allocation of time: empirical findings, behavioral models and problems of measurement', *Journal of Economic Literature*, 29: 471–522.
Jutting, J.P. and Laiglesia, J.R. (2009) 'Employment, poverty reduction and development: what's new?', in J.P. Jutting. and J.R. Laiglesia (eds), *Is Informal Normal? Towards More and Better Jobs in Developing Countries*, Paris: OECD.
Kapelyushnikov, R., Kuznetsov, A. and Kuznetsova, O. (2011) 'Diversity within capitalism: the Russian labour market model', *Employee Relations*, 33, 4: 395–412.
Kapelyushnikov, R., Kuznetsov, A. and Kuznetsova, O. (2012) 'The role of the informal sector, flexible working time and pay in the Russian labour market model', *Post-Communist Economies*, 24, 2: 177–190.
Karakhanyan, S., Van Veen, K. and Bergen, T. (2011) 'Educational policy diffusion and transfer: the case of Armenia', *Higher Education Policy*, 24: 53–83.
Karpuskiene, V. (2007) 'Undeclared work, tax evasion and avoidance in Lithuania', Paper presented at colloquium of the Belgian Federal Service for Social Security on Undeclared Work, Tax Evasion and Avoidance, Brussels, June.
Katsimi, M. and Moutos, T. (2010) 'EMU and the Greek crisis: the political-economy perspective', *European Journal of Political Economy*, 26, 4: 568–576.
Kaufmann, D. and Kaliberda, A. (1996) 'Integrating the unofficial economy into the dynamics of post-socialist economies: a framework for analyses and evidence', in B. Kaminski (ed.), *Economic Transition in Russia and the New States of Eurasia*, London: M.E. Sharpe.
Kharkhordin, O. (1998) 'First Europe–Asia lecture: civil society and Orthodox Christianity', *Europe–Asia Studies*, 50: 949–968.
Kiblitskaya, M. (2000) 'Once we were kings: male experiences of loss and status at work in post-Communist Russia', in S. Ashwin (ed.), *Gender, State, and Society in Soviet and Post-Soviet Russia*, New York: Routledge.

Kim, B.-Y. (2002) 'The participation of Russian households in the informal economy: evidence from the VTsIOM survey', *Economics of Transition*, 10: 689–717.

Kim, B.-Y. (2003) 'Informal economy activities of Soviet households: size and dynamics', *Journal of Comparative Economics*, 31: 532–551.

Kiseleva, L. (2004) 'Otdaite nam to, chto my zarabotali' *Argumenty i facty. Dolgozhitel*, 13.

Kitchin, R. and Tate, N. (2001) *Conducting Research in Human Geography: Theory, Practice and Methodology*, London: Prentice-Hall.

Klimova, A. and Ross, R. (2012) 'Gender-based occupational segregation in Russia: an empirical study', *International Journal of Social Economics*, 39, 7: 474–489.

Klugman, J. and Braithwaite, J. (1998) *Poverty in Russia During the Transition: An Overview*, Washington, DC: World Bank Research Observer.

Koen, V. and Phillips, S. (1992) *Price Liberalization in Russia: Behavior of Prices, Household Incomes, and Consumption During the First Year*, Washington, DC: International Monetary Fund.

Koleva, P., Rodet-Kroichvili, N., David, P., Marasova, J. (2010) 'Is corporate social responsibility the privilege of developed market economies? Some evidence from Central and Eastern Europe', *The International Journal of Human Resource Management*, 21, 2: 274–293.

Kolodko, G. (1999) 'Transition to a market economy and sustained growth: implications for the post-Washington Consensus', *Communist and Post-Communist Studies*, 32, 3: 233–261.

Kolot, A. (2012) *Social Responsibility: Development of Theory and Practice*, Kyiv: KNEU.

Kostera, M. (1995) 'The modern crusade: the missionaries of management come to eastern Europe', *Management Learning*, 26: 331–352.

Krantz-Kent, R. (2009) 'Measuring time spent in unpaid household work: results from the American Time Use Survey', *Monthly Labour Review*, July: 46–47.

Kuhlbrandt, C., Basu, S., McKee, M. and Stuckler, M. (2012) 'Looking at the Russian health care system: through the eyes of patients with diabetes and their physicians', *British Journal of Diabetes and Vascular Disease*, 12, 4: 1–4.

Kulikov, G. and Blyzniuk, V. (2010) *Impact of the Financial and Economic Crisis on Wages, Income Distribution and the Tax System* Geneva: ILO.

Kurinko, R. (2011) *Implementing CSR: Simply about Complicated*, Kyiv: Raduga.

Kuzio, T. (2006) 'Is Ukraine part of Europe's future?' *Washington Quarterly*, 29, 3: 89–108.

Kuznetsov, A. and Kuznetsova, O. (2003) 'Institutions, business and the state in Russia', *Europe–Asia Studies*, 55, 6: 907–922.

Kuznetsova, O. and Kuznetsov, A. (1999) 'The state as a shareholder: responsibilities and objectives', *Europe–Asia Studies*, 51, 3: 433–445.

Lacko, M. (1999) 'Electricity intensity and the unrecorded economy in post-socialist countries', in E.L. Feige and K. Ott (eds), *Underground Economies in Transition: Unrecorded Activity, Tax Evasion, Corruption and Organized Crime*, Aldershot: Ashgate.

Lane, D. (2000) 'What kind of capitalism for Russia? A comparative analysis', *Communist and Post-Communist Studies*, 33, 4: 485–504.

Lane, D. (2007) 'Post state socialism: a diversity of capitalisms?', in D. Lane and D. Myant (eds), *Varieties of Capitalism in Post Communist Countries*, London: Palgrave, London.

Lane, D. (2011) *Elites and Classes in the Transformation of State Socialism*, Piscataway, NJ, and London: Transaction.
Lane, D. and Myant, M. (eds) (2006) *Varieties of Capitalism in Post-Communist Countries*, Basingstoke: Palgrave Macmillan.
Langfelt, E. (1989) 'The underground economy in the Federal republic of Germany: a preliminary assessment', in E.L. Feige (ed.) *The Underground Economies: Tax Evasion and Information Distortion*, Cambridge: Cambridge University Press.
Latouche, S. (1993) *In the Wake of Affluent Society: An Exploration of Post-Development*, London: Zed.
Lavigne, M. (2000) 'Ten years of transition: a review article', *Communist and Post-Communist Studies*, 33: 475–483.
Ledeneva, A. (1998) *Russia's Economy of Favors: Blat, Networking and Informal Exchange*, Cambridge: Cambridge University Press.
Ledeneva, A. (2006) *How Russia Really Works: The Informal Practices that Shaped Post-Soviet Politics and Business*, London: Cornell University Press.
Ledeneva, A. (2008) 'Blat and Guanxi: informal practices in Russia and China', *Comparative Studies in Society and History*, 50, 1: 118–144.
Lee, R. (2000) 'Shelter from the storm? Geographies of regard in the worlds of horticultural consumption and production', *Geoforum*, 31, 1: 137–157.
Lee, R. (2006) 'The ordinary economy: tangled up in values and geography', *Transactions of the Institute of British Geographers*, 31, 4: 413–432.
Lee, Yeon-Ok and Lee, Raymond M. (2012) 'Methodological research on "sensitive" topics: a decade review', *Bulletin of Sociological Methodology/Bulletin de Méthodologie Sociologique*, 114, 1: 35–49.
Lefebvre, H. (2006) *Critique of Everyday Life: From Modernity to Modernism (Towards a Metaphilosophy of Daily Life): Vol. 3*, London: Verso Books.
Lehmann, H. and Muravyev, A. (2012) 'Labour market institutions and labour market performance: what can we learn from transition countries?' *Economics of Transition*, 20, 2: 235–269.
Lehmann, H. and Terrell, K. (2006) 'The Ukrainian labour market in transition: evidence from a new panel data set', *Journal of Comparative Economics*, 34: 195–199.
Lemaitre, A. and Helmsing, A. (2012) 'Solidarity economy in Brazil: movement, discourse and practice analysis through a Polanyian understanding of the economy', *Journal Of International Development*, 24: 745–762.
Leonard, M. (1994) *Informal Economic Activity in Belfast*, Aldershot: Avebury.
Leonard, M. (1998) *Invisible Work, Invisible Workers: The Informal Economy in Europe and the US*, London: Macmillan.
Lerche, J. (2012) 'Labour regulations and labour standards in India: decent work?', *Global Labour Journal*, 3, 1: 16–39.
Levin, M. and Satarov, G. (2000) 'Corruption and institutions in Russia', *European Journal of Political Economy*, 16: 113–132.
Lewis, A. (1959) *The Theory of Economic Growth*, London: Allen and Unwin.
Lewis, W. (1954) 'Economic development with unlimited supplies of labor', in A. Agarwal and S. Singh. (eds), *The Economics of Underdevelopment*, London: Oxford University Press.
Leyshon, A., Lee, R. and Williams, C.C. (2003) (eds) *Alternative Economic Spaces*, London: Sage.
Loayza, N. and Rigolini, J. (2011) 'Informal employment: safety net or growth engine?' *World Development*, 39: 1503–1515.

London, T. and Hart, S.L. (2004) 'Reinventing strategies for emerging markets: beyond the transnational model', *Journal of International Business Studies*, 35: 350–370.
Lovell, S. (2003) *Summerfolk: A History of the Dacha, 1710–2000*, New York: Cornell University Press.
Low, N., Butt, S., Ellis Paine, A. and Davis Smith, J. (2008) *Helping Out: A National Survey of Volunteering and Charitable Giving*, London: Office of the Third Sector.
Luxton, M. (1997) 'The UN, women and household labour: measuring and valuing unpaid work', *Women's Studies International Forum*, 20: 431–439.
Lyon, D. and Glucksmann, M. (2008) 'Comparative configurations of care work across Europe', *Sociology*, 42, 1: 101–118.
Macafee, K. (1980) 'A glimpse of the hidden economy in the national accounts', *Economic Trends*, 2, 1: 81–87.
McAuley, A. (1979) *Economic Welfare in the Soviet Union: Poverty, Living Standards, and Inequality*, Madison, WI: University of Wisconsin Press.
McCarthy, D.J. and Puffer, S.M. (2003) 'Corporate governance in Russia: a framework for analysis', *Journal of World Business*, 38: 397–415.
McCarthy, D.J. and Puffer, S.M. (2008) 'Corporate governance as a foundation for corporate social responsibility in transitioning economies: the Russian experience', *Thunderbird International Business Review*, 50, 4: 231–243.
McCarthy, D.J., Puffer, S.M., Dunlap, D.R. and Jaeger, A.M. (2012) 'A stakeholder approach to the ethicality of BRIC-firm managers' use of favors', *Journal of Business Ethics*, 109: 27–38.
McCleery, R. and De Paolis, F. (2008) 'The Washington Consensus: a post-mortem', *Journal of Asian Economics*, 19, 5–6: 438–446.
McCracken, G. (1998) *Culture and Consumption*, Bloomington, IN: Indiana University Press.
McDowell, L. (2005) *Hard Labour: The Forgotten Voices of Latvian Migrant Volunteer Worker*, London: UCL Press.
McFarlane, C. and Waibel, M. (2012) *Urban Informalities: Reflections on the Formal and Informal*, Aldershot: Ashgate.
Maier, P. (2007) *Do We Need the IMF to Resolve a Crisis? Lessons from Past Episodes of Debt Restructuring*, Bank of Canada Working Paper 2007-10.
Maloney, W. (2004) 'Informality revisited', *World Development*, 32: 1159–1178.
Marcelli, E., Williams, C.C. and Joassart, P. (eds) (2010) *Informal Work in Developed Nations*, London: Routledge.
Martin, R. and Sunley, P. (2001) 'Rethinking the "economic" in economic geography: broadening our vision or losing our focus?' *Antipode*, 33: 148–161.
Massey, D. (2005) *For Space*, London: Sage.
Mathews, M. (1986) *Poverty in the Soviet Union: The Life-styles of the Underprivileged in Recent Years*, Cambridge: Cambridge University Press.
Matsaganis, M. (2012) 'Social policy in hard times: the case of Greece', *Critical Social Policy*, 32, 3: 406–421.
Matthews, K. (1982) 'The demand for currency and the black economy in the UK', *Journal of Economic Studies*, 9, 2: 3–22.
Matthews, K. (1983) 'National income and the black economy', *Journal of Economic Affairs*, 3, 4: 261–267.
Matthews, K. and Rastogi, A. (1985) 'Little mo and the moonlighters: another look at the black economy', *Quarterly Economic Bulletin*, 6, 1: 21–24.
Mayorova, O. (2008) 'Social capital and institutional transition: regional context for

network use in job search in Russia, 1985–2001', unpublished PhD Thesis, University of Arizona.
Meadows, T.C. and Pihera, J.A. (1981) 'A regional perspective on the underground economy', *Review of Regional Studies*, 11, 1: 83–91.
Mendelson, S.E. and Gerber, T.P. (2007) 'Activist culture and transnational diffusion: social marketing and human rights groups in Russia', *Post-Soviet Affairs*, 23: 50–75.
Meriküll, J. and Staehr, K. (2010) 'Unreported employment and envelope wages in mid-transition: comparing developments and causes in the Baltic countries', *Comparative Economic Studies*, 52: 637–670.
Meurs, M. (2002) 'Economic strategies of surviving post-socialism: changing household economies and gender divisions of labour in the Bulgarian transition', in A. Rainnie, A. Smith, and A. Swain (eds), *Work, Employment and Transition: Restructuring Livelihoods in Post-Communism*, London: Routledge.
Mintel. (2002) *The DIY Consumer*, London: Mintel.
Mintel. (2005) *DIY Review 2005*, London: Mintel.
Mintel. (2006) *DIY Retailing – Europe*, London: Mintel.
Mishler, W. and Rose, R. (1997) 'Trust, distrust and skepticism: Popular evaluation of civil and political institutions in post-communist societies', *Journal of Politics*, 59: 418–451.
Mitchell, T. (2003) *The Properties of Markets: Informal Housing and Capitalism's Mystery*, Institute for Advanced Studies in Social and Management Sciences, University of Lancaster, Cultural Political Economy Working Paper No. 2, (www.lancs.ac.uk/ias/polecon/index.htm, accessed 8 February 2009).
Mojić, D. (2012) 'Means of getting ahead in post-socialist Serbia: perceptions and preferences of young people', *Sociologija*, LIV, 2: 303–314.
Morgan, M. and Knuuttila, T. (2012) 'Models and modelling in economics', in U. Mäki (ed.), *Philosophy of Economics*, New York: North Holland.
Morton, H. (1980) 'Who gets what, when and how? Housing in the Soviet Union', *Soviet Studies*, 32, 2: 235–259.
Munro, M. and Leather, P. (2000) 'Nest-building or investing in the future? Owner-occupiers' home improvement behaviour', *Policy and Politics*, 28: 511–526.
Murgatroyd, L. and Neuburger, H. (1997) 'A household satellite account for the UK', *Economic Trends*, 527: 63–71.
Myant, M. and Drahokoupil, J. (2012) 'International integration, varieties of capitalism and resilience to crisis in transition economies', *Europe–Asia Studies*, 64, 1: 1–33.
Natale, S. and Doran, C. (2012) 'Marketization of education: an ethical dilemma', *Journal of Business Ethics*, 105, 2: 187–196.
NCRU. (2005) 'President states solving problem of Ukrainian economy's shadowization as incumbent authority's prime objective', *National Radio Company of Ukraine* (http://nrcu.gov.ua/index.php?id. 148&listid-10721, 12 March 2010).
Neef, R. (2002) 'Aspects of the informal economy in a transforming country: the case of Romania', *International Journal of Urban and Regional Research*, 26, 299–322.
Newman, S. and Jahdi, K. (2009) 'Marketisation of education: marketing, rhetoric and reality', *Journal of Further and Higher Education*, 33, 1: 1–11.
Nikitina, I. (2009) 'K voprosu o praktike registratsii obshchin korennykh malochislennykh narodov (prodolzhenie)', *Pravovoye obozreniye*, 6, 92, (www.uckpa.ru/newspaper/92/atcl6, accessed 15 April 2010).
Nordhaus, W. (1990) 'Soviet economic reform: the longest road', *Brookings Papers on Economic Activity*, 1: 287–318.

Nwabuzor, A. (2005) 'Corruption and development: new initiatives in economic openness and strengthened rule of law', *Journal of Business Ethics*, 59: 121–138.

O'Brien, D., Wegren, S. and Patsiorkvosky, V. (2011) 'Poverty, inequality and subjective quality of life in rural Russia during the transition to a market economy: 1991–2006', *Poverty and Public Policy*, 3: 2.

Oberemko, O. (2006) 'Household spending on preschool education and upbringing', *Russian Education and Society*, 48, 12: 38–63.

OECD (2002) *Measuring the Non-Observed Economy*, Paris: OECD.

OECD (2003) *Labour Market and Social Policies in the Baltic Countries*, Paris: OECD.

OECD (2011) *Towards a Better Understanding of the Informal Economy*, Paris: OECD.

OECD (2012) *Reviews of Health Systems: Russian Federation*, Paris: OECD.

Ofer, G. (1987) 'Soviet economic growth: 1928–1985', *Journal of Economic Literature*, 25, 4: 1767–1833.

O'Hearn, D. (1980) 'The consumer second economy: size and effects', *Soviet Studies*, 32, 2: 218–234.

O'Higgins, M. (1981) 'Tax evasion and the self-employed', *British Tax Review*, 26: 367–378.

Orrù, M., Biggart, N. and Hamilton, G. (1997) *The Economic Organization of East Asian Capitalism*, London and Thousand Oaks, CA: Sage.

Osipian, A. (2010) 'Corrupt organizational hierarchies in the Former Soviet Bloc', *Transition Studies Review*, 17, 3: 822–836.

Osipian, A. (2011) 'Economics of corruption in doctoral education: the dissertations market', *Economics of Education Review* (http://dx.doi.org/10.1016/j.econedurev.2011.08.011, 10 March 2012).

Osipian, A. (2012) 'Education corruption, reform, and growth: case of post-Soviet Russia', *Journal of Eurasian Studies*, 3: 20–29.

Paglin, M. (1994) 'The underground economy: new estimates from household income and expenditure surveys', *The Yale Law Journal*, 103, 8: 2239–2257.

Pahl, R.E. (1984) *Divisions of Labour*, Oxford: Blackwell.

Pallot, J. and Moran, D. (2000) 'Surviving the margins in post-Soviet Russia: forestry villages in Northern Perm' Oblast', *Post-Soviet Geography and Economics*, 41, 5: 341–364.

Park, T. (1979) *Reconciliation Between Personal Income and Taxable Income (1947–1977)*, Washington, DC: Bureau of Economic Analysis.

Parker, M. (2002) *Against Management*, Cambridge: Polity.

Patico, J. (2002) 'Chocolate and Cognac: gifts and the recognition of social worlds in post-Soviet Russia', *Ethnos*, 67, 3: 345–368.

Pavlovskaya, M. (2004) 'Other transitions: multiple economies of Moscow households in the 1990s', *Annals of the Association of American Geographers*, 94: 329–351.

Peck, J. (2010) *Constructions of Neoliberal Reason*, Oxford: Oxford University Press.

Pender, J. (2001) 'From "structural adjustment" to "comprehensive development framework": conditionality transformed?' *Third World Quarterly*, 22, 3: 397–412.

Perlman, F. and Balabanova, D. (2011) 'Prescription for change: accessing medication in transitional Russia', *Health Policy and Planning*, 26, 6: 453–463.

Perry, G. and Maloney, W. (2007) 'Overview: informality – exit and exclusion', in G. Perry, W. Maloney, O. Arias., P. Fajnzylber, A. Mason and J. Saavedra-Chanduvi (eds), *Informality: Exit and Exclusion*, Washington, DC: World Bank.

Petrov, G. and Temple, P. (2004) 'Corruption in higher education: some findings from the states of the former Soviet Union', *Higher Education Management and Policy*, 16, 1: 83–99.

Pettinger, L., Parry, J., Taylor, R. and Glucksmann, M. (eds) (2005) *A New Sociology of Work?*, Oxford: Blackwell.
Pfau-Effinger, B. (2009) 'Varieties of undeclared work in European societies', *British Journal of Industrial Relations*, 47, 1: 79–99.
Phillips, N. (2011) 'Informality, global production networks and the dynamics of "adverse incorporation" ', *Global Networks*, 11, 3: 380–397.
Pickles, J. (ed.) (2008) *State and Society in Post-socialist Economies*, Basingstoke: Palgrave Macmillan.
Pickles, J. and Smith, A. (1998) *Theorising Transition: The Political Economy of Post-Communist Transformation*, London: Routledge.
Pickup, F. and White, A. (2003) 'Livelihoods in post-communist Russia: urban/rural comparisons', *Work, Employment and Society*, 17, 3: 419–434.
Piirainen, T. (1997) *Towards a New Social Order in Russia: Transforming Structures and Everyday Life*, Dartmouth: Aldershot.
Polanyi, K. (1944) *The Great Transformation*, Boston, MA: Beacon Press.
Pollard, J., Mcewan, C., Laurie, N. and Stenning, A. (2009) 'Economic geography under postcolonial scrutiny', *Transactions of the Institute of British Geographers*, 34, 2: 137–142.
Popovich, L., Potapchik, E., Shishkin, S., Richardson, E., Vacroux, A. and Mathivet, B. (2011) 'Russian Federation', *Health Systems in Transition*, 13, 7: 1–189
Portes, A. (1994) 'The informal economy and its paradoxes', in N. Smelser and R. Swedberg (eds), *The Handbook of Economic Sociology*, Princeton, NJ: Princeton University Press.
Portes, A. and Sassen-Koob, S. (1987) 'Making it underground: comparative material on the informal sector in Western market economies', *American Journal of Sociology*, 93, 1: 30–61.
Powell, W. (1990) 'Neither market nor hierarchy: network forms of organisation', in G. Thompson, J. Frances, R. Lavacic and J. Mitchell (eds), *Markets, Hierarchies and Networks*, London: Sage.
Poznanski, K. (2001) 'Transition and its dissenters: an introduction', *East European Politics and Societies*, 15: 207–220.
PricewaterhouseCoopers. (2009) *Paying Taxes 2009: The Global Picture*, Washington, DC: World Bank.
Putterman, L. (1990) *Division of Labor and Welfare: An Introduction to Economic Systems*, Oxford: Oxford University Press.
Ram, M., Edwards, P. and Jones, T. (2002a) *Employers and Illegal Migrant Workers in the Clothing and Restaurant Sectors*, London: DTI Central Unit Research.
Ram, M., Jones, T., Abbas, T. and Sanghera, B. (2002b) 'Ethnic minority enterprise in its urban context: South Asian restaurants in Birmingham', *International Journal of Urban and Regional Research*, 26, 1: 24–40.
Rechel, B., Kennedy, C., McKee, M. and Rechel, B. (2011) 'The Soviet legacy in diagnosis and treatment: implications for population health', *Journal of Public Health Policy*, 32: 293–304.
Reid, M. (1934) *Economics of Household Production*, New York: Wiley.
Renooy, P. (1990) *The Informal Economy: Meaning, Measurement and Social Significance*, Amsterdam: Netherlands Geographical Studies Association.
Renooy, P., Ivarsson, S., van der Wusten-Gritsai, O. and Meijer, R. (2004) *Undeclared Work in an Enlarged Union: An Analysis of Shadow Work – An In-depth Study of Specific Items*, Brussels: European Commission.

Reynolds, P., Bygrave, W.D., Autio, E. and Hay, M. (2002) *Global Entrepreneurship Monitor: 2002 Executive Monitor*, London: London Business School.

Rifkin, J. (2000) *The Age of Access*, Harmondsworth: Penguin.

Rifkin, J. (2001) *The Age of Access: The New Culture of Hypercapitalism, Where all of Life is a Paid-For Experience*, New York: Tarcher.

Rimashevskaya, N. (2006) 'Some problems of social reform in Russia', *Studies on Russian Economic Development*, 17, 2: 115–122.

Rimashevskaya, N. and Onikov, L. (1977) *Family, Labor, Income, Consumption*, Moscow: Nauka.

Rivkin-Fish, M. (2011) 'Rethinking problems surrounding access to care: the moral economies shaping health care work forces in Russia and the U.S.', in P. Watson (ed.), *Health Care Reform and Globalisation: The US, China and Europe in Comparative Perspective*, London: Routledge.

Roberts, K. (2001) 'Unemployment without social exclusion: evidence from young people in Eastern Europe', *International Journal of Sociology and Social Policy*, 21, 4–6): 118–144.

Roberts, K. and Pollock, G. (2011) 'Politics and trust in the South Caucasus, and in the East and West Europe', *Polish Sociological Review*, 2: 167–179.

Roberts, K., Fagan, L., Tarkhnishvili, L., Ivaschenko, E. and Abidekian, A. (2000) 'Employment and social mobility: evidence from Armenia, Georgia and Ukraine in the 1990s', *European Journal of Education*, 35, 1: 125–136.

Robinson, J. and Godbey, G. (1997) *Time for Life: The Surprising Ways Americans use their Time*, University Park, PA: Pennsylvania State University Press.

Rodrik, D. (2006) 'Goodbye Washington Consensus, hello Washington confusion? A review of the World Bank's economic growth in the 1990s: learning from a decade of reform', *Journal of Economic Literature*, XLIV: 973–987.

Rose, R. (1995) 'Russia as an hourglass society: a constitution without citizens', *East European Constitutional Review*, 4: 34–42.

Rose, R. (1996) *Getting Things Done in an Anti-Modern Society: Social Capital Networks in Russia*, Social Capital Initiative Working Paper No. 6, World Bank.

Rose, R. (2005) *Insiders and Outsiders: New Europe Barometer 2004*, Studies in Public Policy 404, Centre for the Study of Public Policy, University of Strathclyde.

Rose, R. (2009) *Understanding Post-Communist Transformation: A Bottom Up Approach*, London: Routledge.

Rose, R. and Haerpfer, C. (1992) *Between State and Market*, Strathclyde: University of Strathclyde.

Ross, A. (2004) *Low Pay High Profile: The Global Push for Fair Labor*, London: The New Press.

Ross, R. (2004) *Slaves to Fashion: Poverty and Abuse in the New Sweatshops*, Ann Arbor, MI: University of Michigan Press.

Rotkirch, A. and Kesseli, K. (2012) 'Two children puts you in the zone of social misery: childbearing and risk perception among Russian women', in H. Carlbäck, Y. Gradskova and Z. Kravchenko (eds), *And They Lived Happily Ever After: Norms and Everyday Practices of Family and Parenthood in Russia and Central Europe*, Budapest and New York: Central European University Press.

Round, J. (2006) 'Marginalised for a lifetime: the everyday experiences of gulag survivors in post-Soviet Magadan', *Geografiska Annaler: B*, 87, 1: 15–34.

Round, J. (2009) 'Transitional economies', in R. Kitchin and N. Thrift (eds), *International Encyclopaedia of Human Geography*, Oxford: Elsevier.

Round, J. and Kosterina, E. (2005) 'The construction of "poverty" in post-Soviet Russia', *Perspectives on European Politics and Society*, 6, 3: 403–434.
Round, J., Williams, C. and Rodgers, P. (2008) 'Corruption in the post-Soviet workplace: the experiences of recent graduates in contemporary Ukraine', *Work, Employment and Society*, 22: 149–166.
Round, J., Williams, C. and Rodgers, P. (2010) 'The role of domestic food production in everyday life in post-Soviet Ukraine', *Annals of the Association of American Geographers*, 100, 5: 1197–1211.
Routh, S. (2011) 'Building informal workers' agenda: imagining "informal employment" in conceptual resolution of "informality" ', *Global Labour Journal*, 2, 3: 208–227.
Roy, A. (2011) 'Slumdog cities: rethinking subaltern urbanism', *International Journal of Urban and Regional Research*, 35, 2: 223–238.
Rutland, P. (2009) *The Politics of Economic Stagnation in the Soviet Union: The Role of Local Party Organs in Economic Management*, Cambridge: Cambridge University Press.
Sachs, J. (1992) 'Privatization in Russia: some lessons from Eastern Europe', *American Economic Review*, 82, 2: 43–48.
Saif, I. (2011) *Challenges of Egypt's Economic Transition*, Washington, DC: Carnegie Endowment for International Peace.
Sakwa, R. (1999) *The Rise and Fall of the Soviet Union: 1917–1991*, London: Routledge.
Samers, M. (2005) 'The myopia of "diverse economies", or a critique of the "informal economy" ', *Antipode*, 37, 5: 875–886.
Sampson, S. (1987) 'The second economy of the Soviet Union and Eastern Europe', *Annals of the American Academy of Political and Social Science*, 493: 120–136.
Santos, J.A. (1983) *A Economia Subterrânea*, Lisbon: Minietrio do trabalho e seguranca social, Coleccao estudos, serie A, 4.
Sarkisyan, S. and Kuznetsova, N. (1964) *Potrebnosti i dokhodsem'I*, Moscow.
Sassen, S. (1996) 'Service employment regimes and the new inequality', in E. Mingione (ed.), *Urban Poverty and the Underclass*, Oxford: Basil Blackwell.
Sassen, S. (1997) *Informalisation in Advanced Market Economies*, Issues in Development Discussion Paper 20, ILO.
Sassen, S. (2009) 'Cities in today's global age', *SAIS Review*, 29, 1: 3–34.
Sassen, S. and Smith, R.C. (1992) 'Post-industrial growth and economic reorganisation: their impact on immigrant employment', in J. Bustamante, C.W. Reynolds and R.A. Hinojosa (eds), *US–Mexico Relations: Labour Markets Interdependence*, Stanford, CA: Stanford University Press.
Sauvy, A. (1984) *Le travail noir et l'economie de demain*, Paris: Calmann-Levy.
Schneider, F. (2001) 'What do we know about the shadow economy? Evidence from 21 OECD countries', *World Economics*, 2, 4: 19–32.
Schneider, F. (2010) 'The influence of public institutions on the shadow economy: an empirical investigation for OECD countries', *European Journal of Law and Economics*, 6, 3: 441–468.
Schneider, F. (2011) *Handbook on the Shadow Economy*, Cheltenham: Edward Elgar.
Schneider, F. (2012) *The Shadow Economy and Work in the Shadow: What Do We (Not) Know?*, IZA Discussion Papers 6423, Institute for the Study of Labor (IZA).
Schneider, F. and Enste, D. (2000) 'Shadow economies; size, causes and consequences', *Journal of Economic Literature*, 38, 1: 77–114.
Schneider, F. and Enste, D.H. (2002) *The Shadow Economy: An International Survey*, Cambridge: Cambridge University Press.

Schneider, F., Buehn, A. and Montenegro, C.E. (2010) 'New estimates for the shadow economies all over the world', *International Economic Journal*, 24, 4: 443–461.

Scott, A. (2001) 'Capitalism, cities and the production of symbolic forms', *Transactions of the Institute of British Geographers*, 26: 11–23.

Seabrook, J. (2003) *The No-nonsense Guide to World Poverty*, London: Verso.

Sedlenieks, K. (2003) 'Cash in an envelope: corruption and tax avoidance as an economic strategy in contemporary Riga', in K.-O. Arnstberg and T. Boren (eds), *Everyday Economy in Russia, Poland and Latvia*, Stockholm: Almqvist & Wiksell.

Seeth, H., Chachnova, S., Surinova, A. and Von Braun, J. (1998) 'Russian poverty: muddling through economic transition with garden plots', *World Development*, 26, 9: 1611–1624.

Settersten, R.A., Furstenberg, F.F. and Rumbaut, R.G. (2008) *On the Frontier of Adulthood: Theory, Research, and Public Policy*, Chicago, IL: University of Chicago Press.

Shafik, N. (2012) *Convergence, Crisis, and Capacity Building in Emerging Europe* (http://blog-imfdirect.imf.org/2012/07/27/convergence-crisis-and-capacity-building-in-emerging-europe, accessed 20 November 2012).

Sharafutdinova, G. (2011) *Political Consequences of Crony Capitalism inside Russia*, Notre Dame, IN: University of Notre Dame Press.

Shaw, D. (1999) *Russia in the Modern World: A New Geography*, London: Wiley-Blackwell.

Shevchenko, O. (2009) *Crisis and the Everyday in Postsocialist Moscow*, Bloomington, IN: Indiana University Press.

Shmelev, N. and Popov, V. (1990) *The Turning Point: Revitalizing the Soviet Economy*, London: I.B.Tauris.

Sidaway, J. and Power, M. (1995) 'Socio-spatial transformations in the "post-socialist" periphery: the case of Maputo, Mozambique', *Environment and Planning A*, 27, 9: 1463–1491.

Sik, E. (1993) 'From the second economy to the informal economy', *Journal of Public Policy*, 12: 153–175.

Sik, E. (1994) 'Network capital in capitalist, communist and post-communist societies', *International Contributions in Labour Studies*, 4: 73–93.

Sil, P. and Chen, C. (2004) 'State legitimacy and the (in)significance of democracy in post-communist Russia', *Europe–Asia Studies*, 56: 347–368.

Slack, T. (2007) 'The contours and correlates of informal work in rural Pennsylvania', *Rural Sociology*, 72, 1: 69–89.

Slack, T. and Jensen, L. (2010) 'Informal work in rural America', in E. Marcelli, C.C. Williams and P. Joassart (eds), *Informal Work in Developed Nations*, London: Routledge.

Slater, D. (1997) *Consumer Culture and Modernity*, Cambridge: Polity.

Slater, D. and Tonkiss, F. (2001) *Market Society: Markets and Modern Social Theory*, Cambridge: Polity.

Slavnic, Z. (2010) 'Political economy of informalization', *European Societies*, 12: 3–23.

Small Business Council (2004) *Small Business in the Informal Economy: Making the Transition to the Formal Economy*, London: Small Business Council.

Smith, A. (2000) 'Employment restructuring and household survival in "post-communist transition": rethinking economic practices in Eastern Europe', *Environment and Planning A*, 32: 1759–1780.

Smith, A. (2002a) 'Culture/economy and spaces of economic practice: positioning households in post-communism', *Transactions of the Institute of British Geographers*, 27: 232–250.

Smith, A. (2002b) 'Rethinking "survival" in austerity: economic practices and household economies in Slovakia', in A. Rainnie, A. Smith and A. Swain (eds), *Work, Employment and Transition: Restructuring Livelihoods in Post-Communism*, London: Routledge.

Smith, A. (2004) 'Regions, territories and diverse economies in the "new Europe"', *European Urban and Regional Studies*, 11: 9–25.

Smith, A. (2010) 'Informal work in the diverse economies of "post-socialist" Europe', in E. Marcelli, C. Williams and P. Joassart (eds), *Informal Work in Developed Nations*, London: Routledge.

Smith, A. and Stenning, A. (2006) 'Beyond household economies: articulations and spaces of economic practice in postsocialism', *Progress in Human Geography*, 30: 1–14.

Smith, A. and Swain, A. (1998) 'Regulating and institutionalising capitalism: the micro foundations of transformation in Eastern and Central Europe', in J. Pickles and A. Smith (eds), *Theorising Transition: The Political Economy of Post-Communist Transformations*, London: Routledge, pp. 25–53.

Smith, A. and Swain, A. (2010) 'The global economic crisis, Eastern Europe, and the former Soviet Union: models of development and the contradictions of internationalization', *Eurasian Geography and Economics*, 51, 1: 1–34.

Smith, A. and Timár, J. (2010) 'Uneven transformations: space, economy and society 20 years after the collapse of state socialism', *European Urban and Regional Studies*, 17: 115–125.

Smith, A., Rochovská, A., Stenning, A. and Świątek, D. (2006) *Social Exclusion and Household Economic Practices in Central European Cities: Petržalka, Bratislava*, summary report presented to Petržalka dissemination workshop, Hotel Niva, Petržalka, 12 July (www.geog.qmul.ac.uk/socialexclusion/pdf/Petrzalkaworkshop.pdf, accessed 15 July 2009).

Smolar, A. (1996) 'From opposition to atomization', *Journal of Democracy*, 7: 24–38.

Smuts, R. (1971) *Women and Work in America*, New York: Schocken Books.

Snyder, K. (2004) 'Routes to the informal economy in New York's East Village: crisis, economics and identity', *Sociological Perspectives*, 47, 2: 215–240.

Sokol, M. (2001) 'Central and Eastern Europe a decade after the fall of state-socialism: regional dimensions of transition processes', *Regional Studies*, 35, 7: 645–655.

Solimano, A. (1998) *Beyond Unequal Development: An Overview*, World Bank Policy Research Working Paper No. 2091.

Southworth, C. (2006) 'The dacha debate: household agriculture and labor markets in post-socialist Russia', *Rural Sociology*, 71, 3: 451–478.

Standing, G. (2005) *Another New Dawn? The Ukrainian People's Security Survey 2004*, Geneva: ILO.

Standing, G. (2011) *The Precariat: The New Dangerous Class*, London: Bloomsbury.

Stebbins, R.A. (2004) 'Serious leisure, volunteerism and quality of life', in J.T. Haworth and A.J. Veal (eds), *Work and Leisure*, London: Routledge.

Stenning, A. (2005) 'Post-socialism and the changing geographies of the everyday in Poland', *Transactions of the Institute of British Geographers*, 30: 113–127.

Stenning, A. and Horschelmann, K. (2008) 'History, geography and difference in the post-socialist world; Or, do we still need post-socialism?' *Antipode*, 40: 312–335.

Stenning, A., Świątek, D., Smith, A. and Rochovská, A. (2006) 'Social exclusion and household economic practices in Nowa Huta', (www.geog.qmul.ac.uk/socialexclusion/pdf/NHreportEnglish.pdf, accessed 23 September 2008).

Stiglitz, J. (1998) 'Towards a new paradigm for development', United Nations Conference on Trade and Development, Ninth Raúl Prebisch Lecture.

Strangleman, T. and Warren, T. (2008) *Work and Society: Sociological Approaches, Themes and Methods*, London: Routledge.

Strayer, R. (1998) *Why did the Soviet Union Collapse? Understanding Historical Change*, London: M.E. Sharpe.

Sturgeon, D. (2010) '"Have a nice day": consumerism, compassion and health care', *British Journal of Nursing*, 19, 16: 1047–1051.

Sundstrom, L.M. and Henry, L.A. (2006) 'Russian civil society: tensions and trajectories', in A.B. Evans, L.A. Henry and L.M. Sundstrom (eds), *Russian Civil Society: A Critical Assessment*, Armonk, NY: M.E. Sharpe.

Suny, R. (1994) *The Revenge of the Past: Nationalism, Revolution, and the Collapse of the Soviet Union*, Stanford, CA: Stanford University Press.

Sutela, P. (2012) *The Political Economy of Putin's Russia*, London: Routledge.

Suzuki, E. (2001) 'The fallacy of globalism and the protection of national economies', *Yale Journal of International Law*, 26, 2: 319–322.

Sýkora, L. and Bouzarovski, S. (2012) 'Multiple transformations: conceptualising the post communist urban transition', *Urban Studies*, 49: 43–60.

Syrinov, A. (2003) *Yroven Zhizni Naselenia Rossii: 1992–2002gg*, Moscow: Goskomstat.

Tanzi, V. (1980) 'The underground economy in the United States: estimates and implications', *Banco Nazionale del Lavoro*, 135: 427–453.

Taylor, R.F. (2004) 'Extending conceptual boundaries: work, voluntary work and employment', *Work, Employment and Society*, 18, 1: 29–49.

Tengblad, A. (1994) *Berakning av svart ekonomi och skatteundandragandet I Sverige 1980–1991*, Stockholm: Arhundradets Skattereform.

Thelen, Kathleen (2012) 'Varieties of capitalism: trajectories of liberalization and the new politics of social solidarity', *Annual Review of Political Science* 15: 137–159.

Thomas, J.J. (1992) *Informal Economic Activity*, Hemel Hempstead: Harvester Wheatsheaf.

Thrift, N. and Walling, D. (2000) 'Geography in the United Kingdom 1996–2000', *Geographical Journal*, 166, 2: 96–124.

Tilak, J. (2009) 'Higher education: a public good or a commodity for trade?' *Prospects*, 38, 449–466.

TNS Infratest, Rockwool Foundation and Regioplan (2006) *Feasibility Study on a Direct Survey about Undeclared Work VC/2005/0276*, Brussels: European Commission.

Tokman, V.E. (1989) 'Economic development and labor market segmentation in the Latin American periphery', *Journal of Inter-American Studies and World Affairs*, 31, 1: 23–47.

Transparency International (2005) *Report on the Transparency International Global Corruption Barometer 2005*. http://transparency.org/policy_research/surveys_indices/gcb.

Turbine, V. and Riach, K. (2012) 'The right to choose or choosing what's right? Women's conceptualizations of work and life choices in contemporary Russia', *Gender, Work and Organization*, 19, 2: 165–187.

Turley, G. and Luke, P. (2010) *Transition Economics: Two Decades on*, London: Routledge.

Urlanis, B. (1966) 'The dynamics and factors of the birth rate in the USSR', *Sov. Zdravookhr*, 7: 8.

US General Accounting Office. (1989) *Sweatshops in New York City: A Local Example of a Nationwide Problem*, Washington, DC: US General Accounting Office.

Venkatesh, S. (2006) *Off the Books: The Underground Economy of the Urban Poor*, Cambridge, MA: Harvard University Press.

Verdery, K. (1991) 'Theorizing socialism: a prologue to the "transition" ', *American Ethnologist*, 18, 3: 419–439.

Vishnevskaya, N. and Kapelyushnikov, R. (2007) 'Inforsment trudovogo zakonodatel'stva v Rossii', Working Paper series 'Problems of Labour Market', Moscow State University-Higher School of Economics, 3.

Volkov, V. (2002) *Violent Entrepreneurs: The Use of Force in the Making of Russian Capitalism*, Ithaca, NY: Cornell University Press.

Wacquant, L. (2012) 'Three steps to a historical anthropology of actually existing neoliberalism', *Social Anthropology/Anthropologie Sociale*, 20: 166–179.

Walker, C. (2010) 'Space, kinship networks and youth transition in provincial Russia: negotiating urban–rural and inter-regional migration', *Europe–Asia Studies*, 62, 4: 647–669.

Walker, C. (2011) 'Re-inventing themselves? Gender, employment and subjective well-being amongst working-class young Russians', in C. Walker (ed.), *Rethinking Class in Russia*, Farnham: Ashgate.

Wallace, C. and Haerpfer, C. (2002) 'Patterns of participation in the informal economy in East-Central Europe', in R. Neef and M. Stanuclescu (eds), *The Social Impact of Informal Economies in Eastern Europe*, Aldershot: Ashgate.

Wallace, C. and Latcheva, R. (2006) 'Economic transformation outside the law: corruption, trust in public institutions and the informal economy in transition countries of Central and Eastern Europe', *Europe–Asia Studies*, 58: 81–102.

Watts, M. (1999) 'Commodities', in C. Cloke, P. Crang and M. Goodwin (eds), *Introducing Human Geographies*, London: Arnold.

Watts, M.J. (2001) 'Wage polarisation and unemployment in Australia', in E. Carlson and W.F. Mitchell (eds), *Unemployment: The Tip of the Iceberg*, Sydney: UNSW Press.

Webb, J., Bruton, G., Tihanyi, L. and Ireland, D. (2012) 'Research on entrepreneurship in the informal economy: framing a research agenda', *Journal of Business Venturing*, In Press.

Wedel, J. (1998) 'Informal relations and institutional change: how Eastern European cliques and states mutually respond', *Anthropology of East Europe Review*, 16, 1: 2–17.

Wedel, J. (2001) *Collision and Collusion: The Strange Case of Western Aid to Eastern Europe*, New York: St Martin's Press.

Wegren, S. (2004) 'Russian peasant farms and household plots in 2003: a research note', *Eurasian Geography and Economics*, 45, 3: 230–239.

Weinberg, E. (1974) *The Development of Sociology in the Soviet Union*, London: Routledge.

White, R. and Williams, C.C. (2010) 'Re-thinking monetary exchange: some lessons from England', *Review of Social Economy*, 68, 3: 317–338.

White, R. and Williams, C. (2012) 'The pervasive nature of heterodox economic practices at a time of neoliberal crisis: towards a "postneoliberal" anarchist future', *Antipode*, 44, 5: 1–20.

Whitley, R. (ed.) (2002) *Competing Capitalisms: Institutions and Economies*, Cheltenham: Edward Edgar.

Williams, C.C. (2002) 'A critical evaluation of the commodification thesis', *The Sociological Review*, 50, 4: 525–542.

Williams, C.C. (2003) 'Evaluating the penetration of the commodity economy', *Futures*, 35: 857–868.

Williams, C.C. (2004a) *Cash-in-Hand Work: The Underground Sector and the Hidden Economy Of Favours*, Basingstoke: Palgrave Macmillan.

Williams, C.C. (2004b) 'The myth of marketization: an evaluation of the persistence of non-market activities in advanced economies', *International Sociology*, 19: 437–449.

Williams, C.C. (2004c) 'A lifestyle choice? Evaluating the motives of do-it-yourself (DIY) consumers', *International Journal of Retail and Distribution Management*, 32, 2: 270–278.

Williams, C.C. (2004d) 'Evaluating the architecture of governance in the UK for tackling undeclared work', *Local Governance*, 30, 4: 167–177.

Williams, C.C. (2005a) *A Commodified World? Mapping the Limits of Capitalism*, London: Zed Books.

Williams, C.C. (2005b) 'Market delusions: rethinking the trajectories of post-socialist societies', *Foresight*, 7, 3: 48–60.

Williams, C.C. (2006a) 'Beyond market-orientated readings of paid informal work: some lessons from rural England', *American Journal of Economics and Sociology*, 65, 2: 383–406.

Williams, C.C. (2006b) *The Hidden Enterprise Culture: Entrepreneurship in the Underground Economy*, Cheltenham: Edward Elgar.

Williams, C.C. (2007) *Rethinking the Future of Work: Directions and Visions*, Basingstoke: Palgrave Macmillan.

Williams, C.C. (2008) 'Rethinking the motives of do-it-yourself (DIY) consumers', *International Review of Retail, Distribution and Consumer Research*, 18, 2: 311–323.

Williams, C.C. (2009) 'Formal and informal employment in Europe: beyond dualistic representations', *European Urban and Regional Studies*, 16, 2: 147–159.

Williams, C.C. (2010a) 'Beyond the market/non-market divide: a total social organisation of labour approach', *International Journal of Social Economics*, 37, 6: 402–414.

Williams, C.C. (2010b) 'Re-thinking the penetration of capitalism in the Commonwealth of Independent States', *Foresight*, 12, 1: 21–30.

Williams, C.C. and Nadin, S. (2010) 'Rethinking the commercialisation of everyday life: a "whole economy" perspective', *Foresight*, 12, 1: 55–68.

Williams, C.C. and Round, J. (2007) 'Beyond negative depictions of informal employment: some lessons from Moscow', *Urban Studies*, 44, 12: 2321–2338.

Williams, C.C. and Round, J. (2008) 'The illusion of capitalism in post-Soviet Ukraine', *Debatte: Journal of Contemporary Central and Eastern Europe*, 16: 331–345.

Williams, C.C. and Round, J. (2010) 'The shallow and uneven diffusion of capitalism in everyday life in post-Soviet Moscow', *Debatte: Journal of Contemporary Central and Eastern Europe*, 18: 53–69.

Williams, C.C. and Windebank, J. (1998) *Informal Employment in the Advanced Economies: Implications for Work and Welfare*, London: Routledge.

Williams, C.C. and Windebank, J. (2001a) 'Acquiring goods and services in lower income populations: an evaluation of consumer behaviour and preferences', *The International Journal of Retail and Distribution Management*, 29, 1: 16–24.

Williams, C.C. and Windebank, J. (2001b) 'Reconceptualising paid informal exchange: some lessons from English cities', *Environment and Planning A*, 33, 1: 121–140.

Williams, C.C. and Windebank, J. (2003) 'Reconceptualizing women's paid informal work: some lessons from lower-income urban neighbourhoods', *Gender, Work and Organisation*, 10, 3: 281–300.

Williams, J.C. and Zelizer, V.A. (2005) 'To commodify or not to commodify: that is not the question', in M. Ertman. and J.C. Williams (eds), *Rethinking Commodification: Cases and Readings in Law and Culture*, New York: New York University Press.

Williamson, J. (1990) 'What Washington means by policy reform', in J. Williamson (ed.), *Latin American Adjustment: How Much has Happened?* Washington, DC: Institute for International Economics.

Willis, P. (1991) *Common Culture*, Milton Keynes: Open University Press.

Wilson, A. (2005) *Ukraine's orange revolution*, New Haven, CT: Yale University Press.

Winiecki, J. (2012) 'Russia and China facing the 'Great Wall': how to succeed in the second structural transition', *Post-Communist Economies*, 24, 3: 309–325.

Wolff, J. (1985) 'The invisible flaneuse: women in the literature of modernity', *Theory, Culture and Society*, 2, 1: 37–46.

Woolfson, C. (2007) 'Pushing the envelope: the 'informalization' of labour in post-Communist new EU member states', *Work, Employment and Society*, 21, 3: 551–564.

World Bank. (2009). *Doing Business Survey, 2009*, Washington, DC: World Bank.

Yakubovich, V. (2005) 'Weak ties, information, and influence: how workers find jobs in a local Russian labor market', *American Sociological Review*, 70, 3: 408–421.

Yeon, O., Lee, Y.-O. and Lee, R. (2012) 'Methodological research on "sensitive" topics: a decade review', *Bulletin of Sociological Methodology*, 114: 35–49.

Yeung, H. and Lin, G. (2003) 'Theorizing economic geographies of Asia', *Economic Geography*, 79, 2: 107–128.

Yurchak, A. (2002) 'Entrepreneurial governmentality in post-socialist Russia: a cultural investigation of business practices', in V. Bonnell and T. Gold (eds), *The New Entrepreneurs of Europe and Asia*, New York: M.E. Sharpe.

Žabko, M.A. and Rajevska, F. (2007) 'Undeclared work and tax evasion: case of Latvia', paper presented at colloquium of the Belgian Federal Service for Social Security on Undeclared Work, Tax Evasion and Avoidance, Brussels, June.

Zaslavskaya, T. (1987) 'The role of sociology in accelerating the development of Soviet society', *Sociological Research*, 26, 3: 7–25.

Zaslavskaya, T. (2004) *Sovremennoe Rossiyskoe Obschestvo: Sotsial'nyy Mekhanizm Transformatsii* (*Contemporary Russian Society: The Social Mechanism of Transformation*), Moscow: Delo.

Zdravomyslova, O. (2003) *Family and Society: Gender Dimension of Russian Transformation*, Moscow: Editorial.

Zdravomyslova, Elena (2010) 'Working mothers and nannies: commercialization of childcare and modifications in the gender contract (a sociological essay)', *Anthropology of East Europe Review*, 28, 2: 200–225.

Zelizer, V.A. (2005) *The Purchase of Intimacy*, Princeton, NJ: Princeton University Press.

Index